WHY WE ARE RESTLESS

NEW FORUM BOOKS

Robert P. George, Series Editor

New Forum Books makes available to general readers outstanding, original, interdisciplinary scholarship with a special focus on the juncture of culture, law, and politics. The series is guided by the conviction that law and politics not only reflect culture, but help to shape it. Looking at questions that range from political equality to poverty and economic development to the international legal and political order, New Forum Books seeks to explain—not explain away—the difficult issues we face today.

For a full list of titles in the series, go to *https://press.princeton.edu/series/new-forum-books*.

Why We Are Restless

On the Modern Quest for Contentment

BENJAMIN STOREY

AND

JENNA SILBER STOREY

PRINCETON UNIVERSITY PRESS

PRINCETON AND OXFORD

Published by Princeton University Press
41 William Street, Princeton, New Jersey 08540
6 Oxford Street, Woodstock, Oxfordshire OX20 1TR

press.princeton.edu

All Rights Reserved
ISBN 978-0-691-21112-1
ISBN (e-book) 978-0-691-21113-8

British Library Cataloging-in-Publication Data is available

Editorial: Rob Tempio and Matt Rohal
Production Editorial: Jenny Wolkowicki
Text design: Karl Spurzem
Jacket design: Amanda Weiss
Production: Erin Suydam
Publicity: Amy Stewart and Maria Whelan
Copyeditor: Jennifer H. Backer

This book has been composed in Arno Pro

Printed on acid-free paper. ∞

Printed in the United States of America

10 9 8 7 6 5 4 3 2 1

For three great teachers:
Larry Goldberg, Leon R. Kass, and Peter Augustine Lawler

CONTENTS

We Restless Souls

She has done everything the college has asked of her, only better. The star student of two departments, she has notched impressive summer internships, spent several semesters abroad, founded one club, served as president of another, and collected her Phi Beta Kappa key the previous spring. As graduation approaches, she has come to us to talk about her future. This should be easy.

Law school or a PhD? For years she has had her eye on these goals and is now well positioned for either. But then the options she puts before us start to diverge: maybe teaching (plausible), maybe farming (not so plausible), perhaps a year abroad, perhaps a return home, perhaps more schooling, perhaps an end to all schooling. She wants to do good in the world and speaks passionately about her pet political causes, but she is also nostalgic and speaks wistfully about family, retreat, and quiet. As she detects the discordance of the possibilities she is contemplating, she is unnerved. The tightness of her face, the finger picking at the plastic tabletop, the skittish darting of her eyes, make her look less like a very fortunate person choosing from the bountiful banquet she has earned the right to enjoy than a terminally ill patient choosing from a grim variety of palliatives.

She has made the most of her American birthright—to pursue happiness wherever it leads—and her very success has left her at a loss. Years of steady progress have culminated in a strange and restless paralysis.

We would like to help her but are not at first sure how. Discussing her predicament soon leads us to see, however, that her unease is not unfamiliar. We, too, have much to be grateful for: the blessing of children, the gift of students, the shared work of thinking, a comfortable home. We spend our days tending to these gifts—teaching, studying, and going to meetings; helping the young ones with spelling, math, and science; ferrying them to piano, aikido, and dance; sitting down at last to family dinner and a family bedtime story—then once again back to the laptops to respond to the incoming flak of email and arrange another such day. Although we shake our heads at our students' frenetic dedication to extracurriculars, we see that we have made our own days full, often fuller than we can handle. The restlessness we observe around us can also be seen within.

We should be grateful to have such problems, and we are. But as Blaise Pascal pointed out long ago, even the fortunate can be unhappy. And their unhappiness can be particularly persistent, for when people seem to have solid reasons for feeling better than they do, they often believe themselves obliged to let their unhappiness go unexamined. Such an absence of self-reflection can make them prone to do senseless things—for they are already doing all the sensible things and are still unhappy.[1]

For our country's sake, we wish this restlessness were confined within the gates of leafy campuses like the one where we teach. But its symptoms pervade American life: in our love for the screen, with its diversions and distractions; in our demand for endless variety in what we eat, drink, and wear; in our appetite for mind-altering substances, from pot to Prozac to Pinot Grigio; in our fascination with crises in almost every area of human life. True, restlessness may be particularly acute among the privileged. But the privileged, by definition, lead the country. Justly or unjustly, their aspirations and problems shape everyone's lives.[2]

Such restlessness cannot help but have political consequences. As Plato wrote long ago, the passions that shape our common life do not arise from an "oak or rock" but "from the characters of the people who live in the cities." Political communities derive both their strengths and their disorders from the virtues, longings, failings, and fears of the human beings who give them life. Successful Americans are energetic people who work relentlessly and enjoy an astonishing plenitude of honors, opportunities, and comforts as their reward. But when those goods fail to make us happy, we sometimes find ourselves entertaining strange and radical thoughts that belie the pragmatism for which Americans are famous.[3]

A Frenchman noticed this peculiarity of our national character long ago. Touring America in 1831, Alexis de Tocqueville discovered that "the most free and most enlightened men placed in the happiest condition in the world" were not content with what they had—that they were "restless in the midst of their well-being." Beneath their successful pursuit of prosaic goods—adding new rooms to their houses, extracting more profit from lines of trade—they were profoundly uneasy. His lesson, not only for America but for the whole modern world, was that the achievement of an unprecedented degree of freedom, equality, and material prosperity would not guarantee steady lives or a stable social order. For free, equal, and prosperous people may think about their lives in a way that makes such steadiness impossible.[4]

Tocqueville's genius for observation is justly famous. But his ability to see into the hidden unease of American souls owes as much to his education as to his talent. From a very young age, Tocqueville steeped himself in a tradition of French writers who made the restlessness of the human soul their special object of study. Those writers thought about restlessness as part of a larger conversation about what we are and how we should live. Though it might seem counterintuitive to turn to old French philosophers in our effort to understand the disquiet that haunts contemporary souls, these classic thinkers have much to teach us. For they are intimately familiar with the way of pursuing happiness that has helped define modern life from its outset.

Four French Thinkers on the Modern Quest for Contentment

Every human society is animated by an assumed understanding of the nature and purpose of human life. This is true, as Tocqueville points out, even of liberal societies—societies that self-consciously avoid making such assumptions explicit and enshrining them in law. Whether or not we make these assumptions official, we cannot avoid relying on them: human life is busy, thinking things through is difficult, and the pressure of circumstance often requires that we take the answer to the question "How should I live?" for granted and get down to the business of the moment. While every society has its dissidents—oddballs, independent minds, and temperamental contrarians—the very possibility of the dissident is defined by the existence of a standard way.[1]

The vision of human flourishing that animates modern life received distinctly powerful articulation in sixteenth-century France. As it came to fascinate the imagination of increasing numbers of men and women, this vision became a subject of intense debate for generations of French writers. The writers who engage in this argument belong to France's tradition of *moralistes,* or "observers of men." We have here selected four of the *moralistes* for special attention: Michel de Montaigne, Blaise Pascal, Jean-Jacques Rousseau, and Alexis de Tocqueville. Each of these authors possesses the uncanny capacity for spelling out one of the few basic modern alternatives for thinking about happiness. Sometimes developing the premises of modern philosophic anthropology, sometimes attacking those premises at their roots, these authors give voice to thoughts that occur to every modern mind from time to time but with a power few of us can hope to match. Here, we seek to borrow that power and put it in the service of our own self-understanding.[2]

The story of the *moralistes* begins in the midst of France's sixteenth-century religious wars, with the great essayist Michel de Montaigne (1533–1592). Although he lived in a world most different from our own, Montaigne lays out the modern vision of contentment with all its basic elements, exercising immense influence on subsequent generations of thinkers in the modern West. Anyone who dips into his book for an hour or two will understand why. As one recent critic has formulated the experience of centuries of readers, "I defy any reader of Montaigne not to put down the book at some point and say with incredulity: 'How did he know all this about me?'" If we want to understand ourselves, we should come to know Montaigne.[3]

In the unforgettable prose of his semi-autobiographical *Essays,* Montaigne articulates the most basic aspiration of his moral philosophy: to "loyally enjoy" the human condition. "When I dance, I dance," Montaigne writes, "when I sleep, I sleep": he finds his happiness by disdaining no aspect of the human condition but partaking joyfully of all of it—books and horses, travel and love, food and art, talking with his daughter, playing with his cat, tending to the cabbages of his unfinished garden. Although he is remembered as a skeptical individualist who debunks the idea of a universal human good so as better to appreciate humanity's manifold variety, the practical consequence of his skepticism is this new and particular ideal of happiness—an ideal we call *immanent contentment*. The formula for Montaignean immanent contentment is *moderation through variation*: an arrangement of our dispositions, our pursuits, and our pleasures that is calculated to keep us interested, "at home," and present in the moment but also dispassionate, at ease, and in balance.[4]

As Montaigne's life shows, this ideal also has a social dimension, which one pursues by presenting to others the variegated and balanced self one has fashioned in the hope of receiving their complete, personal, *unmediated approbation*: the affirmation that we are lovable, not merely for the pleasure, utility, or even nobility of our company but because we are who we are— irreducibly distinct human wholes, worthy of the esteem, affection, and attachment of others. Such approbation, when reciprocated, can be the heart of a friendship such as Montaigne depicts in his story of the bond he shared with his own great friend Etienne de la Boétie.[5]

Taken together, the personal and interpersonal aspirations that make up the ideal of immanent contentment constitute an affirmation of the adequacy of human life on its own terms. By elaborating this new standard of human flourishing as an alternative to the heroic ideals of happiness he inherited from the classical and Christian traditions, Montaigne offers his contemporaries what Charles Taylor has called an "affirmation of ordinary life." Montaigne promises that if we know how to attend to it properly, life simply—not the philosophic life or the holy life or the heroic life, but simply *life*—can be enough to satisfy the longings of the human heart. That revolution in our understanding of ourselves implies a revolution in our understanding of politics, laying the groundwork for a liberal political order that takes the protection and promotion of life so understood to be its aim.[6]

In the decades after Montaigne's death, a new class will rise to prominence in France, one that distinguishes itself more by wealth, education, and accomplishment than by noble birth or feats of arms. That class naturally seeks a new moral vision to replace the chivalric ideal of the warrior aristocracy they have begun to supplant. Calling themselves *honnêtes hommes*, they celebrate Montaigne as the principal exemplar of this new ideal, which they call *honnêteté*. With these *honnêtes hommes*, the ideal of immanent contentment gains a newfound social significance as it begins to shape the aspirations of the seventeenth century's ascendant human type—a type that prefigures many of the attitudes that will come to characterize the modern moral outlook in centuries to come.[7]

This new style of living does not please everyone. The great polymath Blaise Pascal (1623–1662) frequents the circles in which the ideal of *honnêteté* has currency, studies its adepts closely, and comes to believe that they are fooling themselves. Beneath the surface of the charming and variegated arts of living by which they arrange their days, he sees that the *honnêtes hommes* are secretly unhappy. Their ideal of moderate worldly contentment denies but does not change the truth about the human soul, which is both greater and more miserable than Montaigne had imagined. To be human, for Pascal, is to be haunted by longing for a wholeness we feel we have somehow lost. Learning to die, the fundamental lesson of Montaigne's moral art, is not as easy as the *honnêtes hommes* imagine. Indeed, Pascal believes it is a lesson only a God could teach us. The search for unmediated approbation in social life that Montaigne encourages is, at bottom, a tyrannical quest to have others recognize us as the center of the universe. There is no such thing as immanent contentment; the basic choice of modern man is one between sadness papered over with diversion and the anguished but clear-eyed search for God.[8]

Pascal's intransigent criticism of the ways of the modern world is not calculated to flatter anyone, and it does not go over well with powerful people in his own age. The Roman Catholic Church brands the Jansenism of Pascal's friends and collaborators a heresy and puts his writings on its Index of Forbidden Books; Louis XIV razes the convent that had been the Jansenists' headquarters and desecrates their tombs. These attempts to erase Pascal's sad wisdom from modern memory are not without effect. As the great French literary critic Charles-Augustin Sainte-Beuve puts it, the eighteenth century seems to forget the seventeenth century ever existed, and simply picks up where the sixteenth left off.[9]

The Montaignean ideal of immanent contentment will enjoy unprecedented prestige in the age of Voltaire, when the expansion of trade, the flourishing of the arts, and the spread of learning made it a more widely available possibility than ever before. But the Enlightenment also gives rise to a dissident philosopher, Jean-Jacques Rousseau (1712–1778), who understands that Pascal discerned something true about the secret sadness of those seeking to live in the light of the Montaignean moral model. Rousseau will launch his own, semi-Pascalian critique of the ubiquitous human type of his time, the *bourgeois*—an old epithet to which he gives new meaning. Beneath his veneer of pretentious pleasures and pleasing manners, Rousseau writes, the restless heart of the bourgeois is full of envy and anger; he is an empty and divided nonentity with no substantial self and no real care for anyone else. Rousseau does not, however, encourage his readers to seek their solace in the next world, as Pascal does. He instead provokes them to tighten their grip on this one. Radicalizing the ideal of immanent contentment, Rousseau depicts a variety of highly experimental ways of life designed to realize that ideal more completely than ever before. Divergent as they are, however, all of these ways of life break sharply with what he saw as the socially and psychically intolerable status quo of his era.[10]

Though the life and thought of Rousseau have been heavily scrutinized, reading him as the heir of Montaigne and Pascal, as we do here, can allow us to see his work in a new light: as a transformation of the Montaignean ideal of immanent contentment. In Montaigne's hands, the pursuit of immanent contentment is a way of living with a light touch. Pascal attacks that lightness of touch as shallow, hypocritical, and inhuman. Rousseau seeks to reconcile Montaignean immanence with Pascalian depth. His pursuit of immanent contentment is an ardent and uncompromising quest for immersion in what he calls the "sentiment of existence": the simple pleasure of being alive, which he claims can be enough to satisfy our restless hearts if we will only remember how to feel it. It is also an earnest and insistent cri de coeur for the kind of unmediated social transparency Montaigne enjoyed with La Boétie, which Rousseau earnestly seeks from his own friends and lovers, who inevitably disappoint him. Disappointed though he may have been, Rousseau's enormously popular presentation of this ideal will exercise immense influence over the generation "at once sentimental and violent" that makes the French Revolution. And as the bourgeois social class he critiques rises to dominance in the nineteenth century, Rousseau's radicalization of the ideal of immanent contentment grows ever more influential. For his bohemian dreams are calculated to speak with particular power to the empty and divided heart of the bourgeois he so disdains.[11]

The preoccupations and passions of the bourgeois are on display on an unprecedented scale when Alexis de Tocqueville (1805–1859) arrives for his famous visit to America. There he discovers a society John Stuart Mill called, in a revealing exaggeration, "*all* middle class." While it is not an accurate picture of American socioeconomic relations, then or now, Mill's description captures the monolithic power of middle-class ideals on the moral horizon of modern liberal democracy. For the modern middle class invests with particular intensity in the pursuit of immanent contentment, expending its life in labor so as to secure the material conditions of this form of human flourishing. Moreover, as Tocqueville points out, democracy makes the majority into a moral authority and multiplies the points of contact between this authority and the individual human soul. Our democratic ideals thus impinge upon us with a uniquely pervasive pressure. Achieving happiness, here and now, appears to us not only as a desire but as a duty; immanent contentment becomes a command. This transformation heightens the restlessness endemic to the quest for immanent contentment, for it deepens our unhappiness by transforming it into a form of moral failure.[12]

Americans, Tocqueville observes, end up dispiriting and depressing themselves through their very pursuit of happiness. These free, prosperous, enlightened modern people are also "grave and almost sad, even in their pleasures." That experience of unexpected dissatisfaction drives a restless love of change, as we search for some amelioration of our condition that will relieve the existential unease that afflicts us when prosperity's satisfactions come to seem hollow and when others prove unable to give us the unmediated approbation we so ardently desire. In a democratic society, the restlessness that grows in the shadow of the ideal of immanent contentment becomes a politically decisive phenomenon. That restlessness explains the ritualistic idol-smashing so characteristic of modern societies, as we impose upon ourselves "the psychological equivalent of permanent revolution" in our quest to tear down the social barriers that seem to block our path to the contentment we believe it both our right and our obligation to enjoy.[13]

Tocqueville's admiring portrait of American democracy is thus darkened by a shadow of foreboding, an anticipation of what will become of our inner lives as the restless quest for immanent contentment expands its empire over them, and an intimation of how our disquiet will eventually come to undermine our political institutions. In this book, we seek to address that disquiet by considering the genesis and development of the ideal of happiness to which it is so intimately connected. For it is only when we understand this ideal in terms of the most decent human aspirations to which it speaks that we may begin to assess it dispassionately.

As Tocqueville might have predicted, a basic commitment of many modern societies—the commitment to liberalism—is today coming to seem increasingly questionable. Scholars concerned about this trend have been reexamining the philosophic anthropology that underwrites liberalism, some in order to defend it, others to explain why it has failed. In this book, we attempt to do justice to both sides of this argument, seeking at once to understand the deepest reasons for our attachment to the modern idea of happiness, as well as the thread of restless unease it weaves into the fabric of our common life. In so doing, we strive, like Tocqueville, to see "not differently, but further" than the parties of our time, the liberal and anti-liberal coalitions that are coming to define our moment's intellectual polarity. We hope thereby to point the way to a richer anthropological vantage point from which we might discern how to preserve what is best in our political order while addressing the source of our waxing disquiet.[14]

CHAPTER 1

Montaigne

The Art of Ordinary Life

The Self Emerges from the Wars of Religion

What is a human being? How should we order our personal and political lives so as best to fulfill our nature? These are the questions of philosophic anthropology, which modern peoples answer in a distinctive way. For moderns, a human being is a *self*. Selves organize their lives around a distinctive quest: the quest for immanent contentment. Beneath the quarrels of modern politics—left against right, libertarian against communitarian, liberal against conservative—this anthropology and the aim of life it implies stands as a common, background assumption. Our conflicting political visions are often debates over how best to govern human beings understood as selves and help them achieve the aim that follows from that self-understanding.

The self is not an abstract concept invented in a philosopher's peaceful study and then brought to bear on politics. It is a mode of self-understanding born from history, conceived in the midst of harsh political experience and intended to serve political life. Created during the European wars of religion of the sixteenth and seventeenth centuries, the self was intended from the outset to offer human beings a vision of their lives that would restrain the human tendency to deploy violence in the name of the sacred.

In France, the wars of religion were a particularly nasty three-way conflict, pitting Protestant and radical Catholic factions against one another and against a weak monarchy, alternately brutal and feckless. The wars began when Catholic *ultras* massacred dozens of Protestants in an improvised church at Vassy in 1562. They reached their nadir a decade later, on August 24, 1572: St. Bartholomew's Day, when thousands of Protestants had come to Paris to celebrate the wedding of their champion, Henri de Navarre, to the Catholic princess Marguerite de Valois, a marriage that might have united France's warring factions and brought peace to the nation. Instead, the Protestants were again massacred, this time on the order of the queen mother, Catherine de Medici, and her ineffective son, Charles IX, in what has been called the "Kristallnacht of the French monarchy." Some thirteen thousand were killed in Paris, and the slaughter spread throughout France. That winter, France endured a famine so terrible that men ate one another. The wars would continue, intermixed with bouts of plague, until Henri de Navarre gave up his Protestantism to succeed Henri III on the throne of France, supposedly explaining his change of religious allegiance with the famous quip that "Paris is well worth a Mass." In 1598, he issued the Edict of Nantes, which finally granted toleration to France's Huguenots and an uneasy peace to the nation.[1]

Michel de Montaigne lived through this whole drawn-out catastrophe, which he refers to as "the notable spectacle of our public death." The child of a family of merchants who had made their fortune selling dye, wine, and salted fish in Bordeaux, Montaigne was the first to take the name of the château his grandfather had purchased. Well educated, first at home and later at the College of Guyenne, he began a political career but met with sufficient frustration in that arena that he sold his office in the Bordeaux Parlement and retired to his château at thirty-nine—in 1572, the same year as the St. Bartholomew's Day massacre. He began writing a book, the *Essays*, that makes constant if sometimes indirect reference to the chaos of France's political life. All those swords were drawn, Montaigne writes, over a pedantic academic dispute over "the meaning of that syllable, *hoc*." He refers to the words *hoc est enim corpus meum*, "for this is my body," pronounced by priests at every Mass as the host is elevated, and the question of transubstantiation that was at the heart of the theological controversy. Montaigne suggests that one ought not have one's neighbors roasted alive over just how literally we should take that syllable.[2]

Against this backdrop of blood and fanaticism, Montaigne's book presents us with a charming depiction of a self engaged in the successful pursuit of immanent contentment. This contrast between the rich intelligence of Montaigne's private life and the stupid brutality of France's political life gives the *Essays* its pathos and helps the book resonate down through the ages. That contrast makes the basic case for the self: modern peoples think of ourselves as selves and pursue immanent contentment in part because other ways of thinking about ourselves and our purposes seem to us prone to slip into religious violence.[3]

To his contemporaries, who believed that the fate of their immortal souls hung in the balance of their religious disputes, Montaigne offered a simple if challenging alternative to their whole way of thinking about themselves: he suggests that they learn to die. Reversing the Christian memento mori, which reminds us of the vanity of this life so as to turn us toward the next one, the Montaignean version of "learning to die" rebuffs the transcendent aspirations of the human soul, confining our imaginations within the horizon of immanence. "We are never

at home, we are always beyond," Montaigne writes. "Fear, desire, and hope launch us toward the future, and rob us of the
sentiment and consideration of what *is*, to amuse us with what
will be, even when we will be no longer." He exhorts us to know
ourselves, teaching that we should "take hold of present goods
and settle ourselves into them." For "he who knows himself no
longer takes what is foreign for his own. He loves and cultivates
himself before anything else, refusing superfluous occupations
and useless projects." The human problem, as Montaigne presents it, is a natural but erroneous concern with what lies beyond our natural lives. Self-knowledge corrects nature so as to
bring it back to itself, to settle us into the present, the only time
naturally available to us.[4]

Though the critique of the Christian concern with eternal
life here is hardly subtle, the movement of Montaigne's thought
will carry him far beyond a simple anti-religious polemic. He
criticizes not only the Christian concern with eternity but *every*
movement of the restless human soul that takes us beyond ourselves: the love of knowledge, the love of honor, even the love
of virtue. He challenges us to stay *chez nous*, to learn to be at
home within ourselves and within our world, and to cease mea-
suring our lives against any transcendent goal or standard. He
challenges us to practice the art of immanent contentment.
That art transforms the soul into the self.

The Immanence of Humanism
and the Influence of Montaigne

Montaigne is the emblematic figure of Renaissance humanism
in France. Behind its philology, its antiquarianism, and its novel
artistic techniques, the daring assertion that gives Renaissance

humanism its immense vitality is that the human world, the natural world, can be *enough*: an arena adequate to the satisfaction of our longings, a world less fallen than the biblical story suggests. The fifteenth-century Italian Renaissance writer, architect, and artist Leon Battisti Alberti put the humanist point most sharply: "man is a mortal but happy god." Though Montaigne speaks with a humbler accent than unabashedly Promethean figures such as Alberti and Pico della Mirandola, his art of immanent contentment is of a piece with their humanist assertion of the adequacy of this life—of "nature, complete without grace," as Sainte-Beuve put it.[5]

Humanism is a great opening of our eyes to this world and its possibilities. The descriptive precision characteristic of Shakespeare in English and Montaigne in French implicitly makes the case that the world merits the loving attention their eyes devote to it. We do not need to experience our lives as always pointing toward some great beyond; we do not need to order our institutions with eternity always in mind. With the right adjustment of our societies, our science, and most of all ourselves, we can learn to see this world as our home, not our prison.[6]

There are many versions of this modern ambition to give up on the next world so as to flourish in this one: some are programs of political reform, others are blueprints for technological transformation. But the most personal version of this modern turn is psychological: an inward-focused effort to tame our desire to flee from ourselves and what Montaigne calls *l'humaine condition* so as to learn to loyally enjoy that condition—to find happiness, immanently. It is this psychological turn that brings the modern self into being.[7]

While Montaigne helps the modern self find its voice, the development of the self of course bears the mark of many, sometimes contradictory, influences: books such as Montaigne's but also self-portraits such as Rembrandt's, the Reformation's conception of an intimate, unmediated relationship between the Christian and his God, the growth of widespread silent reading, the perfection of the mirror, the slow replacement of the old feudal order with the new order of sovereign states, market economies, and bourgeois individuals—all of it played a part in this revolution in human self-understanding. Innovations of every sort, both mundane and momentous, have helped make us what we are, and the full list of such contributing causes is inexhaustible.[8]

But books do have influence, and few have more influence than Montaigne's—as was his plain intention. As Douglas I. Thompson points out, "Immediately upon securing a limited printing of the *Essais* in Bordeaux, Montaigne set out for the royal court in Paris, where he delivered copies to Henri III and other notables of the court by hand." The *Essays* helped revive Montaigne's checked social and political ambitions during his life, paving his way to the mayorality of Bordeaux and giving him the status that would allow him to serve as a go-between among France's quarreling princes. They would have a much larger impact after his death, becoming perhaps "the most read book in France and in Europe for the successive generations of the 17th century." French philosophy begins here, as does the tradition of the *moralistes*. Shakespeare also read Montaigne; he seems to have shared a copy of the *Essays* with Ben Johnson, and he may have known Montaigne's first English translator, John Florio, personally. Francis Bacon and Rene Descartes, the fathers of modern science, drank deep at the wells of Montaigne's skepticism and empiricism. Later writers—Voltaire and Diderot in the eighteenth century, Emerson and Nietzsche in the nineteenth, Virginia Woolf and Stefan Zweig in the twentieth—would all warm themselves at Montaigne's cheering fire. And Montaigne's attractions have never been limited to men and women of literary or philosophic inclinations. Herman Melville gave the *Essays* high place among "those books to which every serious mind of superior order occupying any active post of authority in the world naturally inclines." For the *Essays* satisfy the appetite of the serious and busy to read of "actual men and events . . . free from cant and convention," in brief chapters suited for the bedside table or the airport terminal. A book about everything, the *Essays* have succeeded in attracting a train of readers as broad as it is long.[9]

Montaigne has enjoyed this success in part because his art of immanent contentment appeals to and shapes the aspirations of an ever-broadening class that would increasingly come to define the modern world. As Nannerl Keohane writes, "Montaigne was engaged in forging new norms for disoriented individuals in a decaying world" and "depicts a life centered in the self" so ingeniously that he "succeed[s] in making such a self-centered life attractive." In his own time, that effort spoke with particular force to the ambitions of other men like himself, the class of *bourgeois gentilshommes*—wealthy, highly educated, often recently ennobled officeholders who had risen above their third-estate origins but were still forced to endure the disdain and occasional violence of sword-dragging *gentilshommes de race*. For them, the *Essays* helped "invent an ideal of the noble life" that was both "different and better" than the military ideal of the class they sought to displace. The ascent of these *bourgeois gentilshommes*, however, was only the beginning of a much larger shift in class dominance—a shift that would eventually see the ideal of the *gentilhomme* set aside altogether in favor of the ideal of the *bourgeois*. As Philippe Desan notes, "It is possible to see Montaigne as one of the best representatives of a bourgeois ethic" that would become dominant with the rise of the modern market and modern politics. The Montaignean self and its art of immanent contentment powerfully align with the basic social currents of modern life.[10]

Montaigne's influence, direct and indirect, has helped us come to understand ourselves, and the happiness we seek, in a distinctly modern way. Although his work is sprawling, self-consciously disordered, and at times, by his own admission, contradictory, he remarks in the midst of a particularly disjointed chapter, "It is the lazy reader who loses my subject, not I." Montaigne has a unified intention and self-consciously leads his reader through "an unprecedented genre of spiritual exercise" so as to alter that reader's self-understanding. His view is powerful, plausible, and presented in prose so lively that Emerson could remark, "Cut these words and they would bleed." With the aid of all the other currents that help fashion the modern self, he gives us the anthropology that stands in the background of modern politics.[11]

The Soul and the Self

Becoming a self requires a transformation of our desires, so that we might come to see immanent contentment as the proper and adequate aim of human life. To do so, we must practice an art of living Montaigne describes in an image of *circumscription*:

> The course of our desires must be circumscribed and restrained to the tight limit of the closest and most contiguous good things. Moreover, their course should be directed not in a straight line that ends up elsewhere, but in a circle, of which the two points grasp one another and meet in ourselves by a brief contour.[12]

Our desires do not naturally run in any such circular course. We are by nature restless: our desires run in a straight line that ends up elsewhere, as the authors of the classical and Christian traditions in which Montaigne is steeped testify. Augustine cries out to his God that "you have made us for yourself and restless is our heart until it comes to rest in you." Socrates describes *eros*—the needy, never-satisfied longing for immortality and wisdom—as the vital center of the human soul. The Torah tells the story of a homeless people wandering in the wilderness, a story that Christianity will transform into its vision of human life as a pilgrimage, a voyage through a foreign land on the way to our eternal home. These stories and images go with the grain of a self-consciously mortal animal, who knows that nature condemns him to die, resents it, and gives voice to his longing to transcend nature's limitations in everything from philosophy to psalms. The Montaignean art of moral naturalism cuts against this grain. Nature must be transformed so as to bring it back to itself.[13]

To effect this transformation, Montaigne relocates the standard of nature. Both the classical tradition and the Bible place human beings at nature's apex, arrogating to them what Montaigne calls an "imaginary kingship." Montaigne seeks to lower our sights and humble our self-image. The longest chapter of the *Essays*, the "Apology for Raymond Sebond," begins with an enormous catalog of the marvelous powers of animals, which Montaigne deploys to combat the presumption that leads us to believe that we rightly exercise dominion over creation. What do we know about where we really stand in the order of things? We cannot, after all, enter into the minds of animals or decipher their language. We know they possess powers we do not, from the sonar of the bat to the sting of the jellyfish; we can only guess at what their senses might reveal to them that is totally unknown to us. "When I play with my cat," Montaigne asks, "who knows whether she amuses herself with me more than I do with her?"[14]

Such wonder at the animal world stands opposed to humanity's pride as nature's "master and emperor." That pride emerges most starkly in the hunt, which Montaigne's contemporaries celebrated as the sport of kings, and which he detests. As Rousseau would later point out, the hunt does indeed develop human courage, patience, and cunning, but only at the price of making our first true experience of self-consciousness an experience of gory dominance over the beasts we kill. The hunt makes human beings into animals both bloodthirsty and impressive. As Leon Kass has written, "The aspiration to live better than cows and pigs seems to come along with the appetite to eat them." Montaigne, who cannot bear to see a chicken's neck wrung without distress, and thinks our attempts to rise above our own animality breed self-loathing and derangement, does not think the bargain worth the price.[15]

Whereas classical philosophy finds in reason both the faculty that sets us apart from the animals and the faculty that should guide us, Montaigne argues that it is our unruly imagination, rather than our reason, that marks us off from the other animals—to our detriment. For from man's imagination "are born the principal sources of the troubles that oppress him: sin, illness, irresolution, trouble, and despair." The human problem lies not in our failure to cultivate our distinctively human faculties but in our misbegotten and doomed attempts to rise above ourselves. We realize our nature not in differentiating ourselves from the animals but in following them: "Our wisdom learns from the beasts themselves the most useful teachings for the greatest and most necessary parts of our life: how we must live and die, manage our goods, love and care for our children."

Instead of the exalted examples of human flourishing celebrated by the tradition, Montaigne points us to animals and peasants—the most humble of human beings—as closer to nature than we are. For both beasts and peasants corrupt themselves less with the unruly activity of the imagination.[16]

Montaigne's art of immanent contentment teaches a human being to seek happiness like a cat lying in the sun. The full novelty of this understanding of human flourishing becomes visible only when we compare it to the models of the good life put forward by the tradition Montaigne inherits and transforms.

How Mere Life Becomes the Good Life

For all the internal disagreement among the authors who constitute the classical and Christian tradition Montaigne inherits, they tend to agree on one central point: the existence of some "one thing needful," a single form of perfection that gives meaning and happiness to human existence. In their contrasting ways, the authors of this tradition often insist that successfully approaching some such transcendent standard is what makes human life worth living.[17]

Socrates, who famously tells an Athenian jury that "the unexamined life is not worth living for a human being," is the greatest single standard-bearer of the philosophers in this tradition. For all their doctrinal differences, the ancient philosophers usually reflect his view that the activity of philosophy itself is the indispensable activity, in the absence of which one is better off dead. Sparta's Leonidas and Rome's Brutus embody another ideal of the best way of life, the ideal of the citizen. Citizenship is to them what philosophy is to Socrates: the thing that makes life worthwhile. To a Roman such as Cato the Younger, the only alternative to citizenship is slavery, a fate worse than death; Cato preferred to die gruesomely at his own hands rather than accept that alternative. For Christians, by contrast, the Kingdom of Heaven is the pearl of great price, which one should sell everything to possess. The call to live as Christ lived entails the willingness to take up one's cross in pursuit of that pearl, in the manner of the martyrs if necessary. Life without Christ is hell on earth and damnation hereafter.[18]

Montaigne contests the common principle that binds these contrasting ways of life together. In spite of his immense learning in classical and Christian texts, Montaigne does not step forward under any of the traditional standards—philosophic, political, or religious. "Authors communicate themselves to the people by some particular and foreign mark," he writes. "I am the first to do so by my universal being, as Michel de Montaigne, not as a grammarian or poet or jurist." Montaigne does not speak to us as a man of this or that profession, an exemplar of this or that well-trodden way. He does not speak to us as a philosopher, a citizen, or an aspiring saint. Instead, he speaks to us simply as a human being. "Mon métier et mon art, c'est vivre," Montaigne writes: "my work and my art is living." Living "human life in conformity with its natural condition," without seeking after any other condition. Montaigne answers the old debate's central question, "How should I live?" by saying simply, "Live."[19]

The presentation of a simply human life as the good life—an unspecialized life, a life that does not seek to live up to *any* transcendent standard—marks what is perhaps the most significant moral innovation of Montaigne's momentous era. As Pierre Manent points out, two of the era's most recognized innovators, Niccolò Machiavelli and John Calvin, both seek to reform existing spheres of life: Machiavelli argues for an expansion of the moral latitude of politics; Calvin argues for a reformation of the

Church and our relationship with God. Montaigne, by contrast, brings a new stratum of human life into view: mere life, life for its own sake, life without the orienting norms of philosophy, politics, or faith. For Socrates, for Cato, and for St. Augustine, and for the whole Western world that was shaped by these models, life without these orienting norms is not worth living; it is subhuman, it is *no life at all*. Montaigne reminds all of them that before they are philosophers, citizens, or saints, they are human beings. His great originality is to exemplify *life simply as the good life*, and thereby to bring the value of such a life into our vision.[20]

One of his countless aphorisms captures this perfectly: "We are great fools: 'he has passed his life in idleness,' we say, 'I have done nothing today.' What, have you not lived? That is not only your fundamental occupation, but your most illustrious one." This sentiment has become common sense, even a platitude. But the very currency of such a platitude implies a widespread rejection of the classical and biblical dispositions. For all the variety of their ambitions, the heroes of the classical and Christian traditions all refuse to accept the limits of time and death. A philosopher such as Plato strives to merge his mind with the eternal truth. A conqueror such as Alexander the Great lives for the sake of immortal glory. A saint such as Augustine seeks to rest his own heart in the very bosom of the God who created the universe. It seems in the nature of such souls—and indeed of human life as such—to seek to transcend our mortal human plane, just as sparks fly upward. But to become a self, to seek one's happiness immanently, is to bring us back home to ourselves by setting all these traditional aspirations aside so as to discover the richness of life in its ordinariness.[21]

Doing so entails a transformation of our whole intellectual and moral lives, beginning with a profound reconceptualization of *what we are.* That transformation begins with a dramatically new version of the quest for self-knowledge at the heart of philosophy.

From Knowledge of Man to Knowledge of Me

How do we come to understand ourselves? Philosophy, Montaigne writes, "draws our soul out of us" in its quest after truths that do not change. The concepts it discovers mediate our knowledge of ourselves: we consider what we are in the light of an ostensibly universal understanding of virtue, happiness, and human nature. Can we really transcend ourselves in this way, though? Philosophers have spent centuries seeking answers to such universal questions, and they have failed to find them. Their quests to understand human nature have led them to define man as everything from a rational and political animal to a bird with two feet and no feathers. Their inquiries into the nature of virtue have led them to undermine every moral law, from the prohibition on cannibalism to the incest taboo. Their searches for happiness, for the summum bonum, have produced at least two hundred and eighty-eight rival conceptions of it. Their attempts to live out these visions of the good life have often proved absurd, from the stargazer Thales tumbling into a well to the cynic Diogenes making his home in a barrel. And yet no proof of the failures of their enterprise has been sufficient to bring them to self-knowledge and detach them from their gratifying self-image as the sole human beings to have discerned the secret of living well.[22]

Montaigne chronicles the follies of the philosophers at great length in the "Apology for Raymond Sebond." The case he makes there for philosophy's failure forms the background of his effort to reconceive how we should seek self-understanding and what we find when we do. "Because philosophy has been unable to find a way to tranquility that is good for all," he writes, "let each man seek it individually!" His art of circumscription individualizes the quest for self-knowledge. "I study myself more than any other subject," he writes in the midst of a highly particular account of his bodily habits, "that is my physics, that is my metaphysics." He transforms self-knowledge from knowledge of man into knowledge of *me*.[23]

In French, the term "the self"—*le moi*—is an abstraction formed by placing the definite article before the first-person pronoun. Although the always concrete Montaigne does not coin that abstract term by bringing *le* and *moi* together (a distinction that seems to belong to Pascal), his decision to write so extensively about himself—*moi*—is a major break with tradition and helps legitimate the self as an object of speech and thought. On his first page, Montaigne writes, "Je suis moy-mesmes la matiere de mon livre" (I am myself the subject of my book), and tells us that we should not waste our time on a subject so vain and frivolous. From an older point of view, such vanity and frivolity are real moral problems: human beings are all too prone to be vain and frivolous when they should be humble and serious. The need to avoid these dangers justified "the traditional interdiction weighing on the first person." Montaigne violates that traditional interdiction more than eight thousand times over the course the *Essays*. He makes himself the *Essays'* exclusive subject. Though he talks about everything, he does so merely to reveal himself more fully, using the stimuli the world offers to his mind to prompt the activity of his judgment and the revelation of his nature. He talks about the poems of Homer and the exploits of Epaminondas, the songs of the cannibals and the arms of the Parthians, because doing so allows him to show us something about *him*.

The failure of the search for the truth about humanity in general makes speech about oneself fittingly modest. For it is modest about what we can know.[24]

Montaigne circumscribes the great Platonic quest of philosophy to discern the forms of the good and the beautiful into the more modest, personal quest to discover what he calls his *forme maistresse*, his master pattern, a "natural form" that is entirely particular. That mistress form is an immanent true self, at once natural and built up through experience, an enduring unity of character that "fights against education and against the tempest of the passions which oppose it." Montaigne offers examples of it at work in himself across his life: the precocious independence of mind with which he judged great matters for himself while still a child, the Latin—his first language—that bubbles up from his entrails in moments of shock, the long-set habits that define him in old age, from sleeping alone to rubbing his teeth with a napkin. It is a thing he continually discovers, for any new accident of life can reveal Montaigne to himself more fully.[25]

As these examples indicate, Montaigne's *forme maistresse* cannot be reduced to pure, inborn nature, long-standing habit, an accident of fortune, or a work of art created through the act of self-fashioning. It is all of those things: Montaigne both speaks of a "natural form" and asks that we "call the habits and condition of each of us *nature*"; he tells us that part of him was produced by something so accidental as a cough and that, in making his book, he "paints himself in colors clearer than my original ones." He can reveal the concoction of nature, habit, fortune, and art that constitutes a self only by means of the *Essays* as a whole, a book he describes as "consubstantial with its author." To seek to write *the whole* of oneself down, as Montaigne does in the *Essays*, is to engage in a quest for unmediated self-understanding. For Montaigne strives to write himself down without the mediation of philosophy's general terms: he does not sort himself into parts passing and permanent, laudable and reprehensible, natural and artificial, low and high. He offers the self-portrait his quest produces to his reader without theorizing himself, in an act of unmediated self-revelation.[26]

The *Essays* thus constitute a new mode of self-understanding, autobiographical rather than theoretical, individual rather than general. But they also constitute a new kind of moral gesture—an act of self-revealing authenticity. That act signals a new conception of virtue, or rather a reconception of moral life that will largely dispense with the term "virtue" as such. Understanding ourselves as selves rather than souls, immanent beings rather than beings oriented toward the transcendent, necessarily entails such a fundamental reconsideration of the nature of moral life.

Immanent Virtues, or "Non-Reproachable Qualities"

If, with Montaigne, we take the internal standard of the mistress form as our basic moral touchstone, our conception of moral life contracts and turns inward. An immanent conception of what we are entails an immanent conception of morality. The soul's vaunting aspirations to walk in the footsteps of God, to outdo death through immortal deeds, to exercise that intellectual part of ourselves that Aristotle called most divine, is replaced by the determination to be faithful to our particular human selves. We seek to be "neither an angel nor Cato" but a man—and an individual man, with a proper name, at that.[27]

By means of this substitution of being true to oneself for being close to the immortal, Montaigne helps create the modern moral standard of what Lionel Trilling calls sincerity:

Who would not wish to be true to his own self? True, which is to say loyal, never wavering in his constancy. True, which is to say honest: there are no subterfuges in dealing with him. True, which is to say, as carpenters and bricklayers use the word, precisely aligned with him.

Montaigne, who never claims to be wise, heroic, or holy, does claim to be sincere. The self-revelatory project of the *Essays*, he remarks, needs only fidelity to its subject to succeed, "and that is in it, as sincere and as pure as can be found." He is a man unified in appearance and substance: "my face gives me away immediately," he writes; I am what I seem. He speaks the same language to everyone, even princes, to whom he does not "refrain from saying anything, however grave or burning." He never makes extravagant promises—not to the women he loved, not even to the kidnappers who held him for ransom during one particularly tense moment of the religious wars. He does not allow what he is willing to say to outstrip what he is willing to do. The immanent, self-referential standard of sincerity dedicates the self to a distinctive form of integrity.[28]

Fidelity to oneself is a virtue that any man, in principle, may master. It does not require great brilliance or austerity or daring; it requires only the willingness and determination to match our words to our deeds and our deeds to our words. We become willing to say what we think and do what we say when we circumscribe ourselves, giving up our habit of taking ourselves too seriously. Montaigne's frankness expresses itself in a cultivated carelessness in dress, word, and deed—in one's whole existential attitude. He calls this cultivated carelessness *nonchalance* and compares it to the "disorderliness that one sees in the dress of our youth," who wear their cloaks like scarves and leave their stockings ill-arranged on purpose, not unlike the students of our own age who believe the proper place for flip-flops is everywhere. Montaigne can be careless in his dress because he puts on no airs; he can be free with his words because he has nothing to hide. "I speak to the page," he writes, "like I speak to the first person I run into." Honesty is here the offspring of the absence of pretense.[29]

This nonchalance must be learned, because taking oneself too seriously comes quite naturally to human beings. Montaigne describes a man of his acquaintance who thought it a cosmic injustice to find himself on his deathbed before he could compose his history of this or that king. Montaigne thinks we are all a little like that and must teach ourselves to let go of our passionate self-importance. It is a lesson worth learning, for to learn to be nonchalant is to learn to be free. It allows us to cope with fortune by being neither her master nor her slave. Montaigne's self-portrait shows us a man who both delights in every human pleasure and stomachs distress, disorder, and disease with firmness; it shows us a man grateful for good when it comes and able to do without when need be. He learns to be nonchalant in the face of death itself: "I want death to find me planting my cabbages," he tells us, "but nonchalant about her, and still more about my unfinished garden."[30]

This nonchalance is the moral reflection of Montaigne's understanding of man's place in the universe. "When the vines freeze in my village," Montaigne writes, "my priest argues that it is the ire of God on the human race, and judges that the cannibals already have the pip." All of us tend to read will into the vagaries of nature, to believe that it has us in mind both when the sun shines upon us and when the hail comes down:

But whoever presents to himself, as in a painting, this great image of our mother nature in her entire majesty; who reads in her face so general and constant variety; who remarks himself therein, and not only himself, but a whole kingdom, as a dot made with a very fine brush: he alone estimates things according to their true proportions.

To immanentize our self-understanding is to learn to take ourselves as little seriously as the universe does. Doing so helps us fend off what Nietzsche calls the "greatest danger of spiritual unfreedom": "the sentiment of personal providence." "Is there any more dangerous seduction," Nietzsche writes, "that might tempt one to renounce one's faith in the gods of Epicurus who have no care and are unknown, and to believe instead in some petty deity who is full of care and personally knows every little hair on our head?" In Montaigne's words, proud, self-pitying man imagines that the "admirable motion of the celestial vault, the eternal light of those torches rolling so proudly above his head, the fearful movement of that infinite sea, were established and have lasted so many centuries for his convenience and his service." Nature is not made for us, nature does not punish us; nature takes no interest in the personal fate of men, whose passing is no different in her eyes from the passing of oysters or daisies. To suppose otherwise gives cosmic license to our ubiquitous self-obsession.[31]

Montaigne's juxtaposition of his nonchalant attitude toward human existence with that of his priest is pointed. While many Christians understand better than Montaigne's priest the difficulty of surmising what providence intends in human and natural events, the Christian God is indeed a personal God who counts every hair on our heads, a God to whom the events of our lives matter. Montaigne—who steeped himself in the poetry of Lucretius, the greatest exponent of the Epicurean gods who take no interest in human things—finds rough comfort in "being included where all are included," in seeing himself as cosmically unimportant.[32]

Montaignean nonchalance is rooted in judgment—judgments he has made about himself, about nature, and about his own cosmic insignificance. Montaigne judges things differently than does his priest and makes no apologies for that independence of mind. Indeed, independent judgment is the cardinal intellectual virtue of the circumscribed self and the aim of the self's education. As Rousseau will after him, Montaigne pays the closest attention to education; he imagines a tutor and a pupil to serve as models for his readers and designs a curriculum for them intended to issue in independence of mind, heart, and habits. He would have that pupil read all the great authors of antiquity without ever submitting to their authority. When he finds himself judging as Plato does, he should say that this shared opinion is "no more according to Plato than according to me." Broad reading and experience give our judgment the capaciousness it needs to exercise its function without leading strings.[33]

Judgment replaces knowledge and wisdom in Montaigne's conception of virtue because it makes no pretensions to universality. While Montaigne judges everything, he claims to do so without supposing himself to be a benchmark. "I have not that common error of judging another according to myself," he writes. "[I] consider him simply in himself, without relation, molding him according to his own model." He judges others for their consistency with themselves rather than their consistency with him. Though he does not try to be heroic, he does not doubt the heroism of the Spartans at Thermopylae; though he does not try to be chaste, he does not doubt the chastity of the Capuchin monks of his time. Here, he marks his difference with writers such as Machiavelli and Guicciardini, who thought that no human action was ever motivated by reason or virtue: "It seems to each that the mistress form of nature is in him, the touchstone and reference for all other forms. Movements that do not accord with his are feigned and artificial. What bestial stupidity!" Such men generalize their morally limited selves, making themselves the mediating term in their judgments of others. Montaigne would relate to others as he does to himself: without any such mediation.[34]

Generosity in judgments of others is one of the Montaignean social virtues; humanity and justice are the others. Just as he tips his hat to the excellences of others, he recognizes something of himself even in their vices and judges them with a "marvelous laxity toward mercy and indulgence." Men can sometimes be monsters. But as Montaigne remarks, "I have seen no monster or miracle in the world more evident than myself." The inward regard of the Montaignean self allows us to recognize the monstrous within, to see that it is not really foreign to us. We thereby learn to see the monstrous in others with humanity.[35]

The circumscription that contains us within ourselves and compels us to come to grips with the monstrous within also teaches us justice, for it allows us to let others be. "Whoever sees right into my soul would not find me culpable of anyone's affliction or ruin, nor of vengeance or envy, nor of public offense against the laws, nor of novelty and trouble, nor of failing my word," Montaigne writes. A soul that encloses itself learns in the process to keep its fingers out of other people's pockets, to accept its place in the order of things, and to avoid grasping after goods that it could possess only at the price of harming others. It learns the art of minding one's own business and giving to each his due.[36]

These characteristics—which Montaigne calls "non-reproachable qualities," not "virtues," perhaps in self-conscious retreat from universal and transcendent moral language—are the defining moral attributes of the circumscribed self and stand opposed to what he calls our "ordinary vices": the treachery, disloyalty, tyranny, and cruelty he saw on display around him every day in the bloody, dishonest, and divided France of the sixteenth century. Such vices result from the restless soul's desire to reach out beyond itself, to impose itself, to rule, advance, and climb. The Montaignean movement of circumscription checks these vices at their source.[37]

Having circumscribed those desires, Montaigne concerns himself with the rule of self rather than the rule of others. He estimates the character of Alexander, who knew how to conquer the world, less highly than the character of a man who knows how to live life in conformity to the human condition in private. Alexander's tutor, Aristotle, held that "office shows the man": he thinks our character most tested and best revealed in positions of public power. Montaigne thinks Aristotle has it backward. "Any man can play his part in the farce and represent an honest man on the stage," he says, "but inside and in his breast, where all is permitted to us, where all is hidden, to be regulated there, that is the point." The test of office pales in comparison to the test of private, inner life: "There is no one but yourself who knows whether you are cowardly and cruel, or loyal and devout." Others guess at what we are; we can fob them off with pleasant appearances. We alone can peer beneath our own surface. To contain our moral horizon within ourselves is to subject ourselves to the judgment of the one judge really in a position to know.[38]

To circumscribe our restless souls is to turn the psychic energies that animate the philosopher, the citizen, and the saint toward the humbler work of establishing our internal coherence. If we do so, we can speak and act with the nonchalance that comes with having nothing to hide. We can judge every-thing, without servility or self-importance, taking our true mea-sure and learning to live within it. We can be generous, humane, and just toward others, giving to each his due, and sometimes more than his due. We can be whole.

Montaigne articulates these "non-reproachable qualities" with charm and self-deprecation. He makes the moral life of a self attractive by asking his reader to affirm only that such a life should be permissible, not that it should be a model for all. In the intervening centuries, however, these moral qualities have come to be such a model and to predominate over the virtues of the premodern tradition: while we still admire wisdom, holi-ness, and heroism, they do not seem to us required to make a life worth living. Inauthenticity, self-abasement, presumption, hypocrisy, inhumanity, and injustice, however—these are real and damning vices, failures to meet the human minimum. For the Montaignean moral qualities—frankness and nonchalance in our speech and deeds, independence and generosity in our judgments, humanity and justice in our conduct—are within the reach of everyone; their opposite vices wholly avoidable failures to do our duty to ourselves and to others.[39]

The Arts of Immanent Contentment, Solitary and Social

The summit of Montaigne's effort to reconceive what we are, how we know ourselves, and the moral standards by which we should live is a new understanding of happiness: happiness un-derstood as immanent contentment. He depicts his pursuit of happiness so understood as an art of presence, balancing, and self-containment, through which he achieves what Virginia

Woolf calls "a miraculous adjustment of all the wayward parts that constitute the human soul." That art is designed to keep the self feeling interested in life yet free of constraining attachments, engaged with others yet complete in itself.[40]

"When I dance, I dance," Montaigne writes. When he dances, he does not allow his mind to wander off and brood over his struggles as a writer, his quarrels with his steward, or the political intrigues brewing around him. He does not consider his partner's lineage or her wealth, though he might well admire her beauty. He does not haunt himself with the thought that dancing might be sinful. He just dances. To dance when we dance, talk when we talk, and eat when we eat is to apply the art of circumscription to the question of happiness. It is to know how to be where we are, keeping the soul at home and engaged in our activities and pleasures; it is to live more fully because we do so with our whole selves. The Montaignean art of immanent contentment seeks presence, or what has come to be called mindfulness. It allows us to enjoy the "sentiment of our own existence," in Rousseau's language: the simple goodness of being alive.[41]

This art teaches us to take pleasure in solitude—a condition most human beings are too restless to endure, much less enjoy. Montaigne himself experiences the difficulty of solitude when, upon reaching middle age, he sells his office in the Bordeaux Parlement, retires to his estate, and begins passing the bulk of his days in his library. Without any concrete project, his mind bolts like a runaway horse, giving itself more trouble than it ever took for others and begetting a frightening succession of "chimeras and fantastic monsters." To deal with the strange thoughts to which his soul gives birth in his solitary idleness, Montaigne writes them down, with the intention of making his mind ashamed of itself. But shame never comes. Instead, his self-reflective art teaches him to marvel and laugh at himself, to become his own companion: "We have a soul that can turn in on itself; it can keep itself company." Solitude brings the self's internal resources to the surface; Montaigne's art of immanent contentment deploys those resources so as to teach the self to experience the presence of its own thoughts and dreams as fullness rather than ennui.[42]

To open this space within ourselves and fill it with imaginative activity is to build for ourselves an *arrière-boutique*, a back shop of the soul, in which we may establish our "real liberty and principal retreat." Therein, we should "hold our ordinary conversation between us and ourselves, and so private that no acquaintance or foreign communication finds a place there; there we must discourse and laugh as if without wife, without children and without goods, without retinue or servants so that, when the occasion arrives for us to lose them, it will be nothing new for us to do without them." To experience our inner lives as a form of fullness is to establish a psychic retreat in which we may live as if without any human tie.[43]

This paean to solitude can sound harsh. Should a man with a wife and a child really talk to himself as if they didn't exist? The ability to keep oneself company in this back shop, to find even in one's stranger musings matter for reflection rather than dread, however, offers comfort for the inevitable loss of those we love, as it quiets the fear of being alone. It also allows us to overcome our self-alienating desire to step outside of ourselves. It thereby makes our contentment truly immanent—locating happiness not only within the confines of the world but within the confines of the self.[44]

The Montaignean art of immanent contentment does not, however, sentence us to solitary confinement. Rather, it allows Montaigne to bring his attitude of nonchalance to bear on all the self's external engagements: "In household management, in study, in hunting and in every other exercise, we must go up to the last limits of pleasure, and but guard ourselves from engaging still further, where it begins to be mingled with pain." Montaigne takes what one might call a "balanced" approach to running his household, neither obsessing over everything nor letting it all go to seed. While he loves books, he loves only "pleasant and easy" ones, "which entertain me, or those that console me and counsel me to regulate my life or my death": Plutarch and Ovid, not Aristotle and Aquinas. Though a most curious man, he never allows that curiosity to morph into the pedantic pride of the scholar or the Promethean ambition of the philosopher. While his curiosity drives him to travel and discover the ways of men of other lands, he travels without the exalted purposes of the pilgrim or the explorer. All such ambitions—to perfect a home or a mind, to be sacred or to be first—take us away from ourselves.[45]

The balance Montaigne seeks to strike between engagement and restraint, presence and self-containment, comes strikingly to the fore in his meditations on sex and love. Montaigne takes a frank, natural, bodily interest in beauty and sexual pleasure and discusses the matter with an effrontery sufficient to have caused his most erotic chapter, "Of Some Verses of Virgil," to be torn out of the copies of the *Essays* that were furnished to convents in the seventeenth century. Lampooning those who would hold themselves aloof from this natural human need— "let us see them square the circle while they are topping their wives!"—he gives us a frank, free, affectionate, and playful picture of erotic life. He does not see a glimpse of the divine in the eyes of his beloved, as does Plato. A beautiful young body is a beautiful young body—why does it need to be anything more? To spiritualize love is to betray it, and to wish that both those we love and we ourselves were something other than we are, capable of a more perfect and enduring union than that to which nature pleasantly invites us. In keeping the soul at home, attentive to its desires, the body teaches the soul a counterintuitive form of moderation. For to keep love grounded, checking its tendency toward celestial flight, is to constrain *eros* within the confines of immanence.[46]

To give the body and its pleasures their place in our lives both moderates the mind's desires and does justice to the truth about our nature. Our happiness cannot be an exclusively mental experience, for there is more to the self than the mind. "I hate to have people order us to keep our minds in the clouds while our bodies are at table," Montaigne writes: when we eat, we should eat. If we hold our minds back from the satisfactions of the body, we do an injustice to half of our being. We should not wallow at table, but we should "attend" to it, "sitting at it, not lying down on it." The art of being where we are is an art of maintaining our equilibrium—attentive to food, drink, and company, appreciative of them, as free from the tyranny of aloofness as from the tyranny of desire. The pleasures of the body can be gifts we gratefully receive, not fetters we flee and fear, if we make moderation the servant rather than the enemy of our immanent desires.[47]

The Montaignean art of happiness finds contentment in moderate attentiveness to both the pleasures of the body and the pleasures of mind, to both solitude and sociability. The distinctive character of the social elements of that art lead Ann Hartle to credit him with nothing less than "the invention of society." He praises what he calls "commerce" with friends, women, and books, and offers rich encomiums to the social arts of conversation and correspondence. In so doing, he is describing a novel kind of social world—a world that the *Essays* themselves, as one of the first common reference points of France's emerging class of readers, help bring into being. Social life, self-consciously restrained and set apart from politics, family, and religion, becomes an end in itself, a thing we pursue for the pleasures intrinsic to it. It thereby departs from the traditional forms of human association: city and kingdom, family and church. In all of those forms, social ties are bound by the serious stuff of law, blood, and God; the social is a point of contact with the sacred. Sociality in the service of immanent contentment does not seek to sanctify itself.[48]

Society so understood makes sense as part of a model of human contentment that is, above all, self-contained. The human goods, as understood by the thinkers of old, always launch us on some flight: toward God, toward glory, toward the abiding form of the beautiful. Montaigne shows us how the human world can be reimagined as a whole unto itself. Reimagining contentment in this way does not immobilize the self; it rather sets it free to wander and seek variety, oscillating between solitude and society, pleasures to delight the body and curiosities to intrigue the mind. It is proper to indulge this questing movement, indeed to encourage it. Dilettantism becomes a kind of moral requirement, for the danger is not in flitting hither and thither but in digging too deep.

Montaigne thus shows us how a skeptic seeks happiness. In the following century, John Locke will famously remark that trying to find a single summum bonum, one highest good that can make all men happy, is like trying to satisfy all men's palates with cheese or lobsters. Since no such summum bonum is known to us, Locke will develop the political philosophy of liberalism, designed to let everyone choose the good for him- or herself. Here, though, Montaigne already depicts in a life the practical reality of the pursuit of happiness as undertaken by a skeptic with no prejudice in favor of austerity. Such a man does not choose between the cheese and the lobsters—he orders both. To the ancient adage "nothing too much" he adds the modern corollary "nothing too little." Multiplying and varying one's pleasures and pursuits allows one to remain nonchalant about all of them.[49]

Friendship as Unmediated Approbation

There is, however, a single, pointed exception to the studied nonchalance with which Montaigne pursues immanent contentment. In one of the *Essays'* most famous chapters, he tells the story of his friendship with Étienne de la Boétie, with whom he formed a tight and precipitous bond when the two were young magistrates in the Parlement of Bordeaux. That friendship endured until La Boétie died, with Montaigne at his bedside, four years later. It was an exceptional union, he tells us, involving the entire mind and will of each partner, something fortune accomplishes only once every three centuries. No common quality, no shared pleasure, can account for a friendship so total. Montaigne explains it with what Alexander Nehamas calls "the most moving statement about friendship ever made": "because it was he, because it was I."[50]

The union of friendship surpasses all other social ties in its freedom and wholeness. All other forms of human association—ties between brothers and sisters, parents and children, lovers and spouses—are less chosen, more encumbered by entanglements of law and property, and more riven with passion and rivalry. Playing on the title of his friend's most famous writing, *De la servitude volontaire* (On voluntary servitude), Montaigne describes theirs as a union formed by *liberté volontaire* (voluntary liberty) and uses words derived from *liberté* and *volonté* some twenty-five times in the twelve brief pages of his essay.

Our love of our friends is not pressed on us by insistent desire or clouded by the will to pass on or inherit; the pall of institutionalized permanence does not enshroud it. We love our friends not for their beauty, their wealth, or even their intelligence but for some "quintessence of all this mixture": we love them because they are who they are, the companions with whom we freely share our whole human experience. We experience that sharing as a good in itself.[51]

Montaigne exalts friendship in spite of his habitual suspicion of the exalted because friendship is the social expression of his loyalty to the human condition. Friends form a whole; the union does not look beyond itself. As Nehamas points out, Montaigne steadfastly refuses to say why he and La Boétie were friends; for to give a reason would be to introduce a third term into their bond and thus begin to look beyond it. If we say, "I love my friend for his wit," we open ourselves to the possibility of finding someone wittier; if we say, "I love my friend for his honesty," we open ourselves to the possibility of finding someone still more honest. Montaigne goes to extremes in affirming the wholeness and even mystery of his union with La Boétie because that wholeness and mystery keeps human affection off the Socratic ladder of love, which leads from the beauty of a single beloved to the unchanging, disembodied form of the beautiful. Socrates's ladder could be thought to lead us to the divine and eternal only at the cost of leaving the human behind. Montaigne never sets foot on it.[52]

The friendship Montaigne attributes to himself and La Boétie takes the form of unmediated, complete, personal approbation. It is unmediated—there is no reason, no abstract good, that links the two men involved, who are instead tied directly to one another, self to self. It is complete—it encompasses the whole of each man's being. And it is personal—an act of one situated, particular, mysterious, willing, and intellectual being toward another. In this, Montaignean friendship partakes of a "creatural realism [that] has broken through the Christian frame in which it arose." In such friendship, one friend offers the whole of himself up to the other; his gift is gratefully received and reciprocated in the other friend's gift of self.[53]

Montaigne emphasizes the rare and extraordinary character of this friendship, which is an exceptional escape from the more ordinary ties of blood, utility, and pleasure. But his chapter expresses a longing that will capture the modern imagination. Modern human beings hope to experience, with other human beings, the extraordinary intimacy the Psalmist experiences with his God: a God who knows his every thought, sin, and desire, and nonetheless loves him as His own. But where the God of the Psalms at once judges the sin and forgives the sinner, modern human beings want such intimate knowledge without any such judgment or need for forgiveness.[54]

This extraordinary social tie, like the rest of the Montaignean art of immanent contentment, lies beyond the boundaries of the political. The life devoted to friendship and happiness so understood, however, not only permits but demands a new understanding of our political attachments.

Montaigne's Conservatism of Convenience

To understand the aim of human life as immanent contentment puts politics in its place—and religion together with it. The two are inseparable in Montaigne's world; he refers to this complex unity as "notre police ecclesiastique" (our politico-religious order). Montaigne's basic stance toward that politico-religious order is conservative; he repeatedly affirms his loyalty to his king, the laws of France, and the Catholic Church. But he makes that affirmation from the vantage point of the distinctive anthropology he articulates in the *Essays*—his novel understanding of our nature and its fulfillment. He thereby alters the meaning of such allegiances even as he professes them, exemplifying the novel bearing toward political and religious institutions that modern philosophic anthropology underwrites.

The *Essays* expound a theological-political conservatism born from the experience of civil war. Montaigne tells us that he is "disgusted with all novelty, whatever face it wears, and with reason, for I have seen very harmful effects of it." Though he details the crimes of his own, Catholic side in the wars of religion in both direct and indirect ways in the *Essays*, he lays the blame for initiating the wars at the feet of the Protestants. In a *police ecclesiastique* such as sixteenth-century France, the Huguenots' religious innovations necessarily implied political upheaval. Montaigne is conservative in both religion and politics because innovation, however justified, can mean blood. But the ground of his conservatism is fundamentally innovative.[55]

This paradox is most acute in Montaigne's apparently contradictory attitude toward Catholicism. He vows that he sincerely and completely submits "not only my actions and my writings, but also my thoughts," to the "Catholic, apostolic, and Roman church, in which I will die and in which I was born." That Catholicism hovers unobtrusively in the background of the life he describes in the *Essays*: in the chapel at the base of the tower where Montaigne does his writing; in the Angelus bell at the top of its stairs, sounding the Ave Maria twice a day. Montaigne is baptized in the Church and married there; he stays loyal to it throughout the wars, when incentives to defect abounded for a broad-minded man with friends and family on both sides, residing in a heavily Huguenot neighborhood. He dies during a Mass he requests when he senses that his end is near. In his travel journal, we observe Montaigne going to Mass frequently, enjoying the homilies, and visiting the sacred sites of Catholicism. He even has an audience with the pope and kisses the papal slipper.[56]

And yet he wrote a book that teems with impieties. Assessing Montaigne's thoughts on death, Pascal calls them "entirely pagan." Montaigne rejects repentance, so central to Catholicism, writing that "if I had to live my life over again, I would live as I have lived": a line that expresses the achievement of immanent contentment with admirable succinctness but that Pascal's Jansenist friends describe as "horrible words, marking the extinction of all religious feeling." He suggests that the Eucharist smacks of cannibalism, that virgin births are quite common in Islam, that there might be a naturalistic explanation of the resurrection, and that no just God would accept the blood of the innocent as payment for the sins of the guilty. He speaks of fortune constantly; he hardly mentions providence. When he considers the proper condition of the soul for prayer, he demands a purity alien to the Christian encounter between a sinner in need of grace and a merciful God who offers it. Not without reason did the *Essays* spend almost three hundred years on the Index of Forbidden Books.[57]

Why is a man so skeptical in his religious thought so conservative in his religious practice? As Emerson noted long ago, in marrying in church, paying his respects to the pope while in Rome, and having Mass said on his deathbed, Montaigne does no more than adhere to the customs of his time and place. "We are Christians by the same title we are Perigordians or Germans," he writes; religion is an accident of geography and history, and this includes *his* religion. But Montaigne's particular brand of skepticism does not lead him to dogmatic or open contempt of religion. On the religious question, he seems to say, "This is how things are done in my country. Do I know better? Am I convinced enough of some alternative to turn my family, my country, my whole world upside down in its pursuit?" His life answers these questions in the negative.[58]

His deepest reasons for creating this strange amalgam of skepticism and orthodoxy are the human and natural reasons of his anthropology, not properly religious reasons. As he does in his description of the self's "mistress form," Montaigne self-consciously blurs the distinction between nature and custom in his consideration of theological-political questions, calling custom a "second nature, and no less powerful." Nature, he writes, "enfolds in the terms of her ordinary progress, like all other things, also the beliefs, judgments, and opinions of men," which "have their revolution, their season, their birth, and their death, like cabbages." In following Catholic custom, Montaigne follows nature, for man's nature situates every individual amid the customs of a particular time and place. "Just as she has given us feet to walk with, [nature] has given us wisdom to guide us in life," and that wisdom guides us to respect custom rather than rebel against it. Montaigne remains Catholic because Catholicism is the natural religion of a Perigordian Frenchman of the sixteenth century.[59]

But had he been born in Brazil—where men "pass their lives in an admirable simplicity and ignorance, without letters, without law, without king, without any religion whatsoever"—he would have been a good Brazilian. For all his professed Catholicism, Montaigne does not make arguments that might lead anyone—Protestant or atheist, Muslim or Jew—to convert to his religion. To be a Christian is to be a "fisher of men," to proselytize; such proselytization is utterly contrary to the spirit of the Montaignean self. For Montaigne, conversion is "an abdication of moral and psychological responsibility," as Mark Lilla writes, a self-betrayal rather than a rebirth, fruitful only in inauthenticity, hypocrisy, and self-delusion. Better, in Nietzsche's phrase, to "become what we are"—what we already are and have always been. So Montaigne remains always who he is: a skeptic seeking his contentment immanently, adhering to the religion of his birth because doing otherwise would be both presumptuous and spectacularly inconvenient.[60]

Montaigne articulates a similar attitude—conservatism elaborated on the novel grounds of his modern anthropology—on properly political questions. He consistently affirms his allegiance to law, king, and country. But his conservatism has little in common with the Burkean conservatism of the Anglo-American tradition. Burke supposes there to be a "latent wisdom" in received customs—the accumulated insights and arguments of many generations that have shaped existing ways of doing things, however arbitrary those ways may seem at first glance. Montaigne, by contrast, in investigating one of the customs of his time with the intention to defend it, finds its foundation so feeble that he "almost became disgusted with it" himself. He cannot discern the latent wisdom of custom, even when he sets out with the express intent to do so.[61]

Moral and political law, Montaigne suggests, do not in fact have any rational foundation. No matter—they have no need for one: "The laws remain in credit not because they are just, but because they are laws. That is the mystic foundation of their authority; they have no other. Which serves them well." And so, in spite of his conservatism, Montaigne never offers a reasoned defense of the laws or social order of his time; he never extols the political advantages of monarchy or the intrinsic justice of aristocracy. Arguments about the right form of government, taken seriously, are pregnant with chaos. Though "we are prone to be discontented with the present state of things," "to wish for the government of a few in a democratic state, or another type of government in a monarchy, is foolish and wrong." And so he leaves the question of the best regime almost entirely untouched.[62]

There is a strange kind of radicalism inherent in conservatism so understood. After all, the daring, Machiavellian view that politics should aim at the conquest of fortune has a commonsense appeal that Alexander Hamilton expressed in the *Federalist Papers*, when he argued that human beings reasonably prefer to be ruled by "reflection and choice" rather than "accident and force." Montaigne is almost shockingly content to leave fortune in charge. "Whatever position you set men in," he writes, "they pile themselves up and arrange themselves by moving and crowding together, like ill-matched objects that one puts in a bag without order find for themselves the way to join and place themselves among one another, often better than art could have disposed them." Such accidental arrangements can maintain a body politic as well as the most beautiful regimes imagined by Plato or Aristotle. Not even revolt against out-and-out tyranny is justified, for "good does not necessarily succeed evil; another evil may follow it, and a worse one. . . . The French, my contemporaries, could tell you a thing or two about it." Better to draw back from politics and build up that part of life untainted by its venom.[63]

The Montaignean desire for immanent contentment encourages such a withdrawal. His experience of civil war reminds us of just how dangerous political passions can be; his low estimate of the capacity of human reason, art, and effort to order or reform our common life reminds us just how grateful we should be for whatever measure of peace and order we happen to enjoy. By relocating the aim of our sociable desires from the political world to the social world, from a world of ruling and conquering to a world of freedom, conversation, and the sharing of interests and pleasures, he seeks to divert the restless passions that so convulsed his world into more peaceable pursuits. He meets with some success. As Marc Fumaroli has written, the "liberal" aristocracy Montaigne helps to shape "no longer aspires to being a jealous caste: through the life of books, arts, conversation, travel and spiritual curiosity, it opens itself up to the most varied forms of humanity, of the past, present and elsewhere." Real life is to be found there, in that life of curiosity, conversation, and appreciation of the beautiful—not in the chambers of court or on the fields of battle.[64]

And so while Montaigne serves two terms as mayor of Bordeaux, and is an able practitioner of shuttle diplomacy between the warring factions of France, he never thinks of his political activity as essential to his humanity. His father, by contrast, was mayor all the way down, carrying the preoccupations of office home with him and incorporating them into his very being. In his own case, Montaigne insists that "the mayor and Montaigne have always been two, and very clearly separated." The freedom Montaigne cares about can be protected in part simply by restraining our own ambitious striving: "Essential and effectual subjection," he writes, "only regards those among us who welcome it and love to honor and enrich themselves by such service." Political involvement is the enemy of freedom, not its essence, even in turbulent times and under tyrannical monarchs: "In truth, our laws are free enough, and the weight of sovereignty hardly touches a French gentleman twice in his life." Political activity has no essential place in the contentment of the Montaignean self.[65]

This sensibility, so alien to the tradition of political and military republicanism passed down from Greece and Rome, has grown apace with the class invested in the pursuit of the ideal of immanent contentment Montaigne embodies. Immanent contentment requires no political engagement, but it does require freedom from political interference in one's private life. Modern peoples thus tend to prefer Benjamin Constant's private "liberty of the moderns" to the ancient liberty of political self-determination. Readers have long seen in Montaigne the seeds of the liberal political philosophy that would be born in the late seventeenth century, and some have gone so far as to describe Montaigne as "the philosopher who invented liberalism." For the pursuit of immanent contentment inclines us to draw back from politics and into the realm of our private pleasures, friendships, and thoughts, where life may be honest, free, and real.[66]

Montaigne's Political Anthropology and the Debates of Modern Politics

Montaigne describes a new way of life: life oriented by the quest for immanent contentment, for psychic equilibrium in our inner lives and unmediated approbation in our social lives. In the background of all our political divisions, this vision of the good life often stands as a shared anthropological assumption, orienting the arguments of both the right and the left. The case our right makes for free-market economics assumes that perpetual economic growth is self-evidently good, an assumption little challenged by human beings accustomed to thinking of happiness in terms of immanent contentment, to which an ever-proliferating variety of goods and services is useful. When our left argues for the redistribution of the same kind of resources, its position often rests on similar assumptions about

the kind of flourishing our political arrangements should support. Similarly, the social aim of unmediated approbation frequently underlies both the celebrations of familial intimacy
dear to the right and the defenses of free erotic connection dear
to the left. Both sides champion authenticity and denounce
hypocrisy—the moral standards correlative to an immanent
conception of happiness. A substantial unspoken consensus
about the constituent elements of a life well lived enframes our
boisterous public disagreements.

Though many of the debates of modern politics can be understood as arguments about the political vision that best
serves the individual pursuit of immanent contentment, others
spring from more fundamental doubts about modern philosophic anthropology. Can human beings adequately understand themselves as selves? Is psychic equilibrium really the key
to individual happiness? Is unmediated approbation truly the
aim of social desire? Is politics properly judged as a more or
less convenient framework within which to pursue an apolitical
vision of the good life? Or are all varieties of politics that
take immanent contentment as the de facto purpose of human
life mistaken in their assumptions about what we are and how
we flourish?

Such questions have haunted modern philosophic anthropology almost from its outset. In the century after Montaigne's
death, they would be raised with extraordinary power by his
greatest and most critical reader, Blaise Pascal.

CHAPTER 2

Pascal

The Inhumanity of Immanence

Montaigne in the Seventeenth Century

"There is a bit of Montaigne in every man," Sainte-Beuve writes. Montaigne speaks up for universal human interests—curiosity and the love of pleasure, joyful worldliness and forthright doubt. He promises that these interests can be safely liberated, as long as they remain within the capacious boundaries set by the modern moral standards of frankness, humanity, and lightness of touch. Few who come to know him are completely immune to the charms of his gruff yet cosmopolitan nonchalance.[1]

Montaigne's sophisticated tranquility will hold particular attractions for the French of the seventeenth century, when his literary acclaim reaches its first peak. Though the civil wars that bedeviled Montaigne's France officially end with the Edict of Nantes in 1598, they are replaced in the decades thereafter by widespread, sometimes violent resistance to the determined consolidation of royal power under the Bourbons and their hard-nosed first ministers, Cardinals Richelieu and Mazarin. France's discontents culminate in the Fronde, a "revolution manqué" that breaks out during the minority of Louis XIV, which will turn out to be the final, failed attempt of France's old nobility to resist the rising tide of monarchic centralization.[2] In the midst of this tumult, a new moral ideal gains ascendance, one that arises precisely "in response to the high melodrama of the Fronde and the boorish behavior that has often been associated with rough aristocratic heroism." The new ideal was that of the *honnête homme*, which Damien Mitton—a wealthy, worldly man of letters, friend of Blaise Pascal, and royal apparatchik—put on paper in his "Description of the Honest Man." Mitton's *honnête homme* is "indulgent, humane, helpful, and sensitive to the misfortune of others." He seeks to be happy, but in a way that lets others be happy as well. His curiosity is boundless, but he is circumspect and modest; his conduct is relaxed, sometimes even negligent, and he has no fantasies about knights in shining armor. As Leszek Kolakowski describes him, the *honnête homme* is "a polished, polite member of the educated upper classes, pleasantly conversing with his peers, moderate in his opinions, avoiding obduracy and strong partisan spirit." For Mitton and many others, Montaigne brilliantly exemplifies this new moral style, a style that seems well suited to replace the rough tastes of the moribund warrior aristocracy whose unwillingness to go gently into that good night makes for nothing but useless tumult.[3]

Some wonder, however, whether Montaigne and his growing number of followers have not drawn the confines of life too narrowly—whether they have not accepted fleeting pleasure as a poor substitute for solid happiness. Nonchalance might be much less than moral life demands of us, and might go along far too easily with the ruses of power. The desire for our friends' unqualified approbation might be something darker than an innocent wish for human confirmation of our individuality. On this view, Montaignean diversion might distract us not only from fruitless obsessions with a death we cannot avoid and truths we cannot know but from the reality of what we are. If so, then gliding lightly over the surface of life comes to look like less than truly living. The art of circumscription comes to look less like a healthy constraint of our restless desires and more like a self-alienating truncation of our god-seeking souls. Montaigne's humanistic pursuit of immanent contentment comes to seem, paradoxically, inhuman.

No one has given more powerful voice to such suspicions of Montaignean moral modernism than Blaise Pascal. At modernity's outset, Pascal examines its meaning in all of its dimensions, with a penetration few have been able to match. Pascal not only understands modern physics but helps create it, and he describes the Hobbesian realities beneath the surface of modern political life more starkly than Hobbes himself. He witnesses the living truth of the modern quest for immanent contentment in the lives of the *honnêtes hommes* around him and sees that, in spite of his contemporaries' impressive efforts to arrange artful and pleasant lives that win their friends' approbation, the restlessness of the human heart Augustine described in antiquity remains alive within them. To Pascal, it must be so, for *l'homme passe l'homme*: "man transcends man." Human beings are quite simply incapable of resting content on the plane of humanity. Indeed, the quest for immanent contentment leaves the restless human heart more anxious than ever, for modernity's very success in remaking the world in man's image allows us to see, with terrifying clarity, that a human life is not the sort of problem a psychological stratagem can solve. In Pascal, the restlessness that is truly modern—the restlessness of the soul that tries and fails to hold itself within the confines of immanence—finds its first and most powerful voice.[4]

Modern Physicist, Augustinian Christian

Pascal's restless heart burns through many of the most honored endeavors of modern life—several of them before he even reaches adulthood. François de Chateaubriand summarizes his brief but incandescent trajectory in one long but brilliant sentence:

> There was a man who, at twelve years old, with *bars* and *rounds*, created mathematics; who, at sixteen, wrote the most learned treatise on conics which had been seen since antiquity; who, at nineteen, reduced a science that exists entirely in thought to a machine; who, at twenty-three, demonstrated the phenomena of the weight of air, and destroyed one of the great errors of ancient physics; who, at that age when other men are just being born, having completed the circuit of the human sciences, perceived their nothingness, and turned his thoughts toward religion; who, from that moment until his death, which came in his thirty-ninth year, always infirm and suffering, fixed the language which Bossuet and Racine spoke, and gave the model of both perfect wit and the strongest reasoning; finally who, in the short intervals of his illnesses, resolved, by abstraction, one of the highest problems of geometry, and threw onto paper thoughts that held as much to God as to man: this frightening genius was named *Blaise Pascal.*[5]

To fill out the elements of Chateaubriand's summary that may be obscure: Born in Clermont, France, Pascal is raised by a father deeply devoted to his education, who homeschools him with a gentle attentiveness reminiscent of Montaigne's "On the Education of Children." Himself a serious mathematician, Étienne Pascal senses that his son will be captivated by mathematics, fears that this infatuation will cause him to neglect his Latin and Greek, and therefore withholds mathematical instruction during Pascal's earliest years. But Pascal overhears the talk of his father and the mathematicians who frequent their home and begins to work at it on his own, inventing a private geometric vocabulary of *barres* and *ronds*. According to his sister, Étienne Pascal discovers his son's clandestine mathematizing when he enters the twelve-year-old's playroom one day to find the boy deriving Euclid's 32nd proposition for himself. Étienne has a change of heart and begins to instruct Blaise formally. The young man will soon make significant contributions to the history of mathematics, not only with his works on conics and the cycloid but also with his treatise on what he calls "the arithmetic triangle"—known to history as "Pascal's Triangle"—which forms the basis of probability theory. At the age of nineteen, he invents and presides over the manufacture of the world's first functioning calculator, capable of adding, subtracting, multiplying, and dividing numbers of as many as eight digits. A handful of these so-called *Pascaliennes* survive to this day, in good working order. At twenty-five, he designs experiments on the void and atmospheric pressure that destroy the ancient scholastic commonplace that "nature abhors a vacuum." At thirty-three, he writes his *Provincial Letters*: daring, uproarious satires of the most powerful churchmen in France, the Jesuits, and one of the greatest best sellers of the ancien régime. He then sets to work on an enormously ambitious *Apology for the Christian Religion*. Even though illness and early death will keep him from making so much as a first draft of the book, his undigested notes, collated and published by his friends as the *Thoughts of M. Pascal on Religion and Several Other Subjects, which were Found after his Death among his Papers*, will become a classic of French moral philosophy and one of the most important works of Christian apologetics ever written. Finally, at the end of his life, he collaborates with his friend Arthus de Roannez to give Paris the world's first system of public transportation, the five-cent carriages, donating all profits to charity.[6]

Pascal's mathematical and scientific genius, his literary and philosophic brilliance, and his technological and philanthropic contributions to the great Baconian project for the improvement of the human condition are the unimpeachable credentials of a first-order modern mind. But Pascal is no standard-issue modern innovator, however brilliant. For although he never completely forsakes science (Chateaubriand is mistaken about this), he perceives the disturbing existential consequences of the modern scientific revolution as few have before him, or since. To Pascal, the universe revealed by modern physics is a boundless vacuum in which man finds himself at sea, prisoner of a meaningless nature that is utterly silent in the face of the human demand for the wisdom we need in order to live well. The Montaignean quest for immanent contentment, intended to vindicate nature, takes place in the context of a universe that science relentlessly demonstrates to be no home for man. Truly thinking scientific modernism through intensifies rather than blunts our need for transcendence.[7]

Pascal's scientific genius, and the unflinching candor with which he draws the existential consequences of science's discoveries, is one side of his extraordinary character. The other takes shape through an encounter with an austere and demanding religious sect that was making both impressive converts and powerful enemies in his century. By combining the uncompromising Augustinianism of these so-called Jansenist Christians with his acute consciousness of the predicament of a humanity set adrift by the results of its own scientific inquiries, Pascal will formulate a distinctive account of the human situation that responds to Montaigne point for point.[8]

The Pascal family shows little more than conventional religious devotion until 1646, when Étienne Pascal slips on the ice of Rouen in January and breaks his leg. The brothers Deschamps, expert bonesetters, move in to treat him. They are disciples of the Abbé de Saint-Cyran, the most important French follower of Cornelius Jansenius, eponym of the Jansenist sect. Jansenius's book, *Augustinus*, attempts to recover the austere and heroic core of Christianity, which he and his followers believe the Catholic Church has mistakenly ceded to the Protestants. The Deschamps talk much of religion with the brilliant young Blaise and lend him the books of Jansenius and Saint-Cyran. With Blaise taking the initial lead, the whole family moves in the direction of a deeper and more demanding Christianity. Pascal's sister Jacqueline eventually takes orders at the Abbey of Port-Royal, home to a sisterhood of intense Cistercians led by Mère Angelique Arnauld. The formidable Mère Angelique had been made an abbess at the age of ten and found the sisters over whom she was placed deeply corrupt. Over the years, she reformed her order with astonishing success. Together with her brother, the theologian Antoine Arnauld, Mère Angelique eventually transforms Port-Royal into a great center of revivified Catholic Augustinianism.[9]

The demanding Augustinianism of the Jansenists soon comes into disastrous conflict with the most potent force in French Catholicism in the seventeenth century: the Jesuits. The Jesuits rise rapidly to a position of dominance in the forty years following their reintroduction into France in 1603. They build dozens of schools around the country and are said to have some thirteen thousand students in their charge in Paris alone; from 1604 onward, one Jesuit succeeds another as the king's personal confessor. These astute and learned churchmen know how to read the signs of the times, and they see that the Montaignean quest for immanent contentment is in the air. Everything from libertinism to deism to historical criticism is conspiring to lead souls away from the Church. The Jesuits respond by seeking to adapt the Church's teaching to the needs of the moment— a "field hospital" strategy meant to prevent Catholicism from losing influence over countless souls in times of pervasive temptation.[10]

The Jansenists see Jesuitism as Catholicism lite, at best—and at worst something much darker. Pascal's entry into the quarrel on the Jansenists' behalf will lead him to see how sharply the culture of his officially Catholic country is diverging from Augustine's original Christian vision. In taking up the Jansenists' quarrel, he draws a vivid contrast between the moral tendencies of modern life and the demands of the human heart for solid truth, happiness, and holiness. Pascal sees this radically Christian perspective, however, not as a break with modern science but as its complement. In his view, the truths of both religion and science drive us to see that our quest for immanent contentment is bound to fail.

Of Permissiveness and Power: The Spirit of Montaigne Meets the Spirit of the Gospel

At the moment Pascal intervenes in the Jansenist-Jesuit quarrel, his Jansenist friends are losing, badly. The Church has ruled five recondite theological propositions heretical and affirmed that those propositions can be found in the work of Jansenius, which the Jansenists deny. Both Rome and the French monarchy— which is edging toward the revocation of the Edict of Nantes and detects a whiff of the Calvinist in Jansenism—are bent on forcing the Jansenists to renounce their position. Antoine Arnauld is on the verge of expulsion from the Sorbonne. At their wits' end, the Jansenists decide to make their case to the public, in an attempt to win the *salons* to their side. Arnauld, whose character has been described as "one part impeccable logic and two of caustic disdain," is not the man for a job that requires winsomeness above all. But he thinks the brilliant young Pascal might be.[11]

Taking up the task, Pascal conceives a rhetorical strategy that turns on revealing the divide between the modernizing attitude of the Jesuits and Christianity's Augustinian core. The Jesuits, who seek to deal with the spreading desire for immanent contentment by incorporating it into Christianity, paper over the stark divergences between the spirit of Montaigne and the spirit of the Gospels, just as Montaigne himself does. In the Jansenists' view, the opposition between the attitude of the Jesuits and the attitude of Port-Royal was an opposition between "the spirit that would make truth pleasing to mankind, and the spirit that would make mankind pleasing to Truth."[12]

Pascal sees that the writings of Jesuit casuists contain a streak of moral permissiveness that can make an honest reader think twice: they justify dueling; they promote "devotions made easy," such as paving one's way into heaven by saying "hello" to the Virgin Mary each morning, and telling her "goodnight" before bed; they invent arguments to allow a priest to remove his vestments before visiting a brothel. Pascal intuits that, if exposed in just the right way, this strain of Jesuit casuistry might well make readers laugh, for it contains "a startling contrast between the thing looked for and the thing looked at," which he identifies as the nerve of comedy. And so, while the Jesuits are Pascal's target throughout *The Provincial Letters*, he does not exactly argue with them. Instead, he gives them a mouthpiece and lets them speak for themselves, in extensive quotations Arnauld and another Jansenist theologian, Pierre Nicole, help him cull from Jesuit books of casuistry, arranging this material for devastating comic effect.[13]

Pascal's work takes the form of a series of anonymous, open letters to a fictitious friend in the provinces, purporting to explain the quarrel, which is the talk of Paris, and indeed of all of France. They recount imaginary dialogues between his narrator, an impartial yet curious figure he will later call Louis de Montalte, and a cast of imaginary Jesuits, Dominicans, and Jansenists. They are an immediate and smashing success. The Jesuits respond, leading Pascal to drop the fiction of the provincial friend and write six more letters addressed to them directly. He has the audacity to address the final two letters to Père François Annat, personal confessor of Louis XIV, by name.[14]

The Provincial Letters are designed for popular appeal. While the quarrel has hitherto been conducted in Latin, Pascal writes in French. He subjects the most powerful priests in France and all of Europe, who have the ear of both the king and the pope, to ridicule. The *salons* eat it up, and delight in the game of trying to guess the identity of the *Provincials'* author—a game that sometimes takes place in Pascal's presence. Outside Paris, too, the *Provincials* strike a nerve; country priests begin reading them aloud from their pulpits. They appeal to everyone who has been burned by the Jesuits' power games or simply enjoys seeing overweening priests mocked. That turns out to be a lot of people.[15]

The daring of *The Provincial Letters* is literal. Pascal and his allies have them printed at night, in small type to minimize the number of pages, and in special, fast-drying ink that shortens the time the pages need to be laid out to dry—a moment of dangerous exposure. Each link in the chain of their distribution knows only his immediate contacts in the network, to preserve the author's anonymity; Pascal himself moves around as he writes. These measures are not paranoia. Louis XIV's chancellor, Pierre Séguier, has something like an apoplectic fit while reading the first letter. The authorities imprison several booksellers for selling the *Provincials* and mount an extensive search for their author. A messenger from a Jesuit who has guessed the writer's identity once enters Pascal's home to warn him to desist while copies of the seventh letter are drying on his bed.[16]

Pascal draws the ire of the authorities in part because he exposes the political advantage the Jesuits accrue from their theological position. How, after all, have they managed their meteoric ascent in France since the beginning of the seventeenth century? The Jesuits have a good racket: they are in the business of allowing ambitious, worldly, passionate people to do most of what they want to do while remaining Catholics in good standing. A little laxity, they know, can be most useful to a priest seeking to extend the influence of his order among men and women with interests and desires to protect. Indeed, they go so far as to teach that the love of God is not necessary for salvation, making eternal life compatible with religious indifference. The Jesuits are permissive moral authorities. Powerful people—great men with mistress trouble, enterprising sorts who make a lot of money on the margins of morality—have long found such authorities useful.[17]

Pascal causes his reader to raise an eyebrow at the excessive convenience of this arrangement. He reminds Christians of their ancient belief that the quest for eternal life demands the ardor of the Apostles, not religious indifference; he reminds priests that the salvation of souls depends on bringing those souls to love God. In so doing, he shines a most unflattering light on Jesuit permissiveness. The political cunning of the Jesuits makes plain that they are no innocents. Worse, they openly pray for the damnation of their enemies, such as the author of the *Provincials*. One wonders if those who pray that others might go to hell ever had any interest in the salvation of souls in the first place. For Pascal, the word that most properly describes their activity—the corruption of the Church's sacred power of binding and loosing so as to secure the ascendancy of a faction of prelates who teach doctrines that lead men to their damnation—is *diabolical*.[18]

Few will follow Pascal that far. Nonetheless, Pascal's argument, which favors an austere Christian morality with little to flatter men's vanity, has a profound if counterintuitive power— perhaps particularly with those who know from experience that our pleasures are not always our friends and that those who wink at them are not really our allies. In the nineteenth century, the dissolute Sainte-Beuve will dedicate twenty years of his life to the study of the austere sisters and solitaries of the Port-Royal community from which *The Provincial Letters* emerged and make a literary masterpiece of this material. Austerity fascinates him, and he knows it can fascinate readers. For in a society that prides itself on being free and easy, austerity is the only fruit that remains forbidden.[19]

The enduring appeal of *The Provincial Letters* derives from their forceful suggestion that the modern alliance of permissiveness and power does not succeed in making men happy. Modern human beings can follow their passions and pleasures, indulge idle or even voyeuristic curiosities, accumulate wealth and achieve ambitions with less shame or need for apology than their forebears. But doing so seems only to add to the mounting pile of evidence that the decisive obstacles to immanent contentment do not lie in the laws and moral norms modern peoples so relentlessly critique and overturn. The unhappiness that remains when such liberations have succeeded must have its source not in our laws but in ourselves.

This insight into the inner source of modern man's abiding unhappiness provides the ground upon which Pascal will build his next project when he suddenly abandons *The Provincial Letters* at the height of their literary success. He does so because he has concluded, prophetically, that "eloquence amuses more people than it converts." While Pascal writes *The Provincial Letters* to defend Jansenist Augustinianism against Jesuit modernizing, they owe their place in France's literary canon in part to the efforts of Voltaire, who simply delights in the effective satire of priests. Making converts will require a different and more serious kind of book, one that seeks to show, with extraordinary power, why immanent contentment cannot be enough.[20]

Self-Knowledge for Modern Man:
Diversion and Misery

The *Provincials* succeed because Pascal knows his audience. He keeps company not only with Jansenists but with men of the world such as Mitton and the Chevalier du Méré—another exponent of the art of *honnêteté*, with no pretensions to piety. For a man with Pascal's talents, amusing such men is easy, for they enjoy being amused. Getting them to question their very taste for amusement, to look hard at themselves and upend their self-satisfied lives—that is difficult. The great project of Pascal's final years will be a book intended to do just that, a book that has been called "Christianity for modern pagans."[21]

Pascal will never finish that book. He makes extensive notes, speaks to friends about it, and gives a presentation of his work at Port-Royal des Champs, sometime in 1658. When he dies, after laboring intermittently through four more years of often terrible suffering, his friends and family collect his fragments, put them in some (much disputed) order, and print them, as one of the first collections of posthumous literary fragments ever published.[22]

In his preface to that first edition of the *Pensées*, Étienne Périer, Pascal's nephew, describes his uncle's rhetorical plan for the book: he sets out to paint a picture of human life, intended for a reader who has always lived in "indifference with respect to everything, and above all with respect to himself." Properly provoked, such a reader might "at last come to consider himself in this portrait, and to examine what he is." He seeks to bring such a reader to see the mysterious and painful contradictions of his own existence, and thereby to spur him to seek in anguish for an answer to that mystery. As Pascal himself explains his rhetorical approach to man:

> If he exalts himself, I humble him.
> if he humbles himself, I exalt him.
> and continue to contradict him
> until he comprehends
> that he is an incomprehensible monster.

Neither exaltation nor misery is proper to us on its own, for we are both "great and miserable." If Pascal can bring his reader to see this contradictory truth about himself, he can induce a kind of horrified wonder—wonder directed not at some strange external marvel but at himself. To do so, he must shake the indifferent soul free from its strange lethargy. He thus upends Montaigne, for while Montaigne seeks to help restless souls achieve a state of nonchalant contentment, Pascal begins with such self-satisfied souls and attempts to awaken them and set them in motion.

Where Montaigne seeks to circumscribe the soul, Pascal seeks to crack it open.[23]

Pascal aims to show human beings who think themselves happy—people who live by the moral code of the *honnête homme*, which seems to serve them well, allowing them to enjoy all life's satisfactions without becoming obnoxious to others—that they are secretly miserable. To do so, he steps out to meet Montaigne, the great exemplar of that moral code, on his own territory: the territory of diversion. Montaigne recommends a healthy dose of diversion and prides himself on his conversational art of leading sad or angry souls step by step away from thoughts of grief or vengeance. Pascal sees the efficacy of the Montaignean solution; diversion, he writes, is "the only thing that consoles us for our miseries." But that diversion alone consoles us is, for Pascal, merely "the greatest of our miseries." Why would diversion itself be to him a misery? Why is it not, as it is for Montaigne, enough?[24]

Pascal seeks to understand just what the soul enjoys in diversion—in being "turned aside," as the etymology of the word suggests. He takes as his examples hunting and gambling (the latter was the favorite pastime of his friends Méré and Mitton). Give the hunter his prey, the gambler the stake he might win in his game, asking only that he forsake his beloved activity, and you will make him unhappy. For it is the hunt and not the kill, the game and not the stake, that he seeks. And yet, should you allow him the chase without the quarry, the game without the stake, the charm of the thing will be equally lost. In the heat of these activities, we imagine that what we really want is the rest following the kill, or the wallet flush with winnings at the end of the game. Effective diversion must include both the hunt and the kill, for neither satisfies alone. Put the soul at rest, and it longs for activity; put the soul in motion, and it longs for rest. In neither does it find contentment.[25]

Our love of diversion motivates not only our amusements but our most serious activities, including politics. Pascal describes royalty as "the finest position in the world"; when he has the opportunity to participate in the education of a young prince, he attends to his duties with intense dedication. Nonetheless, when he examines the nature of the satisfactions inherent in political responsibility, diversion proves decisive: "What is it to be superintendent, chancellor, prime minister, but to have a position in which a great number of people come each morning and from every quarter, so as not to leave any of them an hour a day when they can think about themselves?" Power and responsibility flatter our vanity, of course—it is nice to have people treat us as if we matter. But more than that, responsibility takes our minds off of ourselves. A man kept constantly busy with decisions to make, audiences to hold, honors to bestow, has little time for contemplation of his own being. Leave a king or a president alone and unoccupied, however, and he is just like the rest of us, except that his position adds special miseries to the universal human ones: "he will necessarily come to think about the threats facing him, revolts that may occur, and in the end, inevitable death and disease."[26]

We engage in politics, in hunting and gambling, in flirting and text-messaging and much else, in an unceasing effort to get outside ourselves—we "cannot sit still in a room." For when we do, our minds inevitably turn to "the natural unhappiness of our weak and mortal condition, so miserable that nothing can console us when we think about it closely." What is so unhappy about our human condition? "We want truth and find only incertitude in ourselves. We seek happiness and find only misery and death. We are incapable of not wanting truth and

happiness, yet we are incapable of either truth or happiness."
Our consciousness of our own mortality and our awareness of
our own ignorance make us unhappy; we cannot learn to die, or
rest our well-made heads on the pillow of ignorance, as Montaigne
hopes. No psychic equilibrium is possible for a being whose
desires so radically outstrip his possibilities. Misery follows ineluctably from an honest estimate of the gap between what we
want and what we are.[27]

Grief, on this understanding, is the fitting and proper reaction
not only to the human losses we must endure but to the human
condition as such. To long for a truth our limited minds can
never grasp, for a happiness out of all proportion with the limits
of mortal frailty, is to be permanently, naturally bereft. Diversion
can distract us from grief, but if we grieve not only over what has
happened to us but over what we are, to distract us from grief is
to distract us from ourselves. Self-knowledge can begin only
with the honest acknowledgment of our unhappiness.

Social Life and Self-Deception

Our desire to avoid such honesty with ourselves is all-pervasive.
It animates social life, which Pascal sees as a mutually reinforc-
ing architecture of illusions, designed to enlist others in our efforts to deceive ourselves and thereby take our minds off our
miseries. That secret desire for self-deception infects—indeed
motivates—our search for the unmediated approbation of
friendship. In exposing it, Pascal takes aim at the social aspect
of Montaigne's vision of immanent contentment.

Pascal's Christian perspicacity with respect to human affection can still shock, perhaps more than anything else he writes.
In his view, the very thought that human beings can naturally
love one another is one of our principal self-deceptions. Beneath our shared pleasures, social niceties, and the advantages

we find in cooperation, the truth of social life is harsh: "all men naturally hate one another." Indiscretions, which allow one friend to discover what another truly thinks of him, rupture friendships but display the truth: "I set it down as fact that if all men knew what they said about one another, there would not be four friends in the world."[28]

Why do human beings hate one another? Because our vanities and interests conflict, of course, but more than that, because our self-love wants to see perfection within but cannot prevent the self, the object of its affection, from "being full of faults and misery." "It wants to be great, and sees itself small; it wants to be happy, and sees itself miserable; it wants to be perfect, and sees itself full of imperfections." We hate others because they see our vice and unhappiness, and we see that they see it. We secretly know that we deserve their dislike and contempt—that their disdain is a just verdict on our character. Those we call our friends are merely enablers with whom we have entered into an unspoken agreement to abet one another's self-deceptions: to pretend not to see the vices we see, and to pretend to see virtues in what are at best resplendent vices. We make such pacts because they aid us in our unstinting efforts to convince ourselves that the object of our self-love is good, beautiful, and happy. But we need not dig very deep to detect the underlying hatred. Friendship is fragile because it is an optical illusion.[29]

What, then, are we to make of the love we seem to feel for others, and that others seem to feel for us? Pascal's reflections on this question lead him to his most trenchant analysis of the self—*le moi*, an abstraction he seems to have coined:

What is the self?

A man who puts himself at the window to watch the passersby: if I pass by there, could I say that he put himself there to see me? No, because he is not thinking of me in particular. But he who loves someone because of her beauty, does he love her? No, because smallpox, which will kill her beauty without killing her person, will make it so that he loves her no more. But if one loves me for my judgment, for my memory, does one love me? *Moi*? No, because I can lose these qualities without losing myself. Where then is this self, if it is neither in the body nor in the soul? And how can we love the body or the soul, if not for these qualities, which are not at all what makes the self, because they are perishable? Will we love the substance of a person's soul in the abstract, whatever qualities might be in it? That cannot be, and would be unjust. We therefore never love anyone, but only some qualities.

Love that attaches itself to qualities I will lose—a beautiful shape that will age and sag, a brilliant wit that will tire and become repetitive—does not love *me*, the self that endures all such changes. Love that would cling to the self stripped of all qualities is love of an abstraction, which is impossible. Human love cannot naturally rise above the love of qualities; it misses the self at which it aims.[30]

In the light of Pascal's unflinching analysis, Montaigne's refusal to say why he loved La Boétie—his famously poetic non-answer to that question, "because it was he, because it was I," his vague evocation of a mysterious "quintessence" of qualities that brings them together—can look like an evasion. Montaigne cannot say just what he loves in La Boétie because there is nothing in La Boétie—or any other human being—that could constitute a stable object of love. The Montaignean portrait of unmediated approbation, of the love of one whole human self for another such self, seems to rest on a refusal to face the incoherence of our affections.[31]

When we peek beneath our delusions, we know that we cannot satisfy the longing of another human heart: "It is unjust for anyone to become attached to me, even if they do so willingly and with pleasure. I will disappoint those in whom I cause this desire to be born, for I am not anyone's end and do not have the means to satisfy them." To court the love of others, even to allow ourselves to be the object of their affections, is to deceive them. For we know too well that we are full of vice and frailty; we know too well that we will die. While love clouds the eyes of those in its grips, we, their beloveds, know the truth about ourselves and have a duty to undeceive those who mistake us for the answer to their longings.[32]

Once the veils are off, once the search for self-knowledge truly begins, we discover that the self is not only miserable but hateful. Pascal explains this awful judgment of what we are in an imaginary dialogue with Mitton:

> The self is hateful. You, Mitton, cover it up, but you do not take it away. You are therefore still hateful.
> "Not at all, because in acting as we do, obligingly toward everyone, one has no more reason to hate us."
> That would be true if we only hated in the self the displeasure that comes from it.
> But if I hate it because it is unjust and makes itself the center of everything, I will still hate it.
> In a word, the self has two qualities. It is unjust in itself because it makes itself the center of everything. It is inconvenient to others in that it wants to subject them, for every self is the enemy and wants to be the tyrant of all the others. You take away the inconvenience, but not the injustice.

And therefore you do not make it amiable to those who
hate its injustice. You make it amiable only to the unjust
who no longer see in it an enemy. And so you remain
unjust, and can only please the unjust.[33]

Pascal could say as much to Montaigne, Mitton's model.
Montaigne explicitly seeks to make himself the center of his
own world. By painting his own colors so winningly, he makes
a self-centered way of life attractive to many. If Pascal is right,
however, to make the self the center of everything is the height
of injustice, however we may dress injustice up in seemliness
and wit. The truth of the self is tyranny, fear, hatred of truth and
of those who bear witness to it, plus diversion and a conspiracy
of mutual self-deception to close our eyes to it all. There can be
no stoical ataraxia, and no real friendship, for a heart so full of
miseries.[34]

The Desire for Justice

Hateful and fond of diversion though the self may be, some part
of it cannot rest content with its own shabbiness and dishonesty. Though we constantly deceive ourselves, and enlist others
to help us in that effort, we also hate our self-deceptions. We
cannot render ourselves entirely indifferent to justice or truth,
however convenient we might find it to do so. This incapacity
to give up on disappointed hopes and unmet moral standards,
and thereby rest content with our self-deceptions, is particularly acute in politics. It perpetually upsets our attempts to
achieve political order and renders Montaignean nonchalance
about our common life impossible.

Pascal closely follows Montaigne in his initial diagnosis of
our political situation. "Theft, incest, infanticide, parricide, all

have been considered virtuous actions," he writes, and, in text taken almost word for word from Montaigne, "Can anything be more ridiculous than that a man should have the right to kill me because he lives on the other side of the water and his prince has a quarrel with mine, though I have none with him?" Our ideas of justice vary without limit; our wars make killing men who have done us no harm not only licit but honorable. Montaignean moral and political relativism thus becomes the basis for a radical Augustinian dismissal of the entire natural law tradition: "Doubtless there are natural laws, but this fine reason having been corrupted, it corrupted everything." That "most general of human maxims," that "each man should follow the customs of his own country," concedes that the search for true and natural justice fails before it begins.[35]

Ignorant of natural law, men everywhere dispute the meaning of justice. Force, however, is indisputable; one does not argue with bayonets. And yet force needs justice if it will appear as anything other than crime, just as justice needs force if it will be more than lofty and impotent words. How to bring them together? We might like to arm justice, but the dispute over its nature makes that impossible. Justifying force's self-evident power is much less difficult: "and thus, being unable to make what is just strong, we have made what is strong just." As Peter Kreeft has put it, "It is easier to pin a slogan on a cannon than to make a cannon obey a slogan." The exalted talk of politics is an image of justice painted over the reality of force. Political life is tyranny, or at best a madhouse.[36]

The wise know this, and do not find in it cause for despair. They prefer to laugh than to weep over the gap between human pretensions and human realities. If Plato and Aristotle "wrote about politics," they did so "as a game," like men "laying down rules for an insane asylum." And if they pretended to talk about it as something important, it was because they knew that the madmen to whom they were talking thought themselves kings and emperors." Here again, Pascal follows Montaigne closely and seems on the verge of counseling something akin to his ironic withdrawal from politics. Politics may be a madhouse, ruled by arbitrary custom, but what of it? We may take shelter in private life; we may wink and nod and go our own way.[37]

In another fragment, however, Pascal turns sharply away from this Montaignean political irony:

> Montaigne is wrong: Custom should only be followed because it is custom, and not because it is reasonable or just. But the people follow it for the sole reason that they believe it to be just. If not, they would no longer follow it even though it is custom, because one wants to be subjected only to reason or justice. Custom without this passes for tyranny, but the empire of reason and of justice is no more tyrannical than that of delectation. These are the principles natural to man.[38]

If these principles—that is, the desire to be ruled only by reason and justice—really are natural to man as such, and not merely to unwise men, the Montaignean position becomes untenable. The esoteric philosopher, playing along with the games of the madhouse; the ironic conservative, assenting to the laws not because he imagines them to be just but because he wants no trouble—these types are engaged in an inhuman denial of ineradicable human longings. Frustrating though we may find it, human beings want happiness and truth, not supercilious self-satisfaction fenced about with lies. The ironist and the philosopher not only tolerate but indeed participate in the deceptions of public life. Their own lives are self-deceived. For they suppose human beings can somehow give up on the concerns for truth and justice natural to the human heart.[39]

The gap between the human demand for genuine justice and the half measures of customary law lies at the heart of the restlessness of modern politics. In his time, Montaigne had witnessed the political ascendance of a class he described as halfway between the "illiterate ignorance" of peasants and the "doctoral ignorance" of the wise. This middling class, "its ass between two saddles," possesses enough learning to subvert the political order by drawing attention to its feeble or nonexistent foundations in nature but not enough wisdom to see the dangers inherent in undermining an order that, however flawed, is preferable to civil war. Pascal takes over this Montaignean analysis of those he calls the *demi-habile*, noting that their agitation is effective because human beings want to be ruled by reason and justice, not arbitrariness and force, and "readily listen to such discourses." "The knot of the modern social and political drama," as Pierre Manent points out, resides in the ever-increasing political activity of the class of the *demi-habile*, which insistently plucks the string of the human heart that resonates to denunciations of the defects of our justice.[40]

It is particularly difficult for modern people to be at ease with our politics because so many of us are *demi-habile*, and see that our laws have their origin either in a misty past for which we have no reverence or in the consent of human beings as flawed as we know ourselves to be, transmitted through the rusty, inefficient, sometimes corrupt machinery of representative government. Whatever the merits of this system, it does not even pretend to be the rule of pure reason or uncompromising justice. Though we may understand, with Montaigne, that "the lowest step is the firmest," that a political system that settles for reconciling competing interests rather than striving for exact justice may be the least bad of the available alternatives, we cannot help despising the injustices such rough measures necessarily permit. As Pascal shows us, the soul demands more of politics than politics can ever deliver. The Montaignean political irony that seeks to repress these demands does not succeed and may even give rise to a particularly unstable kind of politics.[41]

True Self-Knowledge: Man's Self-Transcendence

Pascal's depiction of the conflict between what we cannot help asking from politics and what politics actually provides is characteristic of his understanding of the human paradox: "man transcends man." The self-transcendence of a being who outstrips all of nature in his capacity for thought, but cannot thereby avoid the mortal fate of all living things, or even understand nature in a way that makes his own place within it intelligible, renders man at once miserable and great.[42]

Our very awareness of the misery Pascal so powerfully describes is the first proof of our greatness. Man is great precisely insofar as "he knows himself to be miserable. A tree does not know itself to be miserable." The tree, though just as frail and mortal as we are, does not experience these things as miseries. We do. Our miseries are akin to "the miseries of a great lord, the miseries of a deposed king." We experience ourselves as living in humiliating privation of what seems to us our proper state: "What is nature in animals is misery in man." The desires, movements, and even the weariness of the body are an embarrassment for "the beast with red cheeks," in Nietzsche's phrase, but for no other beast. We would not want to be caught in something as innocent as sleep by those whose respect we most desire. For we feel ourselves born to be better than we are. Misery marks the enormous gap in our self-consciousness between what we are and what we ought to be. Our very dissatisfaction with ourselves in our present state testifies, however reluctantly, to the possibility of human greatness.[43]

That greatness manifests itself in our freedom. Though he has little faith in philosophers, Pascal acknowledges that they sometimes "tame their passions," which constitutes a remarkable interruption in the causal chain of nature. "What material thing could have done that?" Though he has equally little confidence in our political and economic rules and institutions, he notes that there is something truly admirable in our ability to create great systems—from transportation networks and currencies to sanitation systems and armies—out of our very concupiscence. Human art can alchemize greed and ambition into a "picture of charity."[44]

The ultimate source of our freedom and our greatness lies in thought, which exists in sharp disjunction with the world of material causality and extension: "It is not in space that I must look for my dignity, but from the ordering of my thought. I will get no advantage from possessing worlds. Through space the universe encompasses me and swallows me up like a point; in thought I encompass it." Weak as a reed, so fragile that "a vapor, a drop of water" may kill him, a human being, through his mind, may think the greatest imaginable thoughts: "infinity," "God," "the universe." The universe, so far as we know, never thinks anything at all.[45]

As clear-eyed as Pascal is about the motives of all human endeavor, including thought, he is never tempted to reduce man to mere matter, for materialism is self-contradictory: "If we are simply material, we cannot know anything at all." Materialism is a doctrine, a rational account of how things are, advanced by its adherents with evidence and arguments, on the implicit assumption that other intelligent beings respond to such strange, immaterial stimuli. A consistent materialist would not argue; he would use force. Indeed, a consistent materialist would not think at all, for he would be merely matter. A thinking being is necessarily a more-than-material being. He participates, through his mind, in a world where reasons rather than forces count as causes.[46]

But this acknowledgment of the strange doubleness of the thinking reed only deepens our perplexities. We are "composed of two natures, opposite and different in kind, soul and body." Moreover, the distance between body and mind is "infinite." Man is the meeting point of the world of thought and the world of extension and, as such, the most radically mysterious part of a mysterious whole. "Man is himself the most prodigious object of nature, because he cannot understand what body is, still less what mind is, and less than anything how a body may be united to a mind. This is the culmination of his difficulties, and yet this is his own being." Pascal sees, and brings us to see, the contradiction between material and spiritual at the heart of our being. He offers no solution to it, for to solve the human paradox lies beyond the power of man. To become aware of our monstrosity is to reach the summit of the self-knowledge man can acquire for himself.[47]

"Know then, proud one, what a paradox you are to yourself." We want happiness, love, and approbation, yet wherever we turn in human life, we find ourselves facing another example of our sad and hateful emptiness. We want truth, yet we cannot even grasp the truth of ourselves, for an enormous contradiction lies at the heart of our very being. And yet, try though we might, we cannot stop ourselves from desiring the happiness and truth that perpetually fly from our grasp.[48]

If Pascal has succeeded in bringing us to see the contradiction of our own being and the unfillable gap between what we long for and what we can get, he has accomplished the fundamental educational effort of the *Pensées*: to turn a soul indifferent to religion, indifferent to itself and its own fate, into a soul at the beginning of a quest.

There are only three kinds of people: those who serve God, having found him; those who are busy seeking him, not having found him; those who live without seeking or finding him. The first are reasonable and happy, the last are foolish and unhappy; those in the middle are unhappy and reasonable.[49]

To learn, with Pascal, that the Montaignean harmony between self-knowledge and contentment is illusory does not make us happy. Self-knowledge brings us not sanity and equilibrium but anguish. That anguish, however, may impel us to seek. Such seeking in anguish is the one rational response to a clear-eyed, undistracted assessment of our natural condition. If we engage in that search, we transform our restlessness from an irritable and directionless unease into a determined quest for an answer to the paradox of ourselves.

Searching in Anguish

The Philosophers: Epictetus and Montaigne

If effective, Pascal's exploration of the human condition has put us in motion, seeking an exit from the prison of misery and diversion hiding behind the mask of contentment. It has also led us to see the locus of our dignity in the capacity that allows us to perceive our misery—in reason. Pascal's next step is, logically enough, to cause us to examine those who orient their lives by reason—that is, the philosophers.[50]

Pascal's greatest thematic consideration of philosophy takes place not in the *Pensées* but in a real-life seventeenth-century philosophic dialogue in which he plays the leading role. That conversation takes place at the Jansenists' headquarters at Port-Royal des Champs, shortly after Pascal's arrival for his first extended stay in 1655. His spiritual director, Antoine Singlin, sends him there for a retreat of sorts, perhaps in an effort to remove Pascal from the fog of ambitious intellectual worldliness surrounding him in Paris. When he arrives, Pascal meets with the "indispensable man" of the place, Louis-Isaac Lemaistre de Saci. An impressive scholar and priest who took the lead in the Jansenists' enormously successful translation of the Bible, Saci customarily interviews Port-Royal's many illustrious visitors. Through his subtle conversational art, he seeks to nudge his interlocutors toward a more profoundly religious life.[51]

Pascal arrives at Port-Royal as an intellectual celebrity, almost scandalous to the pious residents of the place because of his dedication to worldly science and philosophy. His meeting with Saci is an event, on which Saci's secretary, Nicolas Fontaine, takes notes. Fontaine will eventually develop those notes into a full-blown dialogue, apparently supplementing his recollections by consulting Pascal's writings. The result shows us a Pascal fully, brilliantly engaged with philosophy and yet driven to transcend its limits—a picture that matches the thinker we come to know in the *Pensées* precisely.[52]

Saci's conversational art consists in engaging his interlocutor on his favorite subject—surgery for a surgeon, painting for a painter. Once his conversation partner has revealed the preoccupations of his heart, Saci leads him ineluctably from wherever he is to God. Sensing Pascal's interest in philosophy, Saci sets him to talking about that. But he will not need to lead Pascal anywhere, for Pascal's philosophic conversation has a self-transcending trajectory all its own.[53]

With his accustomed boldness, Pascal gathers all of philosophy behind two great banners: dogmatism, represented by the ancient stoic Epictetus, and skepticism, represented by the modern Pyrrhonist Montaigne. These, he says, are "the two greatest defenders of the two most celebrated sects in the world"; they speak not just for themselves but for the very possibilities of human thought and morals. Epictetus is the voice of knowledge and rational self-mastery; Montaigne is the voice of doubt and easygoing hedonism. Between them, Pascal creates a *gigantomachia*, a "tournament of champions," as Graeme Hunter calls it, in which the fundamental alternatives of all rationalism confront one another and thereby reveal their limits.[54]

Of all the world's philosophers, Pascal lists Epictetus as the one who "knows man's duties best." Epictetus counsels man to consider God his principal end, persuades him that God rules with justice, and advises him to bring himself to will everything that occurs as the consequence of divine providence. Should we lose a wife or a daughter, Epictetus would have us say "I gave her up": we should willingly relinquish someone we knew had been given to us only on loan and whom we were fated to lose eventually. "You must not, he says, desire that things be done as you would like; rather, you must desire that things be done as they are done." Should man succeed in so conforming his will to the divine will, he will come to "perfectly know God, love Him, obey Him, please Him, heal himself of all his vices, acquire all the virtues, and render himself holy and a companion to God." The efforts of reason and will can perfect, even sanctify, a human life, bridging the gap between man and God by ascending to the divine perspective. That ascent is the secret of human contentment.[55]

Montaigne, by contrast, is an apostle of doubt. In a tour de force précis of the sprawling "Apology for Raymond Sebond," Pascal describes Montaigne's evisceration of every human pretension to knowledge. Montaigne's skepticism is so thoroughgoing that it must be expressed in the form of a question—the "What do I know?" that is his motto. Montaigne "handles reason devoid of faith so roughly and cruelly as to make it doubt whether it is reasonable." He shakes man's pride in his reason to its foundations, making us wonder if we can know anything at all. Morally unable to determine any firm principles, he follows his pleasures and the common way, seeking always after "convenience and tranquility." The ethical application of intransigent skepticism is Montaignean nonchalance; the skeptic achieves contentment by lightening his touch.[56]

These two sects, Pascal claims, "crush and annihilate one another." Intellectually, Montaigne and the skeptics unsettle Epictetus and the dogmatists, with their fixation on our duties, by pointing out that we do not know whether we were created "by a good God, by an evil demon, or by chance." Without such knowledge of our origins, we cannot know whether Epictetus's efforts to conform his will to whatever comes to pass in life is not a self-deluded resignation to capricious fate rather than a noble ascent to the divine perspective. The dogmatists, for their part, may respond that "there has never been a fully effective skeptic": man cannot sincerely doubt everything. While it may be true that we cannot rationally prove our own existence, we cannot honestly doubt it either. Radical skepticism is a disingenuous argumentative strategy deployed exclusively in philosophy classes and barroom debates. We leave it behind the moment we enter the practical world, which constantly demands that we forget our doubts and make decisions, decisions that reveal what we really think more truly than the smoke and mirrors of academic arguments.[57]

The intellectual defects of dogmatism and skepticism have corresponding moral defects. Epictetus, "knowing man's duties and ignoring his impotence, loses himself in presumption"; Montaigne, "knowing man's impotence but not his duty, tumbles into lassitude." Each runs afoul of one of the dangers that attend man's double nature: Epictetus, conscious of man's greatness, falls into a pride that blinds him to his incapacity to fulfill by his own efforts the duties he perceives. Montaigne, so aware of human weakness, loses human greatness from view and falls into a vice more deadly than pride: despair. By destroying the human hope for truth, despair causes us to fall into an apathy that atrophies the soul, as Thomas Hibbs remarks. For the decay of the soul's powers naturally follows when we cease to seek a truth we do not hope to find.[58]

Caught between overweening certitude and unserious doubt, between Promethean pride and self-destructive despair, the philosophic quest to guide ourselves by reason alone consumes itself in the clash of dogmatism and skepticism. Rather than ending the philosophic search for wisdom, however, the mutual annihilation of dogmatism and skepticism opens the way to philosophy's self-transcendence. If Pascal is right that all of rationalism boils down to a contest between dogmatism, which asserts that we can know what we need to know, and skepticism, which questions whether we can truly know anything; if he rightly delineates the objections each of these camps can pose to one another; and if he rightly convicts them of their characteristic vices of pride and despair, which blind us to truth and hollow out our lives, philosophy has good reason to seek to transcend rationalism. That reason alone cannot give us the wisdom we need to guide our lives does not obviate our need for that wisdom.[59]

And so Pascal would guide his discontented seeker to the world's religions, to see if God or the gods might offer guidance that speaks more truly to the whole of what we are.

Pagan, Muslim, and Jew

According to Périer, Pascal intended in his next step to make a capacious survey of the whole range of human understandings of the divine. We know very little of what Pascal would have done here; the section of modern editions of the *Pensées* that corresponds to Périer's description includes fewer than twenty brief fragments. Pascal commented that he would have needed ten years of good health to complete his work as intended; one hopes that much of that time would have been spent in deepening his understanding of the religions of Greece and Egypt, Moses and Mohammed. What we have shows little of Pascal's remarkable ability, so evident in his treatment of Epictetus and Montaigne, to enter sympathetically into the minds of those with whom he disagrees. Nonetheless, his approach to paganism, Islam, and Judaism can help us understand what he takes to be the unique features of Christianity, the ultimate target of his interest.[60]

Paganism, for Pascal, lacks the intellectual heft to satisfy the demands of the human mind. Pagan religions, he writes, "are more popular, for they are external, but they are not for clever people. A purely intellectual religion would be better suited to the clever, but it would not serve the common people." Pascal detects, as had St. Augustine, that the pagan sages themselves preferred a natural religion, such as that of Epictetus, to the risible and barbaric gods of Rome's theaters and temples. And yet the gods of the philosophers were too distant, bloodless, and unconcerned with human things to satisfy many. By the time of

Christ, "the great Pan [was] dead," in the haunting phrase Pascal borrows from Plutarch: the naïve fecundity of pagan mythology had dried up, leaving only a decayed and sometimes demonic husk of superstitions.[61]

Of Islam, Pascal describes its contrast with Christianity as follows: "the two are so opposite that, if Mahomet took the path of succeeding in a human way, Jesus Christ took that of perishing in a human way. . . . since Mahomet succeeded, Jesus Christ had to perish." With a conquering hero for its prophet and a paradise depicted in images of sensual delight, Islam illustrates the ways of the human world, and succeeds by those ways with a success the world can recognize. It is, in this sense, a perfectly natural religion—all too intelligible as the fulfillment of concupiscent human desires.[62]

Summing up his brief account of what "makers of religions" present to the world, Pascal remarks that they have "neither a morality that can please me nor proofs that can convince me"; they offer only the spectacle of cults, beliefs, and morals forever in flux. He then turns to a tiny, oppressed, but ancient and hardy people, the Jews, who offer an insistent alternative to this sad state of affairs. They worship a single God, governing themselves according to a law they claim that God gave them, which teaches a morality that requires them to be honest and self-restrained. They cling tenaciously to the Book that contains this law, as well as their religion and their history, despite that Book's continual denunciations of their stiff-necked ingratitude. That Book, which describes the misery of man without God in moving detail, is full of prophecies of a figure who would come to redeem all of humanity from its wretchedness, prophecies that this people, scattered from its home, spreads throughout the world. When one who claims to be that redeemer comes, some Jews follow him, and some do not. Those who do not are, for

Pascal, of the greatest interest, because they preserve the prophecies without believing that they point to Christ. Christianity is thereby able to base its claims to truth on the testimony of "unimpeachable witnesses": the followers of another religion, who deny the truth of Christianity but nonetheless teach the proofs of it in their own sacred texts.[63]

Of the others, whom he calls "spiritual" or "true" Jews, Pascal aims "to show that the true Jews and the true Christians have but one and the same religion." While Judaism seems to be a religion built on the pillars of "Abraham's fatherhood, circumcision, sacrifices, ceremonies, the Ark, the temple, Jerusalem, and finally in the law and covenant with Moses," Pascal contends that it "consisted in none of these things, but only in the love of God." The God of the Old Testament promises to punish Jews no differently from foreigners if they offend Him; He receives strangers who love Him, just as He receives Jews. In Deuteronomy, Pascal finds the teaching that the circumcision that God really cares about is the circumcision of the heart, not the foreskin; he finds in the prophets' predictions that the priesthood of Aaron will be replaced by the priesthood of Melchizedek, that Jerusalem will be reproved and Rome admitted. A distinction between carnal and spiritual Judaism runs throughout Jewish history: not only did spiritual Jews become Christ's followers upon his arrival, but spiritual Judaism can also rise up at any time from within carnal Judaism, for it is the animating presence of the Torah.[64]

Of Pascal's remarks on paganism, Islam, and Judaism, only those on Judaism have any real depth, and even here he is far from making the best case for the alternative view. Nonetheless, his remarks on other religions reveal the contours of his claims on behalf of Christianity: that it speaks to our whole being, as neither the superstitions of popular paganism nor the abstract god of the philosophers can; that it speaks *to* human nature in its fallenness, rather than *from* that nature, as does Pascal's Islam; that it realizes the promise of spiritual Judaism while shedding the insularity of carnal Judaism. The searching soul now, finally, approaches the decisive question: the question of Christianity, of what it promises, and whether its promises merit belief.[65]

The Wager

Pascal's tour of the religious landscape, had it been completed, would have sought to place his reader in a position analogous to that of the first Christians, who received the Christian proposition as a radical alternative to the all too well-trodden ways of a fallen world, in which man tries and fails to content himself in countless ways that do not answer to the demands of his paradoxical nature. The first piece of that proposition is the promise of eternal life. Pascal describes what it means to be faced with such an offer in the fragment he called "infinity, nothingness" but which has come to be called "The Wager." Perhaps written with his gambling friends in mind, "The Wager" suggests that cold, self-interested mathematical calculation allows us to see the good sense of betting something finite, temporal life, for a chance at an infinite reward, eternal life. Even if it were highly unlikely that the God offering that reward exists, we should still bet, given the vast disproportion between what we are staking and what we might win, just as it would make sense to bet a dollar for a chance at a million dollars even if the prospects of losing were one hundred to one. Precisely because of the immeasurable disproportion between our finite minds and an infinite God, however, reason can determine nothing about God's existence or nature. From our point of view, the prospects of our wager are therefore even; it would be foolish not to take such a bet.[66]

No passage in Pascal draws more readers, or more objections. Alexis de Tocqueville describes its logic as "unworthy of the great soul of Pascal," for it seems to make soul-saving faith the product of sharp-eyed, self-interested calculation. But taken as a single step along the long road Pascal would have his reader travel, "The Wager" can be seen to be more modest in its aims. Beyond the proposition of eternal life itself, "The Wager" offers no defense of the specifically Christian understanding of God. For that argument, we must turn to the rest of the *Pensées*. Moreover, "The Wager" aims to speak only to "seekers in anguish"—human beings already convinced by Pascal's account of human misery and contradiction. Should such readers be willing to bet what remains of their finite existences—roughly, "ten years of *amour-propre*, trying hard to please without succeeding"—for infinite life, truth, and happiness?[67]

The probabilistic reasoning of "The Wager" gives reasons for thinking we should. But what if we accept that much, yet still do not believe—what if we say that while eternal life would be desirable, there does not seem to be any evidence for it? Pascal assumes that his readers will respond in exactly this way. He responds with the suggestion that they act as if they believe, taking holy water and having Masses said, for this will habituate them to believing "naturally and mechanically." Readers have found this suggestion both puzzling and distasteful, for it seems to indicate that we should simply go through the motions of religious practice until our reason is effectively silenced. Indeed, the word Pascal uses to describe this process of habituation suggests that Christian conversation entails "stupefying" oneself. "The Wager" seems to culminate in an argument for the abdication of reason and intentional self-deceit.[68]

What is Pascal up to? As Thomas Hibbs suggests, Pascal here enters into "the mystery of moral transformation." Our vision is colored by our desires, which are in turn shaped by our habits: the foods that look tastiest to some will nauseate others; a library, which looks to some eyes like a treasure house of inexhaustible delights, looks to others like a prison of constraint and boredom. The problem of belief is that, to eyes customarily fixed on tangible goods, material limits, and human honors, the promises of religion seem airy, thin, and implausible. To see them otherwise requires that we transform our vision by transforming our desires—that is, by engaging with the animal, mechanical part of our natures. As Pascal puts it, "At least realize that your inability to believe comes from your passions, since reason brings you to this and yet you cannot believe. Work, then, on convincing yourself, not by adding more proofs of God's existence, but by diminishing your passions." The possibility of altering our habits thankfully allows us to perform this kind of work on ourselves, as anyone who has ever executed a significant project of moral reform, from quitting cigarettes to running marathons, knows. Such efforts at self-transformation turn what reason can see to be good into the heart's desire: what begins as a rational judgment about the importance of health becomes a tangible desire for the good of exercise as the realization of the body's capacities for action. That we can acquire this new desire by acting for a time as if we already possessed it marks our success not in deceiving ourselves but in transforming ourselves.[69]

Christianity posits the existence of another dimension of human life—a dimension of grace or supernature, present if hidden in the Church's sacraments, present if hidden in nature itself. When reason clamors against this claim, the psychic wellspring of its arguments is the intractable belief that what we can see is all there is. Catholic Christianity, with its edible and potable sacraments, its stations of the cross and its rosary beads, its fasts and its pilgrimages, makes belief in the supernatural something human beings can *do*. To silence reason and practice faith opens the eyes to a possibility we must teach the machine to perceive before we can seriously think about it. Should we do so, we expand the range of our perception but see nothing inconsistent with any truth right reason can perceive about the world.[70]

As Pascal states his intention at the outset of the *Pensées*, he hopes to make decent people "wish [the Christian religion] were true," because it "promises the true good." That is, he hopes to make us see that the good Christianity offers is the good we really want: infinite life, happiness, and knowledge. The wager is a device meant to clear away apparently rational objections to this Christian proposition. If we have been previously convinced by Pascal's depiction of our misery, it may lead us to a project of moral reform, which may allow us to begin to experience a different kind of life here and now: the life of one who is "faithful, honest, grateful, beneficent, a sincere friend, and truthful," a life that is a palpable improvement on the life of the hateful self Pascal so poignantly describes. This moral transformation from a life of sad sensuality to a life of gracious joy can be completed only with divine help. But the presence of grace is perceptible only to eyes that wish to see it and are thereby prepared to pierce the veil of divine absence in which the world seems shrouded.[71]

The Hidden God

Seeing the action of grace will require some looking, for there is nothing open and evident about God's presence in the world. Pascal loves to quote a remark to this effect from Isaiah: "*truly you are a hidden God.*" God gives hints but not the sight of Himself; we see at once too much and too little: "Nature offers me nothing that is not matter for doubt and inquietude. If I saw nothing there which indicated a Divinity, I would determine myself in the negative; if I saw everywhere the marks of a Creator, I would repose peacefully in faith." Nature's splendid order seems to speak of God; nature's arbitrariness shows us no God but fortune; nature's cruelty makes us wonder if it is not governed by a gnostic demiurge, who positively delights in our ignorance and suffering. Even God's presence in scripture itself is often veiled. At times, to be sure, the God of the Old Testament appears in blinding majesty; at other times, however, He appears in the guise of a wandering stranger, or in a still, small voice that speaks in the calm that follows a storm. The God of the New Testament hides in plain sight in the very midst of those who have been expecting His arrival for centuries; He is "rejected, despised, betrayed . . . spit upon, buffeted, mocked, afflicted in innumerable ways," all because He is not recognized for who He is. Considered merely as a man, Jesus Christ is a figure so insignificant that contemporary historians take no notice of his appearance. Even in the life of the Church itself, God keeps His promise to remain with man by taking up residence in "the most strange and obscure hiding place of all, which are the species of the Eucharist." For what could be more hidden than a God who presents Himself to man with the appearance, feel, smell, and even taste of plain bread and wine?[72]

Why does God hide Himself? Why not appear in unmistakable majesty before the eyes of every human being in every time and place? God appears beneath veils, Pascal believes, because He is not a boor: He does not wish to force upon those who do not seek Him "a good they do not want." Many would prefer it if God neither existed nor took an interest in human life, for to consider oneself constantly under the gaze of the divine observer can be, to say the least, unsettling. For those who do seek Him, God's veiled mode of appearing serves to draw "the inquirer out of himself and into the quest," as Hibbs puts it. The searcher who follows inquiry beyond rationalism's limits still retains the character of a seeker, then. And the God he pursues has the character not only of a father but of a teacher.[73]

God's divine pedagogy includes, as Hibbs argues, a teacher's irony, which He deploys to egg His students on. In the remarkable fragment known as "The Memorial"—a fragment Pascal sewed into the lining of his doublet, carefully removing it and sewing it into the next one every time he changed that garment for the last eight years of his life—he insists that the "God of Abraham, God of Isaac, God of Jacob" was not the distant and impersonal God postulated by Cartesian reason. Pascal seems to have believed he *met* God on the night of November 23, 1654, in an experience he describes with the words "fire," "certitude," "tears," and "joy." Pascal, who knew well the experience of intellectual discovery, here describes something quite other, something no effort of the human mind could produce on its own. The God of the Patriarchs and the Gospels is a God who not only allows Himself to be discovered by man, as does "the god of the philosophers and the learned," but comes forth to find him, seeking out those open to the disconcerting presence of the divine guest.[74]

The decisive act in God's search for man is the Incarnation. That event not only reveals God to man but reveals man to himself: "Not only do we not know God except through Jesus-Christ, but we do not know ourselves except through Jesus-Christ." Christ in the Garden of Gethsemane, sweating blood in fear and anguish and praying that the cup of crucifixion might pass Him by, is the mirror of human misery; Christ going forth from there to meet His fate without a murmur is the image of human greatness. This most bodily of gods satisfies every legitimate longing of the human mind. The God of the Gospels both shows man to himself and provides the answer to the question of human longing. "Man," as Peter Kreeft remarks, "is like a very strangely shaped lock, with weird protuberances and indentations. . . . Christianity is like a key—an equally strangely shaped key—that fits the lock." Christianity reveals us to ourselves in all the contradictions of our nature. The picture it offers us of ourselves—ever-seeking, suffering even in triumph, stuck with sin and yet, with the help of grace, capable of a greatness that may rightly be called divine—could hardly be more opposed to the image of the contained and contented self offered us by Montaigne. The strangest part of that picture is what Pascal calls the heart—the part of us that, when animated by grace, makes possible a form of love that rivals Montaignean friendship.[75]

The Heart and the Possibility of Love

When Montaigne sought to describe a way of life loyal to our nature, he described a life he called "intellectually sensual and sensually intellectual"—a life fit for both mind and body. Pascal's Christianity, too, speaks to both of these parts of ourselves; it is at once as intellectually inexhaustible as the Trinity and as bodily as bread and wine. But for Pascal, man is not composed of body and mind alone. He locates the deepest stratum of human nature in what he calls the "heart," a part with little place in Montaigne's sensual and intellectual vision of the good life.[76]

"The heart has its reasons which reason does not know"— so runs the most quoted remark in the *Pensées*. It appears at first glance a pithy justification of sentimentality, and Pascal elsewhere tells us that the heart "feels" rather than reasons. But the heart feels strange things: it grasps "first principles, such as space, time, motion, and numbers"—the most unsentimental stuff imaginable. This knowledge of the heart is reason's starting point, not its sentimental antithesis: "The heart feels that there are three dimensions in space and that numbers are infinite, and reason then shows that there are no two square numbers of which one is double the other." All rational knowledge begins from the first principles the heart grasps by "instinct and sentiment," which is indeed knowledge, firmer than any that reason provides.[77]

And yet the heart is an organ of love even more than knowledge. As such, it moves and is moved in a manner most different than reason's: "The heart has its order; the mind has its own, which consists of principle and demonstration. The heart has another. We do not prove that we should be loved by displaying in order the causes of love. That would be absurd." Marriage proposals must impassion, not prove. The language of the heart seeks to move us, with all the decisiveness of our most profound instincts. As the encounter with a beloved may introduce us to aspects of existence we had previously failed to perceive, the language of the heart seeks to show us a new dimension of our lives, as undeniable, once we see it, as our awareness of the passage of time.[78]

Scripture speaks this language of the heart; it seeks to "impassion, not to instruct." Though the figure at its center, Jesus Christ, offers food for both body and mind, He does not catch our attention with either "carnal or intellectual greatness": "he produced no inventions; he did not reign." His greatness was of another order: "he was humble, patient, holy, holy, holy to God, terrible to demons, without any sin. With what great pomp and magnificent splendor did he come to the eyes of the heart, which perceive wisdom!" To perceive that holiness is wisdom is to enter into the perspective of charity—what Pascal calls the Christian "hidden thought" that allows us to see everything in a new light. That perception is faith, given by grace as an intuition of the heart, and as such not at our command. The most we can do is open ourselves to receive it.[79]

Pascal describes the experience of conversion, of the wandering heart touched by grace, in the image of a foot that has spent its life imagining itself an autonomous being and loving only itself, and then suddenly discovers that it is part of a larger whole, from which it receives life and in which it has its function. This larger whole is the Church, or the "Christian Republic," as Pascal calls it, a "body of thinking members" whose animating principle of life and unity is charity.[80]

Charity—the experience of which Pascal calls "fire" and "the greatness of the human soul"—is the one thing needful, for it alone allows us to move beyond the fitting self-hatred we experience when we face the tyrannical, truth-hating character of our human selves. If "the true and unique virtue" consists in hating ourselves, we must then "seek to love a being truly worthy of love." And yet we cannot simply forsake self-love for the love of some being outside ourselves. We must therefore "love a being who is within us, and who is not us. . . . Now only the universal being is like that. The universal good is within us; it is ourselves and not us." The self is not self-contained; the universal being is within it. *L'homme passe l'homme.*[81]

Because the universal being is within me, because, without being the miserable *I*, it is what I most of all *am*, I can come to see everything from its point of view. To do so is to solve the problem of moral perspective Pascal raises in one of the first fragments of the *Pensées*. If we wish to see a painting properly,

Pascal remarks, we cannot stand too near or too far; we must be situated at the one right point, a point determined by the art of perspective. This thought lies at the heart of Pascal's work on conic sections, which solves an intractable geometric problem by considering it from a unified viewpoint. "But who will assign this point in truth and morals?" he wonders. Charity, the perspective of the universal being that dwells within us, assigns the point from which to view all things. Similarly, Pascal contrasts three figures who perceive time's passage differently: for one, it passes slowly; for the other, quickly; but the third man has a watch. The perspective of charity is this moral timepiece. Because it is a perspective from within, it can be our own.[82]

Should we adopt this perspective—or, rather, should we be infused with it, for the true movement of charity is a movement of grace—we solve the problem of our own injustice and misery. "No one is as happy as a true Christian, nor as reasonable, as virtuous, as lovable." We become reasonable and lovable because we have found an escape from the self's unreasonableness and tyranny. We no longer hide from the truth about the self or see the world through its distorting lens, for we no longer make it the center of everything. We are no longer caught in the trap of our finitude, doomed to desire a happiness we cannot acquire. For we live in the hope that we may receive that happiness not as an achievement but as a gift.[83]

Montaigne might say that this perspective of the universal being is but one more diversion, one more way of getting our minds off ourselves and our misery. He suggests as much about eternal life in his chapter "Of Diversion." Here, it seems that the best test of Pascal's proposition is an experiential one. As Hibbs remarks, Pascal assures his would-be wagerer that, "with each step he takes along the road," he "will see more clearly the truthfulness and goodness of the Christian way of life." The wagerer becomes a pilgrim, who understands his life not as an effort to be at home in this world but as an embattled voyage on his way to a home he does not reach in this life. And yet, the rightness of each step that wagerer has taken becomes clear in hindsight, as the withering of the passions clarifies his sight.[84]

Those who have not entered into that perspective must attempt to judge it from the outside, through the testimony of others. Pascal gives regrettably little such first-person testimony. As Gilberte Périer points out, he "never spoke of himself, nor of anything else with regard to himself; and it is known that he wanted an honest man even to refrain from naming himself, from using the words *je* and *moi*." The *Pensées* follow this design; although they peer into the deepest recesses of human fear and sadness, they tell us almost nothing particular about their author's life—a choice about style that signals the whole substantive difference between Pascal and Montaigne. When we attempt to size up the Christian religious experience, we naturally wish, however, that Pascal had given us more of a view from the inside.[85]

In one fragment, however, Pascal breaks his self-imposed taboo on the first person to describe precisely this Christian experience:

I love poverty because He loved it. I love goods because they give me the means to aid the miserable. I keep fidelity with everyone. I do not return evil to those who do me evil, but I wish them a condition similar to mine, where one receives neither good nor evil from men. I try to be just, truthful, sincere, and faithful to all men, and I have a tenderness of heart for those to whom God has united me more closely.

And whether I am alone or in the view of men, I have in all my actions the regard of God, who must judge them and to whom I have consecrated all of them.

Such are my sentiments.

And I bless every day of my life my redeemer who put these sentiments into me, and who, from a man full of weakness, misery, concupiscence, pride, and ambition, has made a man exempt from all these evils by the force of grace, to whom all the glory is due, what comes from me being only misery and error.[86]

Pascal's entry into this perspective allowed him, in his view, genuinely to love others: in his particular attachments to Jacqueline and Arthus de Roannez; in the charity toward everyone that led him, at the end of his life, to house a poor family in his own home and invent the five-cent carriages for the benefit of the poor of Paris. Such charity is not the unmediated, complete approbation of the selves of others; we must hate sins even as we love sinners. It is, instead, the love of the universal being who resides in others as much as in ourselves, who *is* them as much as He, *is* ourselves.[87]

On the night of fire, the moment of his decisive entry into this new perspective on himself and everyone around him, Pascal records "joy, joy, joy, tears of joy." That joy is not contentment—it is fire. Pascal never circumscribes himself into a settled equilibrium. He burns himself up, "prematurely breaking the ties that hold the soul to the body, [dying] of old age before forty years of age," in Tocqueville's words. As Tocqueville comments elsewhere, "Man comes out of nothing, passes through time, and goes to disappear forever into the bosom of God." Such is Pascal's life, if one adds that some human souls give forth prodigious light as they make their mortal passage. If Montaigne figures the life of immanent contentment as a circle, Pascal figures the Christian life as a comet, whose motion, beginning in anguish and culminating in joy, neither comes to rest nor turns in on itself but burns forward straight and bright until it is absorbed into eternity.[88]

Pascal's Legacy: Honest Sadness in an Age of Happiness-Signaling

Whether Pascal's joy is true or whether, as Kolakowski darkly suspects, Pascal's religion is "a religion for unhappy people . . . designed to make them more unhappy" is perhaps an interior secret no outside observer can penetrate. But Kolakowski is right in this much: Pascal's sketch of Christian happiness and virtue is only a sketch—the first few notes of a Christian allegro to relieve the awful if beautiful sadness of his long, Christian adagio. It is the latter that has been the heart of his intellectual legacy. Pascal speaks the truth of human misery with unparalleled immediacy. The importance of his voice only increases in a society such as ours, systematically dedicated to the masking of unhappiness. As Kreeft comments, the truth of human suffering is the truth that Americans and Englishmen most assiduously hide. As if misery were not enough of a burden, we have made it into an object of shame, a disorder. We identify not only success but even normalcy with happiness. That is why we signal happiness so relentlessly, in our Instagram feeds and our holiday cards, in the laughing, smiling pictures of ourselves we strive to put before the world.[89]

Pascal scrubs away this rouge-and-lipstick cheerfulness. No observer more powerfully reveals the restless unhappiness at the core of the modern soul, sadly seeking to absorb itself in a form of contentment not capacious enough to meet the demands of its self-transcending nature. It is a truth we would often prefer not to hear. In the century following his death, Pascal's Augustinian brooding will be almost completely drowned out by the fanfare of Enlightenment optimism. But the memory of the sad truths to which he gave voice with such force will not go away. It will find in one of the Enlightenment's own children a strange and quixotic avenger.[90]

CHAPTER 3

Rousseau

The Tragedy of Nature's Redeemer

Rousseau's Third Way

Pascal's power is also his weakness. His unsparing critique of our pretensions to happiness inspires trust, for one senses that he was as tough on himself as he was on everyone else. But that toughness can also prompt doubts. Is the quest for immanent contentment really such a complete failure? Is human love truly impossible without the mediation of the personal God of the New Testament? Has the fall of nature been so far, leaving the created world with nothing of substance—nothing but the Church?[1]

One might like to forget what Pascal shows us about ourselves. But it is hard to recover one's Montaignean nonchalance once Pascal has brought us to contemplate the abyss of our disquiet. Faced with the choice between the intransigently Christian depth of Pascal and the broad-minded, intentional shallowness of Montaigne, the mind seeks an alternative, a third way. Perhaps it is possible to combine depth and naturalness. Perhaps we can understand our restlessness as something other than the longing for a hidden God who cannot be compelled to show Himself. Perhaps we can find some earthly alternative to a life of meaningless diversion.

Jean-Jacques Rousseau seeks such a third way. This sets him apart from many of his eighteenth-century contemporaries, who counter Pascal's critique of the self-delusions of modern man by simply denying the problem. The Enlightenment's great champion, Voltaire, writes many pages defending our love of diversion as both unavoidable and unregrettable. In his infamous celebration of worldliness, *Le Mondain*, Voltaire tries to show that the wine, women, and song of his beloved Paris are infinitely preferable to the imagined delights of the primordial paradise whose loss so haunted Pascal. Every time he feels ill, however, the aging hypochondriac feels a telling need to argue with Pascal once more. Voltaire's denial of the problems intrinsic to the quest for immanent contentment, which Pascal demonstrates so powerfully, fails to fool even himself.[2]

Rousseau, by contrast, sees that Pascal had touched on truth. Voltaire will come to hate him even more than Pascal because Rousseau uses the kinds of arguments and evidence the Enlightenment has developed to critique the Enlightenment itself. He is, in Voltaire's eyes, a *philosophe* who gives aid and comfort to the priestly enemies of philosophy and liberty. The two engage in a long and nasty quarrel that eventually devolves into frankly avowed mutual detestation. On Voltaire's side, that hatred is truly murderous: he hopes to see Rousseau "beaten to death . . . beaten to death between his *gouvernante*'s knees," and helps stir up a crowd that will stone Rousseau's house in 1765.[3]

It had not always been so. The young Rousseau arrived in Paris in 1742 as a great admirer of Voltaire, determined to make his name in Voltaire's world of art and intellect, power and wealth. There, like so many others, he strives after brilliance: hunting for offices with aristocrats and the Crown; hobnobbing with musicians and writers; paying his court to the city's great beauties and women of influence; contributing articles to the

Encyclopédie. At times he lives in the houses of the great; at times he is reduced to abject poverty. His unstable fortunes introduce him to the full range of human possibilities, "from the lowest up to the highest, except the throne," in the capital of the Enlightenment at its peak.[4]

Then he turns his back on it all. One day, in the grips of a vision he invites us to compare to the illumination of St. Paul on the road to Damascus, Rousseau suddenly sees through all the pretenses of Parisian brilliance. Pascal is right: his celebrated contemporaries are secretly miserable. They seek science purely for the sake of distinguishing themselves; their amusements merely hide their unease. True love and friendship have no place in their glittering society, which is in truth "a society of smiling enemies."[5]

At the moment of his illumination, Rousseau "[sees] another world and [becomes] another man." He quits his lucrative post as cashier to a receiver general of finances and decides to earn his bread as a human Xerox machine, copying music at so many cents a page. He dispenses with all the formal, pseudo-aristocratic accoutrements of his life of social striving: selling his watch, dispensing with his sword and silk stockings, and counting it a blessing when a laundry thief relieves him of forty-two fine linen shirts. Most importantly, he leaves Paris. Rousseau departs the city in 1756, hoping never to return.[6]

Rousseau will come to understand his decision to leave Paris as fatal, for it turns his Enlightenment friends—Denis Diderot, the Baron d'Holback, Friedrich Grimm, and many others—permanently against him. They see in Rousseau's departure a condemnation of their whole way of life. They are right: Rousseau does indeed see the celebrated society of Paris as a web of lies woven in the silk of amour propre. He intends his departure to signal the initiation of a new way of life: an authentic life that dispenses with the formalities and falsehoods of urbane sophistication; a way of life he means to be an example for the world.[7]

Pascal, too, stripped away the veils of social life to reveal the sad hollowness beneath. Rousseau accepts Pascal's diagnosis of the dismal psychic condition that lies behind the sheen of Parisian forms and manners but sees dramatically different causes for that emptiness and hate. And seeing the problem differently, he sees the solution differently. For Pascal, we are unhappy because we are alienated from God. For Rousseau, we are unhappy because we are alienated from ourselves. For Pascal, nature is fallen but can be redeemed by God. For Rousseau, man is fallen but can be redeemed by nature.[8]

Such are Rousseau's principles, principles that lead him to perform a vast imaginative experiment on the human condition in his thought. Because he believes thought and life should be unified, Rousseau also performs an experimental application of his principles on himself. He reimagines the standard of immanent contentment in the light of Pascal's critique of it, reinterpreting the Montaignean standards of psychic equilibrium and unmediated approbation. In so doing, he takes us to the limits of human possibility in an impassioned effort to prove that human nature is not as fallen as Pascal imagines. The stakes of the moral and intellectual experiment of Rousseau's thought and life are enormous, for he tests the question of whether human happiness and love are possible on the basis of modern principles and in the absence of help from the personal God of the Bible.[9]

Rousseau locates the cause of our restlessness in human dividedness. Just like Montaigne, Rousseau imagines human existence on a horizontal axis between the individual and society, and posits that our dividedness springs from our failure to be wholeheartedly committed either to ourselves or to the larger social wholes upon which we depend. Rejecting Montaignean moderation and eclecticism, though, Rousseau hopes that we might become whole again by going "all in" on something: whether solitude, society, or family, what matters is that we give ourselves over without reserve. Rousseau experiments with extremes: he celebrates a form of citizenship that reminds every reader today of totalitarianism; he embraces a form of sentimental individualism that anticipates all the waves of bohemian social rebellion that will sweep over modern social life in the centuries to come. Most radically, in *Émile*, he makes of man a tabula rasa, investigating what he might become if we could set everything we are aside and experiment on our nature with the precise control of the scientist's laboratory. The redemption of earthly existence, in Rousseau's view, requires that we be willing to take the extreme step of transforming our nature, so as to rescue the possibility of human wholeness from the degradations of history.[10]

Rousseau's thoughts are radical, but they are really only the product of consistent effort to draw the consequences of the principles shared by everyone who would like to find a form of immanent contentment equal to the challenge of Pascal's biblical pessimism. Rousseau arrives at his strangeness and extravagance by thinking through principles he shares with more moderate moderns to their necessary if extreme conclusions. In this sense, Rousseau *is* modern self-knowledge.[11]

Rousseau's New Eden and the Exile from Self

Though Rousseau accepts Pascal's assessment of modern emptiness, he reinterprets that assessment so as to give his reader a reason to reject society without rejecting the world. He therefore bluntly denies the most basic principle of Pascal's Christian self-understanding: "there is no original perversity in the human heart," he writes, "man is naturally good." Original sin is out. And yet he stipulates, in the very same sentence, that "men are wicked." The bad men we see around us have, somehow, good natures. Such is the paradox at the heart of Rousseau's thought, and the key to his attempt to attack the ways of the world while redeeming the possibilities of immanence.[12]

In his *Discourse on Inequality*, Rousseau explains this paradox in the form of an unforgettable philosophic fable, a "legend of the fall," as David Gauthier calls it. A novelist as well as a philosopher, Rousseau understands the power of stories to reshape our self-understanding—particularly stories that adopt and adapt the sacred narrative at the heart of his audience's view of itself. Such is Rousseau's constant practice: he writes his *Confessions* to rival the *Confessions* of St. Augustine; he writes *The New Heloise* to rival the old Heloise. In the *Discourse on Inequality*, he goes so far as to retell the story of the Bible itself. Rousseau converts the biblical tale of the mysterious sin that caused our fall from Eden into a story of explicable accidents that caused our fall from nature.[13]

Man once wandered alone through the woods; he was simple, strong, self-sufficient, free, and as content with himself as a rabbit. His pleasures were plain but adequate: rest, nourishment, occasional coupling with the females he encountered in his solitary walks and never thought about in their absence. His most abiding pleasure was the sentiment of his own existence: the delight we can take in simply being alive. He lacked both language and reason, cared nothing for human others, and existed in happy ignorance of his own mortality. With robust capacities and limited desires, he enjoyed a psychic equilibrium that is the Rousseauan standard of immanent contentment.[14]

Whereas characteristic instincts attached each of the other animals to its particular food and way of life, man was happily omnivorous, and free to imitate the ways of every beast he en-countered. His distinctive capacity was his *perfectibility*, his abil-ity to adapt his own nature, to transform himself: fishing like a bird, climbing like a monkey, foraging like a deer, and hunting like a lion. Activated by circumstance and abetted by time, man's perfectibility will eventually make him the master of all of nature—but only at the price of tyrannizing over himself.[15]

Nourished by the easy fecundity of unspoiled nature, popu-lation increases, and men and women see more of one another. Some fatal accident teaches man the use of fire, and with it the beginnings of the arts. Soon huts are built, and families form in them; "the sweetest sentiments known to man," conjugal and paternal love, first touch the human heart. Slowly, mysteriously, the cry of nature man shared with the animals transforms itself into articulate and distinctive human speech. To learn to speak is to learn to reason—to compare and to classify, to create and deploy the abstractions inherent in the most basic words of every language. To think the simple idea "tree" entails gathering the enormously varied shapes of the forest under one, invisible, genre; a sentence as simple as "he runs" entails an astounding mental separation of actor from action. In learning to speak, we cross an enormous divide into an articulated and intelligible world.[16]

To compare is to rank, and as we acquire speech we come to take pride in our place at the peak of nature, dominating the animals, arranging the world around us to make things serve our needs. The taste for ranking soon penetrates the human world: men and women gather in the little assemblies of the first villages; they sing, dance, and speak before the crowd, all hoping to shine. They admire, and first taste the desire to be admired. That desire will soon dominate them utterly.[17]

Men are farming now; agriculture begets property, and prop-erty begets conflict. These conflicts must be resolved, and the clever ones who have something to protect contrive a resolution that will serve their interest. Law is born, to protect the property of all—that is, of all those who have something. With it come the ideas of right and public power. Once protected, property increases, further dividing poor and rich; political power accumulates in the hands of the wealthy, who use it to perpetuate their advantages. Prosperity and misery, oppression and resentment, have entered the human world.[18]

Material changes inflect the soul. Man knows new pleasures, which quickly become new needs. Common life and the division of labor make finding sustenance easier, but we pay for it in our newfound dependence on others. To depend on others is to care for their opinions, and soon to see ourselves through their eyes. The simple and direct love of our own existence, our natural *amour de soi-même*, grows and twists itself into *amour propre*, the desire for others to confirm the significance of our existence. We want to be important, and to be first; others want to be first as well. We need and flatter one another, yet secretly hate one another. All of our arts and enterprises are fueled by this compound of need and loathing.[19]

"Everything is good, coming from the hands of the author of things; everything degenerates in the hands of man." There has indeed been a fall. But what paradise, exactly, have we lost? The old Eden was the garden home of innocent love between man and woman and filial closeness between man and God. The new Eden is a garden of innocent love of self, and the self-sufficiency of a being who never imagines God and yet feels perfectly content. We left the old Eden through a sin of self-destructive pride and caprice; we left the new Eden simply by working to win our sustenance from the world with the one great tool at our disposal: our plentifully malleable selves.[20]

Rousseau allows Pascal this much: the men we know are indeed miserable and full of hatred. They are natural solitaries seeking half-heartedly to be social, too dependent on others to enjoy the goodness that comes with self-sufficiency, and too in love with themselves to be social all the way down. The charming, diverse life Montaigne described, of people flitting like bees through a blooming garden of solitary and social pleasures, is in fact a desperate hunt to find some relief from our terrible inner divisions. Human beings engaged in such a life—those who call themselves civilized, be they the *honnêtes hommes* of Pascal's time or the *philosophes* of Rousseau's—"draw the sentiment of [their] own existence" only from "the opinion of others." Often, they hate themselves for it. That self-loathing is conscience's miserable protest against such worlds of compulsory falsehood.[21]

It need not be this way. Man's fall is an accident of history; indeed, it is the accident that brings history into being. Our misery is of our own making; we are wicked only because we have adulterated ourselves. And yet we knew not what we did. If the hollowness of our being is a contingent consequence of an unnecessary chain of events, in which we ourselves were the primary, if unwitting, actors, we can be otherwise—we can make ourselves otherwise. Perfectibility is the mother of possibility.[22]

Rousseau sketches a whole landscape of such possibilities, one that stretches from the horizon of solitary self-sufficiency with which we came forth from nature to a horizon of complete sociability into which we may enter. It is a landscape of soul transformation. Men do not merely make a world through their history, inventing arts and languages, laws and cities. Men make themselves—they work revolutions upon their own beings.[23]

"Human nature does not go backward"; we cannot return to the forest to live with the bears and dine on grass and acorns. But we can take our history into our own hands. By so doing, perhaps we recover the wholeness we have lost—if not going back to what we once were, then rising above our contradictions. The Montaignean life, which deals with our restlessness by launching us on a never-ending tour of social and solitary life, exacerbates those contradictions and leaves us hollow. Indeed, it dissipates us down to "nothing." We are nothing because we do not know how to be good either for others or for ourselves. But if our nothingness results from the contradiction between our social longings and our solitary ones, perhaps we can become something by being entirely one or the other.[24]

Rousseau's "system" explores a series of such possible resolutions to the contradictions of the human heart. Each of these alternatives to bourgeois emptiness doubles down on one aspect or another of our divided nature, seeking to prove, against Pascal, that it is possible to make an integral and contented whole of a human life, here and now. These experiments aim to restore our psychic equilibrium, either by drawing us sharply away from the social world or by plunging us into it completely. Let us take them up in the order Rousseau did, from the most radically social to the most radically solitary: citizenship, family life, and solitude, in both a moderate and extreme form.[25]

Heroic Immanence

Pascal revealed the emptiness of the quest for immanent contentment as carried out by the Montaignean *honnête homme*. Rousseau vindicates immanence by investing it with heroism. In celebrating the citizen, the first great alternative on his human landscape, he paints a portrait of psychic equilibrium achieved not by circumscribing oneself but by eliminating internal division—annihilating the petty selfishness that dissipates virtue and makes coherence of character impossible. He describes the approbation and belonging we desire as found not in the private pleasures of friendship but in the public dedication of citizenship. He defends immanence by elevating it, and investing it with integrity.

When Rousseau speaks to the public as an author, he does so first in the rebellious tones of a citizen infuriated by bourgeois self-dealing. He writes his first important work of philosophy in response to a question posed in an essay contest by the Academy of Dijon: "Has the restoration of the arts and sciences contributed to the corruption or purification of morals?" He reads this question while walking from Paris to Vincennes, where his friend Diderot had been imprisoned after infuriating the wrong people with his *Letter on the Blind*. The question stops him in his tracks and summons forth a tremendous response. His mounting disgust with Parisian sophistication, his memories of the bucolic innocence of his youthful life in the countryside, the republican pride of a native Genevan—all of it rebels against this potential invitation to Enlightenment self-congratulation.[26]

The first words he writes are in the voice of the Roman consul Fabricius: a model of citizenship of the stern, antique stamp. Resting beneath a tree on the roadside, Rousseau composes a speech for Fabricius—a speech that contains in nuce the whole *Discourse on the Sciences and the Arts*. Fabricius, called "the Just," was a poor yet incorruptible hero of the early Roman Republic. He had won his sterling reputation by rejecting rich bribes, alerting his greatest enemy to a plot against his life, and refusing to be intimidated, even by an elephant. In the speech Rousseau composes for him, Fabricius looks down in fury upon late imperial Rome, with its wealth and artistic splendor. What has become of the rustic huts of old Rome, he asks, of the dwelling places of moderation and virtue? Have Rome's mighty legions triumphed over Greece only to enslave themselves to effete artists, disingenuous actors, and honey-tongued rhetoricians?[27] The voice of Fabricius surges forth from Rousseau's memory of the nights he spent reading Plutarch with his father as a young boy, which permanently inflected his self-understanding:

> Ceaselessly occupied with Rome and Athens; living, so to speak, with their great men, myself born the Citizen of a Republic, and son of a father whose love of the fatherland was his strongest passion, I caught fire with it from his example; I believed myself to be Greek or Roman; I became the character whose life I read.[28]

When Rousseau's illumination strikes him on the road to Vincennes, he *becomes* Fabricius—one of the characters whose life he read as a boy. He will eventually sign his discourse as "a citizen of Geneva." To be Fabricius, to be a citizen of Geneva, is to be something other—something better—than a Parisian, no matter how refined. It is no accident that Rousseau begins to write while walking away from Paris, where he never felt at home. His illumination shows him that the problem is not himself, but Paris, where vanity is ubiquitous and virtue has no weight.[29]

Rousseau steps away from Paris and speaks truths to that city that one can see only from a vantage point beyond its walls— from Rome, from Geneva, from Sparta. His first step beyond the world of the bourgeois is a step into the world of the citizen. It is the beginning of a powerful enthusiasm for virtue, an "effervescence" that would endure for years, which "transforms" him, annihilating vanity and replacing it with noble pride, and allowing him, for the first time in his life, to achieve the integrity of "[becoming] in fact what I appeared to be."[30]

How does Rousseauan citizenship solve the problem of bourgeois dividedness that leaves us so restless and empty? Rousseau attributes to politics both a power and a legitimacy far beyond what we usually imagine. "Everything depends radically on politics," he declares: politics does not merely govern some of life, to some degree—it governs the whole human world, including men's souls. The laws and moeurs of civic life shape men into citizens by taking hold of their most intimate and abiding desire, their love of their own selves. Good political institutions extend the amour propre of each citizen over the whole body politic. They teach us to perceive our own existence only as part of a larger whole and to love it "with that exquisite sentiment which any isolated man has only for himself." In patriotism, the "force of amour propre" can combine with the "beauty of virtue"; pride can annihilate our narrow self-concern and replace it with a generous vision of oneself not as Caius or Lucius but as a Roman. The citizen becomes part of a "body of thinking members," as Pascal had put it; but the body to which the Rousseauan citizen belongs is not the church but the city.[31]

In Geneva, Rome, and above all Sparta, Rousseau sees men living out a human possibility that offers his contemporaries a double-edged lesson in self-knowledge. The citizen shows men what they might be, thereby putting what they are into relief. To men who constantly put on sociable airs, the citizen shows what it means to be *actually* social, to care more for the city than for one's own narrow self. The citizen's courage and integrity also show what it means to be free: that is, to be truly masters of ourselves, and to have the consent we give to law prevail over the petty passions that enslave us. Knowing how "to act in conformity with the maxims of his own judgment, and not to be in contradiction with himself," the citizen stops the restless alternation between individualistic desire and social pretense, and achieves the contented wholeness of public-spirited integrity.[32]

The wholeheartedness of the citizen, the integrity of Fabricius and Cato, the courage of Regulus and Scaevola, ignited the imagination of the young Rousseau with the fire of high human possibility. When that fire reawakens in the mature man, it spurs Rousseau to write so as to awaken his contemporaries from the complacent slumbers of the life of bourgeois comfort and to charm them with an image of a life that finds its contentment in heroic integrity.

For all his evocations of ancient virtue, however, Rousseau's account of the citizen is not a return to a premodern standard. Rousseau knows that the ancient citizen was tied to the pagan gods by the hope that he might seize for himself a glory as immortal as theirs. His own account of citizenship celebrates integrity, not glory. That integrity is modeled on the wholeness of his natural man and is conceived of as an alternative to the dividedness of the bourgeois. It culminates in the life of a human being who is a law unto himself—an "intelligent being and a man" in the place of the "stupid and limited animal" from which he evolved. Beautifully self-regulating, the citizen commands himself from top to bottom, without internal division. His excellence is a tribute to human possibility on the immanent plane.[33]

But the citizen overcomes his dividedness only through the conquest of his own nature. Though the form of the citizen's life is akin in wholeness to the life of natural man, the content of that life consists in nature's utter negation. As Rousseau makes clear in his *Considerations on the Government of Poland*, the creation of citizens requires the complete co-option of their lives. Their education must be public, for fathers will inevitably attach their children to their families rather than their fatherland. Moreover, that education must be total—it must surround the child with an entire moral world beyond which he never looks: "Upon opening its eyes a child ought to see the fatherland and until death ought to see nothing but it. . . . This love makes up all of his existence; he sees only the fatherland, he lives only for it; as soon as he is alone, he is nothing." To escape bourgeois discontent through citizenship entails eliminating even the thought of private life.[34]

The life of the citizen is a constant public spectacle, at which he and his fellows are both observer and observed, all seeking, without respite, the public approval of the nation: "From the effervescence excited by this common emulation will be born that patriotic intoxication which alone can raise men up above themselves, and without which liberty is only a vain name and legislation only a chimera." Even when he waxes most eloquent about the patriotic enthusiasm for virtue, Rousseau always sees that enthusiasm as a form of "intoxication." This intoxication must be kept up in a perpetual performance of the spectacle of public life, in which all are at once actors and audience, drawing themselves into a world of splendid but unnatural illusion.[35]

"Good social institutions are those that best know how to denature man," Rousseau writes in *Émile*, giving, as his example, a Spartan mother who regards it as slavish to mourn the loss of her own children who have died in the service of the fatherland. To find contentment in the integrity of the citizen requires more than the annihilation of petty passions. It requires the annihilation of all human attachments that might compromise our political wholeheartedness. It requires that we become denatured.[36]

Though the spectacle of Sparta intoxicates, it also confronts the reader with a prospect of self-denaturing that Rousseau himself makes more daunting by painting nature in such winsome colors elsewhere in his thought. The price we must pay to achieve contentment by living at the social extreme of Rousseau's vision is high indeed, and Rousseau himself proves unwilling to pay it. Shortly after his illumination on the road to Vincennes, Rousseau follows through on his resolution to quit Paris. At first, he intends to return to Geneva, where he hopes to reclaim his citizenship and give himself over to civic life. Another possibility, however, soon offers itself: the bucolic retreat of the Hermitage, on the grounds of the château of his friend Mme d'Epinay. In the restless struggles of Rousseau's own soul, the romance of nature wins out over the rigors of civic life. For Rousseau's political passions are not his only passions, nor are they his strongest ones. He will seek, at the Hermitage, a sweeter and more natural model of human wholeness. And he will write the work, *Émile*, in which he most completely explores the possibility of overcoming human dividedness not by overcoming nature but by reconciling the natural and the social. In the life of that book's main characters, Émile and Sophie, he will depict the immanent contentment and unmediated approbation achieved by a man and woman raised from birth to form a whole *together*, even as they retain their natural independence from the corruptions of social life.[37]

The Contented Couple

Émile stands at the center of Rousseau's human landscape. It is the story of a "savage made to inhabit cities," of a man raised to preserve as much of his natural independence as possible while engaged with human others. In the *Discourse on Inequality*, Rousseau's account of human history had been the story of the simultaneous development and corruption of our human faculties. In that story, to learn to speak was to learn to lie; to discover the world of beauty was to enter the empire of vanity; to strive after virtue was to taste the love of domination. In *Émile*, Rousseau seeks to describe an alternative human history, this time guided by the "philosophy and experience" so tellingly absent as man bumbled blindly through history's first draft. He presents that alternative history in the form of a bildungsroman, which recounts the education of a single human being, Émile, in the hands of a beneficent and almost omnipotent tutor. That tutor makes it his business to untie the tangled threads of vice and virtue—to cultivate the human faculties without simultaneously corrupting them. He aims to mold a human being whose existence will be infinitely richer and more social than that of savage man, while still sharing in that being's wholeness, independence, and purity. *Émile* is thus Rousseau's most ambitious effort to have it all and presents us with the picture of a contentment that is immanent, social, and natural all at once.[38]

Rousseau hints at the existence of some such possibility even in his first narrative of man's exit from nature in the *Discourse on Inequality*. In the midst of that story, he marks a middle point in our development, halfway between primitive indolence and civilized corruption, as "best for man." In that age, our faculties had been developed to a point where we could truly be called human without yet destroying our psychic equilibrium. We had become social, but social dependency and amour propre had not yet completely enslaved our imaginations. This "happiest and most lasting epoch" was the age of familial happiness.[39]

In his efforts to win his existence from nature, whose original fecundity became less and less adequate as population increased, primitive man develops enough art and foresight to build the first huts. Primitive woman, pressed by need, discerns in this state of affairs a possibility that would alter human history. The increase of population had made sexual encounters more regular and pregnancy more frequent, compromising the natural independence women once shared with men. Looking at the physically resourceful men who had built the first huts with eyes sharpened by necessity, natural woman finds in her own perfectibility the capacity to seize an opportunity. She invents the family.[40]

Rousseau's picture of the original relations between the sexes notes a basic difference between male and female sexual capacities: man's desire spends itself quickly, rendering him at least momentarily impotent, while woman is capable of continual sexual enjoyment. Moreover, she is not subject to the seasons of heat and refusal common to other species. Natural man, for his part, is not particularly interested in sex—the civilized male's obsession with sex is a function of an imagination as yet undeveloped. Were the sexual economy not thus imbalanced, with female demand exceeding male supply, human beings could not be the pacific natural solitaries Rousseau describes. If man were naturally lusty, and woman naturally modest and resistant to his approaches, rape and the murder of rivals would be ordinary occurrences in the pure state of nature, and Rousseau's whole story would collapse.[41]

In sex as in other things, human beings lack the instinctive guidance that makes animal behavior so regular. But we imitate what we find useful in them. Rousseau observes that the females of many species are coquettish. By imitating animal coquetry, natural woman discovers the possibilities she can open for herself by working on the imagination of the human male, which floats freely as it develops. Her practical need for help finding her sustenance while pregnant and nursing teaches her to transform coquetry into modesty, thereby molding the male's desire to win sexual acceptance into a desire for her approval of his being. Feminine modesty is the first true ruling art. Armed with it, woman will transform, educate, and humanize her mate.[42]

Everyone benefits. The tender sentiments born of sexual relations extend sweetly over the common life man and woman now share. Naturally attached to her child by her need to nurse, woman feels her very being enlarged through that attachment. She has every incentive to extend it through time and to expand it to encompass her mate, because doing so allows her to secure both practical help and a satisfying redoubling of her own pleasurable sentiment of existential largeness. The easy sustenance and affection of the household give children the incentive to stay, at least until their own erotic lives attach them elsewhere. Man's projects increase in duration and usefulness as he learns to focus on bringing home the beans, if not yet the bacon. Woman, now become more sedentary, has both the means and the motive to civilize the household with comforts and adornments. Her mate and her children come to enjoy the sentiment of extended being she was the first to know; all experience the deepening of that sentiment which comes when one shares one's life with others. Their selves feel at once larger and fuller; their contentment is as immanent and more truly human than the contentment of a natural solitary.[43]

But the familial happiness that is the jewel in the crown of the golden age undermines itself. By increasing everyone's safety, comfort, leisure, and pleasure, the family facilitates the development of our faculties. It is a warm and nutritive greenhouse in which language and art, reason and imagination, self-awareness and amour propre, all grow with new suddenness and vigor. Agriculture, metallurgy, and property are born. The material concerns always entwined with the family now take on a life of their own, which competes with the affective ties of sentiment that give familial life its sweetness. Coquettish and modest young women work in unwitting concert with their protective and calculating parents to provoke the imaginations of the neighboring young males; those males imaginatively crystallize girls not so different from all the others into jewels of incomparable beauty. Reflecting back on himself, the young man's amour propre becomes highly sensitive to slights, real and imagined; jealousy finds arms in the tools of the hunt and the harvest. Men become jealous flatterers; women enjoy collecting admirers. All come to live in their imaginations, alienating them from the contented circle of tenderness that had once been their home.[44]

In *Émile*, Rousseau seeks to rebuild the familial happiness that was once the greatest sweetness of human life. At the same time, he aims to intensify that sweetness with the aid of the sentimental, moral, and aesthetic sensitivities that come with the cultivation of the mind and to armor family happiness against its tendency to undermine itself. Both man and woman must be educated anew to make this possible. In educating Émile, the tutor seeks to develop his natural powers without granting a toehold to the corrupting forces of the social world; he teaches Émile to bear the blows of necessity with both toughness and resignation. At fifteen, Émile is as strong, intelligent, industrious, self-sufficient, and skilled as possible for a human being of ordinary capacities. His tutor assiduously avoids the precocious stimulation of the erotic imagination he believes endemic to the social world; he keeps the passions silent for as long as possible. But sexuality will come, and with it the searching neediness that will open Émile's soul to the world.[45]

While one cannot make a man love nothing, one can do much to shape the objects of his love—such is the advice Rousseau gives to lawgivers. The tutor heeds that advice, creating for Émile an imaginary beloved, the charming and modest Sophie, who serves as the purifying focus of his inchoate longings well before he has met any woman who bears that name. Meanwhile, her parents are carefully raising a real young woman to meet and even surpass Émile's hopes.[46]

"In everything not connected with sex," Rousseau writes, "woman is man." "In everything connected with sex, woman and man are in every way related and in every way different." It turns out that a great deal is connected with sex, so much so that Rousseau's plan for Sophie's education is much more conventional than the impossibly countercultural education he designs for Émile. She, too, is raised to develop her natural talents to the fullest and with the least possible corruption, but she is also raised to be an agreeable companion to man—not so as to sacrifice her well-being to his but because her capacity for creating agreeable relations with her future husband is decisively important to her own quest for happiness.[47]

Émile's initial education is solitary and physical. His first incentives are cakes rather than praise—he learns to reason from the belly outward. From pleasure, he works his way up to utility; the tutor avoids introducing him to properly moral relations until his burgeoning desires make entry into the social world unavoidable. He receives no religious education at all until at least this point, and what he will think about God rests ultimately with him. Sophie, by contrast, dwells in a moral and religious horizon from the outset. She lives immersed in the interdependent world of family, with its cares, duties, and joys. As a child, she learns to perform all the tasks of the household she will govern as an adult. Her play with dolls, apparently frivolous, allows her to cultivate the arts of adornment that will help her win her empire over Émile.[48]

And yet Sophie is no tyrant. She wants to be adored, but more for her virtues than for her other attractions. Her model is Circe, who gives herself only to Ulysses, the one man her charms cannot reduce to a beast. Émile has deep-seated sentiments of duty and humanity he will not ignore even when they come into conflict with his attachment to his beloved. She loves him because he knows how to prefer duty to desire—even his desire for her.[49]

Together, the pair form a single moral person and enjoy a psychic equilibrium that is shared rather than located in the individual:

> The social relation of the sexes is admirable. From this society results a moral person of whom the woman is the eye and the man the arm, but with such a dependence on one another that it is from the man that the woman learns what must be seen and it is from the woman that the man learns what must be done. If woman could ascend to principles as well as man and man had a mind for details as good as hers, they would be always independent of one another and would live in eternal discord, and their society could not subsist. But in the harmony that reigns between them everything tends to the common end; one does not know who contributes most; each follows the impulsion of the other, each obeys and both are masters.[50]

In the family, Émile and Sophie find a wholeness that extends and enlarges upon their natures; their attachment to one another is deep, their contentment all the sweeter because of their knowledge of the fragility of their shared life. Their educations have been self-consciously crafted to inure them to the corrupting temptations that destroyed the original golden age of family happiness, temptations Rousseau identifies, in his own time, with the cosmopolitanism of great cities. After his search for Sophie has begun, but before he has found her, Émile and his tutor turn their backs on Paris:

Adieu, then, Paris, celebrated city, city of noise, smoke, and mud, where women no longer believe in honor nor men in virtue. Adieu, Paris; we are looking for love, happiness, innocence; we will never be far enough from you.

After he has found her, but before they wed, Émile will travel far and wide over Europe, but he finds no place he could call a fatherland. He and Sophie wed and settle near Sophie's parents: Émile's fatherland is his household. With this picture of happiness realized, *Émile* closes.[51]

Of all the human possibilities Rousseau depicts, the familial contentment of Émile and Sophie perhaps speaks most powerfully to the longings of the modern heart. While citizenship remains attractive to many, and the longing for individual wholeness is evident in our pursuit of authenticity, the desire for the complete and contented household, for the psychic equilibrium of the harmonious couple, has a governing power that reaches into the minutest details of life. The nuclear, love-bonded family is the image of immanent contentment most vivid to the contemporary imagination, its intimacy the form of approbation modern peoples most insistently demand. The erotic longings of the young fixate on the household of the future; the middle-aged brood anxiously over it; the memories of the old dwell on it with the pains and pleasures of hindsight. Even our heated contests over the nature of family testify to the overwhelming significance of this form of immanent contentment in our lives and thoughts.[52]

Rousseau himself, however, identifies two profound obstacles to the search for immanent contentment understood as familial happiness. The first becomes manifest in the unfinished sequel to *Émile: Émile and Sophie, or, The Solitaries*. Its title alone is sufficient to horrify anyone who has been moved by the picture of domestic bliss Rousseau paints in such rich colors at the end of his educational treatise. It takes the form of letters from Émile to his tutor, telling him the story of his sufferings. That story begins with the tutor's departure from Émile's life and the death of Sophie's parents shortly thereafter. Sophie and Émile, on their own and bereft, are then crushed by the death of their daughter. Sophie's grief is inconsolable.[53]

Unable to comfort her, Émile takes her to Paris to divert her. It is an amazingly Pascalian turn of events, in which the connection between death and diversion is the central element. In the city, Émile and Sophie strive to amuse themselves; they drift apart, and Sophie becomes pregnant with another man's child. Their common life sundered, the two are destined to die apart and alone—Émile after a stint of slavery to Barbary pirates. Rousseau seems to have charmed us with his picture of family happiness only to brutally pull back the curtain on the illusion.[54]

Some see in *Émile and Sophie* proof of the failure of Émile's education; some see in it proof of its success, for Émile proves capable of enduring the harshest necessities, even slavery, when they come. For the question of whether we can find our contentment in the family, however, the decisive element is the story's opening. Like everyone with familial attachments, Émile and Sophie are prisoners of fortune. Sophie, who has not had Émile's education in the endurance of necessity, feels that dependency with unbearable sharpness when fortune turns on them. Born and raised to hold a family together, to enliven its duties and ennoble its dependencies, Sophie cannot bear to see it torn apart by capricious death. A soul born to love takes loss necessarily to heart. The Pascalian truth of the incapacity of human beings to bear the weight of one another's love comes home to her with overwhelming force.[55]

The second problem with the marriage of Émile and Sophie as a model of social contentment is that it is a highly mediated affair. Whereas Montaigne and La Boétie love one another for their whole selves, without moralistic, religious, or utilitarian entanglements, Émile and Sophie love one another for their virtues. They have the practical concerns of a household, and perhaps the devotion of a religion, in common; the tutor himself plays a role in their lives so decisive that Émile blames the collapse of their marriage on his departure. We have watched the artful fashioning of both and understand all the experiences that have made them who they are—to the reader, at least, their characters lack the mysterious depths that prompt Montaigne to say "because it was he, because it was I."

In his own life, Rousseau seeks an erotic bond with something closer to the personal, unmediated character of Montaignean friendship, which we must briefly consider to fully grasp his understanding of the nature and limits of the contentment human beings seek in the couple. At fifteen, he has an enchanting encounter with Françoise-Louise de Warens, a thirtyish noblewoman he calls *maman*, who replies in kind by calling him *petit* ("little one"). She will be his protectrice, hostess, and lover, on and off, for a decade. But Rousseau refuses to call their attachment a love affair and insists on its "singular" character, defined by countless "peculiarities." It has elements of friendship but includes sexual desire; although it is sexual, it is "without restlessness, without jealousy." Referring to their liaison as a "sympathy of souls," he remarks that he and Mme de Warens "put [their] whole existence in common." Theirs is "a possession that was mutual and perhaps unique among humans which was not at all, as I have said, that of love, but a more essential possession which—without depending on the senses, on sex, on age, on looks—depended on everything by which one is oneself, and which one cannot lose without ceasing to be." For these two, "You and I are words banished from their language," as Rousseau will later write of the characters of his novel *Julie*.[56]

Rousseau here echoes the hyperbolic language of unmediated approbation Montaigne deployed to describe his friendship with La Boétie, in his own, even more extreme, register. His liaison with Mme de Warens is the decisive, character-determining episode and what he calls the "short happiness" of his life. In the presence of Mme de Warens, he feels his own sentiment of existence redoubled and intensified, and thus enjoys a profound, calm, and self-aware contentment. The impression the experience makes on his character determines who he will be from then on. But it cannot last. The bohemian attachment of *maman* and *petit* includes none of the dutifulness of the marriage of Émile and Sophie. They have no children; both of them take other lovers; eventually, they split. However precious the experience of the free but profound interpenetration of two such irregular characters may be, it cannot weather a life.[57]

The happiness we can know through human attachments is frail indeed. The attempt to find immanent contentment in a couple, be it in the virtuous marriage of Émile and Sophie or the eccentric liaison of *petit* and *maman*, is at best short-lived, for the beings we love are as fragile as we are. Even if our nature is not, as Rousseau contends, solitary, our fate may be. The search for a solitary form of contentment, for a psychic equilibrium less dependent on others, beckons with the voice of necessity.[58]

Moral Self-Contentment

The city can make us whole only by sacrificing our nature. The more we seek completion in the couple, the more we risk being shattered by the brute facts of human vacillation and vulnerability. Perhaps, then, we should seek our wholeness not in the city or the couple but in our individual selves. Perhaps we can find a contentment capable of enduring the vicissitudes of fate by turning inward.

Rousseau's stirring depiction of the effort to return to self has made him into an apostle of authenticity. It lies at the heart of his most sustained meditation on the ultimate questions of God and man, "The Profession of Faith of the Savoyard Vicar." That crucial work, which seeks to find a middle way between the bitterly opposed priestly and rationalist parties of Rousseau's time, will suffer the fate of so many attempts to transcend the dilemmas of one's moment: it pleases few and offends many. Because of the "Profession of Faith," *Émile*, in which it appears, will be burned in the public squares of both Paris and Geneva. Rousseau, forced to flee France, will wander the earth as a vagabond—albeit a famous one—for much of the rest of his life.[59]

If the religious authorities of both cities are wrong to burn the "Profession of Faith," they are right to scent in it a serious challenge. Rousseau's Vicar is a priest who has fled his native parish after a sexual escapade put him out of the good graces of his bishop. As the Vicar explains, had he been a little less scrupulous he could have avoided all scandal, and scandal was the only part of the matter his bishop or anyone else cared about. Rousseau himself is less critical of the immorality of the Vicar's behavior than of the laws of a Church that, in his view, demands that its priests renounce their manhood in order to preach their religion.[60]

It is not the Vicar's behavior, however, but his teaching that draws the Church's ire. For in spite of his clerical robes, the Vicar is neither Catholic nor even Christian. As he understands it, Christianity insults the justice of God and opposes the happiness of man. The Vicar professes a merely natural religion.

Through it, he claims to have discovered the secret of happiness and, in spite of his misfortunes, to have healed the divisions in his own life and made himself content.[61]

Using the Vicar as his mouthpiece, Rousseau offers his most direct response to both Montaigne's religious skepticism and Pascal's existential Christianity. He borrows from both even as he answers them. With Montaigne, the Vicar rejects the possibility that we might rationally come to know the truths about God and ourselves that we need as moral beings. These questions are enmeshed in hopelessly twisted knots of argument that reason alone can never untangle. With Pascal, however, the Vicar argues that no man can be skeptic all the way down: "doubt about the things it is important for us to know," he remarks, "is too violent a state for the human mind. It does not hold out for long, and decides in spite of itself one way or the other." Human beings are practical beings as well as theoretical ones; though our reason can vacillate unceasingly between affirming and denying God's existence, we cannot avoid deciding the questions that orient our moral lives, because we must act. To act with any consistency, to live coherent lives, we must have principles. But where will we find those principles, given the incapacity of reason to discover them?[62]

We will know them when we feel them. To lead himself out of the forest of doubt, the Vicar resolves "to admit as evident everything to which I cannot, in the sincerity of my heart, refuse my consent." Like Pascal, the Vicar holds that the heart, not reason, guides us best on the question of faith. But Pascal's heart and the Vicar's are two decidedly different things. For Pascal, the heart is the locus of faith and love, but also the organ with which we perceive the most basic dimensions of our existence in the world: space, time, motion, and number. For the Vicar, the heart is an organ of feeling. As he remarks on the question of spontaneous motion—motion caused by the will, rather than any antecedent material cause:

> You will ask me . . . how I know that there are spontaneous motions. I shall tell you that I know it because I sense it. I want to move my arm, and I move it without this movement's having another immediate cause than my will. One would reason in vain to try to destroy this sentiment in me; it is stronger than any evidence; one might just as well try to prove to me that I do not exist.

The Vicar uses sentiments such as these to cut through the swirl of arguments about the existence of God and the nature of man. Reasoning from what he feels, he arrives at a simple faith: a faith in an intelligent God who set the world in motion but grants us the freedom of the human mind and will.[63]

The sentiments at the heart of the Vicar's faith, however, concern justice and morals rather than such speculation about spontaneous motion. Taking aim at the doctrine advanced by Pascal's Jansenist friends, that "God owes his creatures nothing," the Vicar remarks that God owes us what He promises us in giving us being. We have been made with an irrepressible longing for happiness and an innate respect for justice. If God Himself is just, then to create beings with such a longing is to give them a promissory note on the object of their desire, conditional on their conduct of their lives: "The more I return within myself, the more I consult myself, the more I see these words written in my soul: *Be just and you will be happy.*" He who wrote that demanding promise on our hearts has implicitly obligated Himself to fulfill His side of the bargain if we fulfill ours.[64]

But how do we know what justice is—what we must do to deserve the happiness we crave and that God, implicitly, promises? Again, sentiment guides the Vicar: "I have only to consult myself about what I want to do: everything I sense to be good is good; everything I sense to be bad is bad. Conscience is the best of all casuists, and it is only when one haggles with it that one has recourse to the subtleties of reasoning."[65]

With this sentimental understanding of conscience, the Vicar teaches us how to make peace with our own minds and rehabilitates nature in the face of both Pascal's Christian account of its fall and Montaigne's moral relativism. Pascal held that the natural laws that guide the conscience were lost to us when we were exiled from Eden. In saying that much, he departed decisively from the natural law tradition. He did so in part because he was following Montaigne's account of the immense variability of human customs—an account Pascal sometimes reproduces word-for-word. On the Vicar's view, however, Montaigne grossly exaggerates the variability of human conceptions of right and wrong in order to establish his proposition that "the laws of conscience, which are born of nature, are born of custom." To this, the Vicar answers:

> O Montaigne, you who pride yourself on frankness and truth, be sincere and true, if a philosopher can be, and tell me whether there is some country on earth where it is a crime to keep one's faith, to be clement, beneficent, and generous? Where the good man is contemptible and the perfidious one honored?

Sentimental conscience lifts the fog of relativism that shrouds the post-Montaignean moral world. Philosophers are driven to embrace such skepticism in the first place, the Vicar suggests, only by their insatiable desire to distinguish themselves: "Where is the philosopher who would not gladly deceive mankind for his own glory?"[66]

But the Vicar does not hear an alternative to the pride-soaked arguments of the philosophers in the pure voice of God that rings out in scripture, as Pascal had. The Vicar raises deep doubts about all holy books, which he sees as books written by ambitious men and deployed by other men in support of their own arrogant desire to subjugate others. The Vicar would have us, instead, listen to ourselves, for the voice of God is most audible when we silence the passions and attend to the quiet, inner summons of conscience.[67]

The Vicar seems to concede, however, that even sincere fidelity to one's own conscience fails to guarantee earthly happiness: "The wicked man prospers; the just man remains oppressed." Reasoning from the felt truths of human freedom and the active character of the human mind, the Vicar has already demonstrated the immateriality of the soul, at least to his own satisfaction. He now argues that the soul survives the body long enough for God to fulfill the promise implicit in the creation of a being who desires happiness and respects justice.[68]

But how long is that, exactly? The Vicar holds that "the greatest enjoyment is contentment with oneself": to be content with one's own conscience is happiness. The Vicar himself claims to enjoy that happiness, in spite of his situation of poverty and exile. As for the wicked, he remarks, "What need is there to go looking for hell in the other life? It begins in this one in the hearts of the wicked," hearts "chewed up by envy, avarice, and ambition." God, the Vicar implies, has ordered the natural world in such a way that justice is its own reward. If that is so, any supernatural world would prove superfluous. The Vicar, then, finds in the economy of human sentiments a natural and immanent substitute for transcendent justice, wisdom, and happiness.[69]

The Vicar's natural religion thus contains an implicit critique of supernatural and revealed religion. He spells out that critique much more directly in the second part of his profession. He there takes aim at a doctrine Rousseau had identified earlier in *Émile* as "the principle of sanguinary intolerance": "*One must believe in God to be saved.*" The doctrine that one must believe not only in God but in the specific revelation of Jesus Christ is of course a principle common to both Catholic and Protestant—a principle definitional of Christianity. In the Vicar's view, however, a God who consigned men to hell for failure to believe in a religion He did not reveal to all of them, equally and immediately, would be "the most iniquitous and most cruel of tyrants." While the Vicar confesses to a certain awe before the man-God of the Gospels, and performs the liturgy with reverence at the ceremonies where he presides, he plainly distrusts what we might call "institutional religion." In his heart, he follows only nature.[70]

The Vicar tells us that he would never breathe a word of doubt about revealed religion to anyone with a calm and stable faith. He does, however, present it to the young Jean-Jacques. In *Émile's* fourth book, Rousseau interrupts the story of Émile's education on the cusp of adolescence to tell the story of a young man most unlike Émile at the same stage of life—himself. The young Jean-Jacques was a wandering teenager without trade or talent, a Protestant who pretended interest in converting to Catholicism so that Catholics would feed him. His introduction to the Roman Church had immediately acquainted him with novel and nasty vices at which priests winked, or worse; the hospice for catechumens where he had been received was to him a prison wherein he could feel only disgust. Having sold his old religion without for a moment believing in his new one, the young man had no principles of conscience to guide him. From the mire of his poverty, he looked with avid eyes on the wealth and pleasures of others; reduced by need and abuse to dishonesty and cunning, the young Jean-Jacques was headed toward "the morals of a tramp and the morality of an atheist."[71]

Though such a moral state might seem exceptional, Rousseau indicates that it is in fact the moral condition of the whole of Europe in his time. Staging an absurd argument between a "Reasoner" and an "Inspired Man," Rousseau shows us what he takes to be the spiritual condition of a world dominated by these rival parties. Between the philosophers' desire to distinguish themselves with novel doctrines, whatever the moral costs to mankind, and the priests' desire to impose their will on others with the sanction of divine authority, no one seriously seeks the truth about God, the world, and human life. Following such examples, the whole public is headed toward the morals of a tramp and the morality of an atheist. The Vicar's sentimental faith attempts to open a different way forward.[72]

The Vicar's path would lead us to immanent contentment understood as moral self-satisfaction. His sentimental theology brings the transcendent God who connects happiness and justice down to earth, naturalizing that connection and locating it within the self. This attempt to find an alternative to self-serving relativism and priestly browbeating has an obvious appeal. But the Vicar's profession of faith ultimately rests on a dubious sanctification of sentiment. If it feels right, do it, the Vicar teaches; strive to see your life not as God sees it but by the less discomfiting standard of your own moral self-regard. And at the same time that it divinizes sentiment, his natural theology depersonalizes God. It lifts God above speaking to man—above dealing with us on all the levels of our complex, embodied beings, amid all the messy particulars of human history. A mere fashioner of harmonious order, the Vicar's God is subject to all the objections to his existence implied by the disorder perceptible in nature. Intentionally less lovable and less terrible than the God of the Bible, the Vicar's God is also, perhaps unintentionally, less plausible.[73]

But from Rousseau's own point of view, the deepest problem with the Vicar's faith is that it relies on God at all. Rousseau's goal is to find contentment by recovering and enhancing human wholeness; dependency on any being other than ourselves, even God Himself, necessarily qualifies that wholeness. The Vicar's faith sits uneasily on the divide between moral life and self-reliance. As morality, it is too self-referential to be trustworthy; as self-reliance, it is too enmeshed with God and duty to be truly self-contained. In his own life, Rousseau seeks to find contentment in a more radical form of self-sufficiency.

Radical Solitude

"Only the wicked man is alone," the irrepressibly social Diderot writes in his *Fils Naturel*, which appears shortly after Rousseau moves to the Hermitage. This line will become the proximate cause of Rousseau's final break with his old friend. For Rousseau understands his choice to quit Paris and dwell at the Hermitage as an existential choice for solitude. He sees himself following a tradition common to the wise men of many times and places, who seek "calm and peace in retirement." His long-running personal experiment with solitude is his final effort to achieve and exemplify happiness.[74]

Solitude had an important place in Pascal's thought as well. For Pascal, solitude was a testing ground of the soul: to be alone and undiverted was to come face-to-face with one's own unhappiness and need for God. To dwell alone contentedly, as Rousseau seeks to do, is to refute Diderot and Pascal, the Enlightenment and Christianity, all at once. In his effort to find contentment by leaving the social world behind, Rousseau seeks relief from his restlessness at the opposite extreme of his human landscape from the wholeheartedly social citizen—in the recovery of the undivided, self-sufficient wholeness originally known to natural man.[75]

Rousseau is not strictly speaking alone at the Hermitage. His long-time companion, Thérèse Levasseur, and her mother live with him. He pays frequent visits to his hostess, Mme d'Epinay—indeed, these obligatory visits occur much more frequently than he likes. In his long, daily, solitary walks, however, he gives himself over to his "chimeras," as he calls them. For as long as those walks last, he utterly forgets the world of men and contents himself completely with the delightful indulgence of his powerful imagination. They quickly become the center of his bucolic existence.[76]

In his fantasies, Rousseau conjures up images of all the women with whom he had flirted and philandered as a young man. Making the charms of these women his palette, Rousseau paints portraits of two enchanting friends, whom he brings to life on the page as the central characters in his *Julie*. He seeks out solitude whenever he can get it in order to plunge himself into the world of these beings more delightful than any of the actual human beings around him.[77]

But these charming beings who live in his imagination alone prove insufficient to him. He feels that his heart is born to love, and longs to see the objects of his love embodied. Thérèse, sweet but uncultivated and incapable of following Rousseau's adventurous thoughts, cannot deeply share his life, as Mme de Warens once did. But a lively young noblewoman, Sophie d'Houdetot, comes to visit him while he is at the height of his fantasies, and all the delights of his imaginary life crystallize around this woman of flesh and blood. The austere citizen of

Geneva falls as madly in love as an adolescent boy. The consequences of his infatuation will destroy his life at the Hermitage, which he will soon feel compelled to leave. A romantic imagination left to itself does not stay within the confines of solitude for long. Rousseau at the Hermitage is a solitary manqué.[78]

He will have another chance. Forced to flee France by the crisis provoked by *Émile* and *The Social Contract*, and with no hope for a better reception in Geneva, Rousseau settles, briefly, in the middle of a Swiss lake, on St. Peter's Island.

He does not do anything much on St. Peter's. Indeed, doing nothing is, for him, the whole point. He wanders over the island, examining plants for no other purpose than to wonder at them. He floats around in a little boat, lost in the country of his imaginings. He sits on the shore of the small, unnamed, uninhabited island next to St. Peter's, listening to the waves beat gently against the shore. These modest activities prompt him to "sense [his] existence with pleasure, without taking the trouble to think." He claims he has never been happier in his life.[79]

What is so fulfilling in these activities? In the midst of them, Rousseau enjoys, more completely than ever before, the sentiment of his own existence. Immersed in that sentiment, he enters a psychic state in which he thinks of neither past nor future; in which he feels neither desire nor fear; in which he thinks of no one else and cares not whether others think of him; in which he delights in the goodness of simply being. Though civilized human beings often forget this fact, being, simply being, is good. Our best chance at immanent contentment rides on our capacity to settle ourselves into the experience of this humble, egalitarian, charming truth.

The sentiment of existence is not a state of moral self-satisfaction, such as the Vicar describes, for Rousseau expresses no concern during these moments for questions of duty or jus-

tice. It need not imply any unity with a larger human whole—
city, family, or romantic pair. It is an experience of amoral, aso-
cial, existential satisfaction, of happiness born from simply
living and sensing with self-conscious but unconcerned delight.
It does not depend on God; rather, those who know how to
experience that sentiment are, at least for the moment, "sufficient unto [themselves], like God." On St. Peter's Island, where
he develops an art of immersing himself in this sentiment, arranging each day for that purpose, Rousseau seems to become
a wholehearted, natural, undivided, and happy human being.
He seems finally to achieve the solitary, fully immanent experience of contentment for which he longs.[80]

Pascal held that man's thoughts, in solitude, naturally turn to the
miseries of his condition: mortality, vice, ignorance. Rousseau's
thoughts do not follow this pattern. A dreamer who "knows
how to nourish himself with agreeable chimeras," Rousseau
finds himself pushed to greater heights of imaginative enjoyment by the splendid surroundings that blend with his reveries
so perfectly that the line separating fiction from reality becomes
lost to him. Moreover, he finds that he can enjoy the reveries of
St. Peter's Island even while living in Paris many years later, for
memory rekindles not only the thought of the sentiment of existence but the experience of it.[81]

And yet Rousseau knows that his reveries are not and cannot
be the full truth of a human life. "I never meditate, I never
dream more deliciously than when I forget myself," he writes.
"I feel ecstasies and inexpressible raptures in melting, so to
speak, into the system of beings and making myself one with
the whole of nature." But of course Rousseau is not one with
the whole of nature—he is a human individual. This truth of his
condition comes home to him when, having drifted in his boat
all afternoon, sunset recalls time to him, and he finds himself

rowing like a galley slave to get back to the island before night-fall. The approach of darkness reminds him of his finitude and vulnerability.[82]

Physically, Rousseau is not in fact alone on St. Peter's; he stays in the home of a tax collector, and he brings Thérèse along with him. In telling the story, Rousseau calls Thérèse alternately *ma compagne* and *ma gouvernante*—"my companion," "my housekeeper," never "my wife," though she is so by the time Rousseau writes the *Rêveries*. Both here and in the *Confessions*, Thérèse often appears as a sad reminder of Rousseau's frailty and his faults: the mother of the five children he placed in the orphanage, sharing his wanderings as an exile, tending to the bodily needs of a frail, needy, caustic, and paranoid man, and described with little respect in his writings. She reminds us that Rousseau can never be self-sufficient in the literal sense.[83]

More than that, Rousseau comes to see that it is possible, even in solitude, to be in one's mind "on the world's stage, preoccupied with making ourselves admired." In the "Seventh Walk" of the *Reveries*, he recalls a botanizing expedition in which he reaches a dark and secluded glade in the forest, a place where he supposes himself completely alone, perhaps even the first human being ever to have set foot there. Solitary yet joyful, he compares himself to another Columbus—the first man ever to land on an undiscovered country of psychic possibility. The amour propre of a man who entertains such thoughts remains very much alive and betrays that he still sees himself through the lens of comparison. A clanking sound awakens him from his reverie, he bursts through the thicket in search of the sound, and he finds a stocking mill churning away, just twenty feet from his undiscovered country. He laughs, chagrined at his puerile vanity and the comic manner in which he has been punished for it.[84]

Although Rousseau claims that he wrote the *Reveries* "only for myself," he edits them, perhaps anticipating publication, and wonders aloud what the "men of this century" will think of the life he describes therein. The amour propre of a writer follows him even when he leaves Paris far behind. His godlike moments of contented, self-sufficient immersion in his own being are only moments, not a way of life. No man is an island, not even if he is on one.[85]

Were Rousseau Montaigne, he might judge that a merely episodic happiness, a life full of compromises and dependencies, is the best we can hope for—and all in all, not so bad. But Rousseau is not Montaigne. He accepts too much of the Pascalian diagnosis of the restless emptiness of the life of the Montaignean modern to rest content with such a life. His own writing powerfully recasts Pascalian discontent in secular terms and launches him on a quest to make himself whole again. His honest revelation of the serial failures of his quest for immanent contentment across the breadth of the modern moral landscape is an invaluable contribution to the self-knowledge of all who live with that goal on their horizon.

The Instructive Tragedy of Rousseau's "Sad and Great System"

Rousseau powerfully articulates the modern quest for happiness, sharpening its contours and bringing its limits clearly into view. He knows, from the inside, the deepest desires of the modern heart: to be at home in nature and at home in the human world; to have a social life that is more than a "society of smiling enemies"; to find the contentment with ourselves, the wholeness, that the modern exaltation of the individual seems to promise. He seeks to satisfy these desires by overcoming our dividedness but proves, perhaps against his own intention, that our dividedness is here to stay.

In both his life and his thought, Rousseau performs a far-ranging experiment that tests the soundness of modern self-understanding. In *The Social Contract* and *Émile*, he imagines what we might make of man, unconstrained by the weight of history and the limits of practical life. In his life, too, Rousseau refuses the compromises essential to a smooth and comfortable social existence. Detesting dependency and the polite fictions of social life, he demands transparent, total, effusive approbation from his companions—with predictably disastrous results. Though he thinks of himself as "born for friendship," Rousseau destroys every friendship he ever has.[86]

Rousseau's experiments, in both his life and his thought, fail. If citizenship is to succeed, it can do so only by completely de-naturing man, and success so defined *is* failure. The sociability of the couple, while less denaturing, leaves us subject to the possibilities of alienation and grief that accompany every human attachment. The wholeness we hope to find with others is at best frail, at worst a mere prelude to misery.

Solitary wholeness is just as elusive. The religious and moral solitude of Rousseau's Savoyard Vicar is tendentious and compromised—too sentimental and self-referential to be truly moral, too dependent on God to be truly self-sufficient. The more radical solitude Rousseau seeks in his own life proves fleeting as well. Though he achieves, for a few precious mo-ments, a contented psychic equilibrium born of an imaginative merger with nature, self-forgetting is not self-knowledge, as the reminders of his frail, proud individuality that break into his reveries continually inform him. Rousseau can never be enough for himself for long.[87]

If the experiments of Rousseau's thought and life fail, however, those failures are instructive. Rousseau is like a chemist in a laboratory whose daring combinations of elements have blown up in his face: the experiment kills its author but leaves a telling residue in his beakers. Rousseau seeks to solve the problem of modern restlessness by conceiving of restlessness as dividedness, a dividedness he maps along a horizontal axis that stretches from the natural and solitary to the social and artificial. He finds that we cannot quiet our restlessness by going to either extreme, as both are only parts of what we are: human beings are as social as we are solitary, as historical as we are natural. Compromise positions between the extremes prove no better for resolving our internal contradictions.

Rousseau was right to call his corpus a "sad and great system." It is great insofar as it is one of the most powerful efforts ever undertaken to think through and live out the immanent principles upon which our modern pursuit of happiness is built. It is sad insofar as it offers us no satisfying way forth from our contradictions. The fall of something great is properly understood as tragic.[88]

The self-knowledge Rousseau has to offer us is thus a tragic self-knowledge. Perhaps inadvertently, he teaches us that all of our attempts to overcome our dividedness by living out our modern principles more consistently will fail to reconcile us to ourselves. He systematically demonstrates that neither wholly consistent sociability nor wholly consistent solitude is possible—nor even obviously preferable to the bourgeois dividedness from which we begin. The modern quest for immanent contentment is destined to leave us as restless as ever, no matter how wholeheartedly we give ourselves to it.

CHAPTER 4

Tocqueville

Democracy and the Naked Soul

To Teach Democracy to Know Itself

Count no man happy until he is dead, said Solon. The misfortunes of a Priam may come at the end, after all, or strike a man's nearest and dearest as he is borne to the grave, turning a life that seemed blessed into a theme for tragedy. Happiness so understood is beyond the powers of any frail, mortal man to give to himself. The premodern tradition often reflects this Solonic sternness, asking us to be heroes or saints, and then telling us that even the most successful efforts of human will and intelligence are not enough. Grace or good fortune must smile on a human life, up to and even beyond its final act, if we are to call it happy.[1]

Montaigne thinks that there is something off in Solon's dark vision: if we may count no man happy until he is dead, "then man is never happy, since he is so only when he is no more." He prefers a happiness measured to our mortality—a happiness we can enjoy here and now, whatever Solon might say. He develops an art of pursuing happiness so understood, which entails not heroism or holiness but self-knowledge, cutting our demands down to the compass of our capacities. That art asks of us only

the intelligent, moderate enjoyment of life's good things—
friendship and solitude, love and travel, art and books, the horse-
back ride and the unfinished garden—which the burgeoning
prosperity of the early modern era put within the reach of a
growing, ascendant class of human beings. This book has been
the biography of this ideal of happiness, happiness made immanent, and of the modern class of people that takes this ideal
for its own.[2]

Like Montaigne, the *honnêtes hommes* of the seventeenth
century sought to find their contentment here and now, by gliding lightly, yet loyally, over life's surface. Pascal grew up sur-
rounded by these *honnêtes hommes* and judged that their *honnêteté* could never answer to the deepest demands of the human
heart. However good and reasonable it might seem to circumscribe what we mean by happiness so as to bring it within our
reach, we cannot cut ourselves off from the depths of human
longing without cutting ourselves off from ourselves. Human
beings are not made to be satisfied by amusements, however
various, refined, and intelligent those amusements might be.
Human beings are made for a serious, even anguished, quest—
the quest for a hidden God, who sometimes gives the gift of
grace that alone can fill the living abyss of the restless human
heart.

To see happiness as the gift of a God who cannot be compelled to give it is a Christian reprisal of Solon's harsh wisdom,
hardly suited to draw crowds of human beings away from more
mundane and cheerful pursuits. Scolds are easy to ignore, especially when prosperity is on the rise, and the Enlightenment
ignored Pascal. With Voltaire as its champion and Paris as its
playground, the ideal of immanent contentment spread inexo-
rably outward in the eighteenth century, becoming the affair of a
decisive segment of European society—the social class Rousseau

lambasts in his portrait of the *bourgeois*. When Rousseau borrows Pascal's exposé of the secret misery of the *honnête homme* to apply it to that class, however, he does so not to divert men from the pursuit of immanent contentment but to change its character. In Rousseau's time, and with his help, immanent contentment, which Montaigne described as the carefree delight of the sophisticated few, becomes the serious demand of the earnest many.

That class and its aspirations are Tocqueville's object of study when he finds, in America, a "world altogether new"—the world Mill would call "*all* middle class." Though Tocqueville knows well that America has its inequalities, economic and otherwise, he sees that the middle-class ideal of happiness reigns in this new world without rival. Immanent contentment becomes the universal standard of aspiration for ordinary, hard-working men and women and takes on the color of their indefatigable, if slightly irrational, striving: "the inhabitant of the United States attaches himself to the goods of this world as if he was assured of not dying, and he throws himself into seizing those that pass within his reach with so much precipitation that one would say that at every instant he is afraid of ceasing to live before enjoying them." Because this class reigns in the American political world "like God over the universe," the democratization of the ideal of immanent contentment not only transforms its character but makes a private preoccupation into an all-pervasive social and political phenomenon.[3]

In American democracy, the possibilities and pathologies of the pursuit of immanent contentment play themselves out on the grand stage of the political life of a vast and powerful nation. Tocqueville's "new political science"—in which he looked to America as a case study, pregnant with lessons for all of democratic modernity—seeks to fathom the politics animated by that pursuit. For as Aristotle pointed out long ago, it is our way of pursuing happiness that makes us who we are, both personally and politically: "it is through hunting for [happiness] in a different manner and by means of different things that individuals create ways of life and regimes that differ." In making a people animated by the pursuit of immanent contentment his central object of study, Tocqueville becomes the great political anthropologist of Montaignean modernity. He shows us what our self-understanding means for our political life.[4]

Tocqueville's engagement with Montaigne himself is indirect, and mediated by Pascal. To the latter, his debts are difficult to overestimate. As his great friend, traveling companion, and coauthor Gustave de Beaumont remarked, Tocqueville studied no one "with more perseverance and more interest than Pascal. The two minds were made for one another." As we have seen, Pascal's distinctive modernity arises precisely from the depth of his engagement with Montaigne. When Tocqueville adopts and adapts Pascal's critique of modern man, he adopts and adapts Pascal's critique of Montaignean man.[5]

It is for this reason that attentive readers can see an uncanny parallel between the modern way of life Montaigne sketches and the democratic way of life Tocqueville observes. The Montaignean view that our common human condition matters more than artificial hierarchies of social status is the precursor of the democratic belief in the "equality of conditions," a belief that defines the world Tocqueville makes it his task to describe. The Montaignean critique of conventional human ties, and his exaltation of the free approbation of friendship, resounds in the individualistic flight from the constraints of place and family so natural to the American, as well as our potent desire for affirmation as particular, irreplaceable persons. Montaigne's delighted unmasking of the pretensions of the mighty and pompous, his deep-seated abhorrence of cruelty, his cheeky defense of man's material and bodily existence—all find their echoes in Tocqueville's portrait of democratic man. Even the unnerving skepticism for which Montaigne is famous becomes, in democratic America, the instinctive intellectual disposition of an entire nation, much to Tocqueville's astonishment.[6]

Tocqueville's admiration for the vigorous, great-hearted animal of American democracy was such that he referred to himself as "half Yankee." He marvels at the proud political energy, the immense economic and industrial vitality, the frank speech, the ready compassion, and the robust moral character of the Americans he presents to his readers as model citizens of the modern world. The first volume of *Democracy in America* offers an attractive portrait of what the pursuit of immanent contentment writ large might mean for the lives of modern peoples.[7]

But just as Pascal detects an existential moan underneath the tinkling laughter of the Montaignean bon vivant, Tocqueville discerns a restless unease beneath the cheerful busyness of the American democrat. Indeed, he sees that the more successful the enterprise of democracy becomes, the more unsettled its citizens will be by this Pascalian malaise. The paradox animating the second volume of *Democracy in America* is that ever-increasing equality and prosperity do not cure restlessness but entrench it: our unease is the product of our success. Tocqueville's effort to "teach democracy to know itself" is an effort to teach democratic human beings the Pascalian lesson that the goods that are their treasure, the justice that is their pride, and the happiness that is their aim can never be enough for a human soul.[8]

Tocqueville reads the prose of American life with the poetry of the French *moralistes* resounding in his ears. If we read his work as the culmination of this French conversation, it can help us plumb the depths of the strange and uneasy combination of satisfactions and discontents experienced by so many in our own time. For the rich anthropological visions of the *moralistes* remind us of the deepest reasons immanent contentment appealed to us in the first place, of the fissures in that standard that appear when we test it under the pressure of life and thought, and of the self-undermining character of every attempt to quiet our souls by doubling down on some version of the project of immanence. By considering in their fullness the arguments of both those who see immanent contentment as the proper human destination and those who see it as a lamentable detour from our true aim, we can cultivate the imagination we need to see our past with gratitude, our present with clarity, and our prospects with sobriety. Moral imagination, so understood, can make a decisive contribution to the political prudence we need to navigate our unsettled age.[9]

The All Middle Class Society?

Tocqueville observes democracy with both the limitations and the virtues of the outsider. That outsider's perspective can help us develop the moral imagination required for genuine situational awareness of our own place and time. Countless studies written by insiders describe more exactly the character of the Puritan founding, the progress of the arts and sciences, the nitty-gritty realities of township government, the ravages of slavery, and the place of women in the America of the 1830s, focusing on the questions of liberty and equality that come naturally to the democratic mind. As an outsider, however, Tocqueville sees the significance of some basic facts of democratic society that insiders are strongly disposed to miss. In the language of Rousseau, he helps us step outside of ourselves so as to "observe once what [we have] seen everyday," for he focuses on the definitive assumptions we make about happiness, justice, and human nature—assumptions that often escape our notice precisely because of their ubiquity.[10]

Tocqueville sees these assumptions and appreciates their significance because he is not one of us. Unlike any American, no matter how wealthy, Tocqueville grows up in a château that bears his name, where his family has resided for centuries. His aristocratic lineage dates back almost eight hundred years, to an ancestor who was listed among the companions of William the Conqueror at the Battle of Hastings. His great-grandfather Guillaume-Chrétien de Malesherbes represented Louis XVI at his trial and was guillotined a few months after the king; Tocqueville keeps a bust of Malesherbes on his desk. The sweet-tempered tutor who raises him, the Abbé Leseur, is an "intransigent Catholic monarchist." So is Tocqueville's mother, whose imprisonment during the Reign of Terror left her slightly unhinged. One of Tocqueville's earliest memories is of sitting with his family around the fireside as she reduced everyone to tears, singing a mournful peasant song about the death of the king. Though Tocqueville himself is a steadfast political liberal who sits on the center left of France's Chamber of Deputies during his years as representative from la Manche, he always feels "more at ease in dealing about some matter with aristocrats whose interest and opinions were entirely different from mine, than with the bourgeois whose ideas I shared and whose interests were similar to my own." With his fellow aristocrats, he shares something deeper than ideas and interests.[11]

A social order alien to democracy, the order of France's ancien régime, lives in Tocqueville's bones. With its three fixed orders of clergy, nobility, and third estate, the ancien régime was a world of deep, mostly hereditary differences in social standing: differences in who had access to political power, in who could marry and who remained celibate, in who could wear what clothes, in who could put battlements on their houses, in who could live a life of leisure and who could work for pay. In that world, dominated by clerics and nobles, what we call the middle class was but one part of the enormous, variegated third estate, the very name of which indicates its status as a social and political afterthought.[12]

When Tocqueville arrives in America, he suddenly beholds a society that is all third estate: a world without titles of nobility or primogeniture; a world where everyone, even the richest, works because the world of work is the locus of all of life's interest; a world where the clergy are overwhelmingly Protestant "businessmen of religion," as Tocqueville calls them, who marry like everyone else; a world of men constantly in motion and on the make, whose defining characteristics are industriousness, the love of material well-being, and the restless hunger for change. Tocqueville calls this basic reality of American life the "equality of conditions" and sees it for what it is: something genuinely new under the sun—a "world altogether new." The human resemblance that it required the full daring of Montaigne's imagination to postulate has taken on flesh as a prosaic reality that shapes the lives of millions. Tocqueville's political science consists in drawing the consequences of this tremendous innovation, which is often as imperceptibly ubiquitous to those on the inside as is water to the fish who swim in it. Because it registers the incalculable impact of the most fundamental yet most easily overlooked fact of the modern social and political world, that science remains indispensable to our self-understanding.[13]

We cannot help but wonder, however, whether Tocqueville's most fundamental observation holds up. In a world where rising inequality constantly makes headlines, can any piece of Tocqueville's analysis, which flows with remarkable unity from the "mother idea" of the equality of conditions, retain its relevance? Given the obvious inequalities of the America he observes in the 1830s, did it ever have any relevance in the first place?[14]

Tocqueville is not blind to American inequality. He devotes the longest chapter of *Democracy in America* to detailing the crimes of the American people and their government toward enslaved blacks and expelled native Americans, and he is unsparing in his assessment of these American forms of majoritarian tyranny. But even our perception of our inequalities is determined, in Tocqueville's view, by the decisive historical novelty that strikes his eye so forcefully: the society utterly dominated by the human type Rousseau called the *bourgeois*. For what we mean when we discuss inequality is precisely exclusion from the opportunities, rights, and risks of bourgeois, middle-class life. The demand for equal pay for equal work assumes the dignity of salaried labor—an assumption foreign to aristocratic society. We worry that mobility is declining because we take the goodness of mobility for granted. The concern that values such as industriousness and thrift are in decline assumes that those bourgeois values are basically correct in the first place. When we note the degree to which our society is not, and never has been, "*all* middle class," we implicitly assume that it can and should be. That assumption reflects a historical experience more unusual than is sometimes understood.[15]

Because we experience equality as an ordinary reality, we perceive inequality as a profound injustice. To illustrate the distinctly democratic character of this perception, Tocqueville extracts passages from the letters of a seventeenth-century marquise, Mme de Sévigné, in which she combines the most refined wit, tenderness, and elegance with unbelievably savage one-liners about local artisans being drawn and quartered because they had the temerity to protest a new tax. "Madame de Sévigné," he remarks, "did not clearly conceive what it was to suffer when you were not a gentleman." She has no compassion for the suffering of an artisan because she does not perceive an artisan as her equal, or indeed in any way akin to herself. "Today," Tocqueville continues, "the harshest man, writing to the most insensible person, would not dare to engage in cold blood in the cruel banter I have just reproduced." Where one finds such talk, one knows one has reached the edges of democracy.[16]

Though the equality of conditions entails equality of political rights, though it feeds upon economic arrangements such as the equal division of estates, its greatest power resides neither in ballots nor in bank accounts but in souls. The equality of conditions is a sentiment: the "sentiment of human resemblance." With no need for the particular genius of a mind like Montaigne's, those moved by the imaginative force of this sentiment recognize the humanity they share in common with others, no matter how far removed from their social situation and place. Tocqueville notes that, in America, householders treat their domestic servants with a respect an aristocrat could only find peculiar. Their relations, defined by contract rather than class, assume that the servant could and probably would move on and up, perhaps becoming a master himself one day. The master, moreover, has probably experienced some change of status in his own life, making it natural to imagine himself in the role of his servant. The broad compassion so characteristic of democratic human beings springs from this capacity for imagining ourselves in the places of others: our own position is rarely so secure as to make another's suffering seem alien to us.

In a democratic society, the abstract proposition of philosophic humanism Todorov describes as the "universality of the they" becomes an immediate and powerful movement of the heart. We see—sometimes even when we would prefer not to—our common humanity with others.[17]

The obverse of this perception of our common capacity for suffering is an idea of happiness measured to capacities just as common. A secure life, lifted above poverty and precarity; a comfortable life, cushioned from the degradations of shabbiness; a prosperous life, the reward of one's hard work. A life recognized by others as significant, and relieved of the loneliness which, as we will see, follows like a shadow on the heels of our mobility. Such is the democratic interpretation of Montaigne's contentment made immanent, purged of the *outré* elements of the life of the aristocratic libertine. The conditions of happiness so understood show up in the numbers, from life expectancy to GDP growth, that are our national pride. The contentment that we suppose to result from these goods seems possible and desirable not just for some human beings but for all human beings. For who is not capable of the ordinary satisfactions of comfort and security? Who does not resemble us in the desire to avoid poverty, anxiety, discomfort, and loneliness?

The very hold the sentiment of human resemblance has over democratic human beings often prevents them from noticing just how remarkable it is. Human difference, after all, is more visible than human resemblance: our eyes see big human beings and small human beings, males and females, dark-skinned and light-skinned, the fine tailoring of wealth and the dishevelment of poverty. We never see a human being simply, which is an abstraction; we always see *this* or *that* human being, who has qualities that differentiate him or her from others. Moreover, as

Rousseau noted, human self-consciousness seems to be inseparable from amour propre, the comparative self-love that fixates
on these human differences. To rank, differentiate, and put ourselves first are as natural to human beings as thinking.[18]

Human resemblance is anything but obvious, and we have
powerful psychic motives for resisting our awareness of it.
Nonetheless, modern, democratic human beings declare it to
be self-evident, and indeed experience it as such. We can see it
at work not only in the democratic compassion and the egalitarian respect we strive to express in our speech and manners
but in our anger on behalf of equal justice and, less admirably,
in our pervasive irritation at those above us on the social scale.
It is a social force of the greatest power, which remakes relations between races and sexes, young and old, students and
teachers. Moreover, its strength grows rather than wanes as it
advances; as Pierre Manent has written, "the more homoge-
nous society becomes, the stronger the desire for homogeneity
becomes."[19]

When Tocqueville perceives this great and growing force
from the vantage point of an aristocrat, he rapidly understands
that the vestiges of the aristocratic world—and with them, the
very form of humanity he knows himself to embody—are
doomed. He accepts this premonition of his own obsolescence
and seeks to persuade his peers among the aristocratic remain-
der of France to submit to it as a "providential fact." He knows
that the sentiment of human resemblance is the soul of democratic justice and that this justice is democracy's greatness.[20]

But as a man whose life straddles the divide between the
"two worlds" of democracy and aristocracy, Tocqueville numbers himself among those who "believe that there is hardly ever
absolute good in laws." No society enjoys all good things; all of
them have their strange caprices that reveal the partiality of

their view of human life. The telling idiosyncrasy of the American democrat is his instinctive hostility to what Tocqueville calls "forms." Tocqueville's observation of this apparent quirk of the democratic mind reveals the determinative thrust of our pursuit of happiness.[21]

Hostility to forms is not in itself new. In a time besotted with forms, Montaigne rebelled against them so as to pursue his happiness in the stripped-down daylight of nature. In the democratic age, however, such hostility to forms becomes an instinctive orientation for millions. Tocqueville analyzes that orientation with his characteristic mix of appreciation and skepticism. In so doing, he both discovers something decisive about the democratic mind and opens a new chapter in this French conversation about happiness.

A World Stripped Bare

Democratic human beings, Tocqueville writes, "despise forms, which they consider as useless and inconvenient veils placed between them and the truth." The meaning of the term "forms," which Tocqueville does not precisely define, emerges from the portrait of the aristocratic society he paints to put democracy into relief. In the aristocratic world, the observation of formalities structured all of social life. One addressed people by their proper titles: "my lord," "my lady," "your grace," "your highness." One went through prescribed motions, from bowing and curtseying in the ballroom to kneeling and crossing oneself in church. One had to dress one's part, and to know one's place in the ranks of men, so as not to dishonor oneself by placing oneself too low or give insult to others by placing oneself too high. Old, sometimes strange rules governed political life, and men prided themselves on the punctilious insistence on the rights and privileges expressed by such formalities. Even within the family, children kept a respectful distance from their fathers and addressed them with the formal *vous*. Aristocracy sought to civilize the human scene by covering it in veils, prescribing its words and deeds, and maintaining dignified separations between its players.[22]

The pursuit of immanent contentment is hostile to forms from the outset. Montaigne writes that "we must tear the mask off of things as well as people"; when we do, we find that "kings and philosophers crap, and ladies too." The beautiful portrait he paints of his perfectly transparent friendship with La Boétie charms us with a vision of human intimacy totally unmediated by the barriers, roles, and expectations of formality. His modern ethical vision sees the untamed flow of life as a stream to be pleasantly followed, not a shapeless mass of matter that habit and reason must mold into a determinate shape. "Life," he writes, "is a material and corporeal movement, an action imperfect and unregulated in its essence. I employ myself to serve it as such." The whole effort of his work is to seek happiness by following the unregulated, formless movement of life so understood.[23]

Until Tocqueville, this suspicion of forms characterizes the whole tradition of *moralistes* we consider here. Though Pascal rejects Montaigne's ideal of immanent contentment, he inherits his distrust of forms; he opens the *Pensées* by lifting the veil of mannered politeness that covers the social world to reveal the misery and hatred beneath. Rousseau, in his turn, will take this hostility to forms, this longing for unmediated spontaneity and transparency, to his wonted extremes. When he quits Paris for a new way of life, he marks the occasion by jettisoning the formal accoutrements of Parisian propriety—the watch, the sword, the linen shirts, all of it. Distrusting the deceptions he believes implicit in the prescribed forms of articulate speech, he looks to tears, gestures, and inarticulate cries as the most authentic revelations of the human heart. He once chooses to make his sentiments known to the staid David Hume by leaping into his lap and bathing him with kisses.[24]

In its egalitarian quest to affirm human resemblance beneath the visible distinctions of outward forms, modern democracy universalizes the suspicion of formality that characterizes this philosophic tradition. Forms often embody the social hierarchies democratic peoples believe it their duty to demolish. To refuse to observe the formalities is to take liberties, and free peoples enjoy taking liberties. There is nothing that strikes their ears more discordantly than being told to "know their place." This instinctive hostility to forms leads them not only to transgress expectations and boundaries but also to strip things down so as to reveal their hidden essences—most notably, their own selves. Democratic human beings engage in pervasive rituals of self-exposure, through which they demonstratively throw off social expectations and encumbrances. In so doing, they often discard intellectual and moral inheritances that their ancestors took centuries to amass. While that heritage can constrain their lives, it can also inform and civilize them.[25]

This constant repulsion of the shaping force of the past, this refusal to be assigned to any known place, thus turns out to present problems of its own. Tocqueville trains his eye on these problems, in a decisive departure from the tradition of the *moralistes* that formed him. In America, he sees that a society that strips away veils, demolishes roles, and annihilates social distance leaves its citizens feeling exposed, helpless, and uneasy. For all of their rigidity, the formalities of aristocratic society taught one how to live. A world without them is a world in which we have both the opportunity and the necessity of making it all up for ourselves. Our hostility to forms leaves us intellectually, socially, and morally naked.[26]

Tocqueville's political science takes as its central object this self-denuding movement of the democratic soul. As we will see, the democratic hostility to forms makes knowledge, particularly self-knowledge, elusive. Without such knowledge, democratic humanity's pursuit of happiness, for all of its impressive energy, lacks determinate form and becomes haphazard and anxious. Moreover, democratic human beings learn the harsh experiential lesson that forms, for all their restrictiveness, have a mediating capacity, in the absence of which the search for love, recognition, and approbation becomes ever more difficult. Eventually democratic politics comes to reflect the anger that wells up under the pressure of unease and loneliness.

The Deformations of Doubt

In *Democracy in America*'s second volume, Tocqueville examines the inner life of the democratic soul from the top down, beginning with the intellect. In so doing, he shows how the desire for immanent contentment shapes the way we think. We are attracted by the satisfactions of immanence in part because we are unnerved by claims about the transcendent. For we know such claims can be made by ambitious men seeking to enlist us into the service of their enterprises. We fear being hoodwinked out of the happiness available to us here and now. That nagging suspicion shapes the way we think about our options.[27]

Jealous of its prerogatives, the democratic soul Tocqueville describes believes in a principle celebrated by Montaigne: the principle Todorov calls the "autonomy of the I." The free, independent, egalitarian American citizen, engaged in the pursuit of happiness enumerated among his fundamental rights, naturally wishes to be as self-sufficient as possible. Intellectually, he wants to guide himself only on the basis of "the individual effort of his reason." He prides himself on accepting the noble challenge of deciphering the world on his own and living by the light of his self-generated convictions. Pragmatic and adept at solving the practical difficulties life presents, the American "conclude[s] that everything in the world is explicable, and that nothing goes beyond the limits of intelligence."[28]

Americans therefore "love to see the matter they are dealing with very clearly." So as "to see it more closely and in broad daylight," they "strip it as far as they can of its covering." Self-reliant people want to see, for themselves, the naked truth of things; to get to the heart of the matter, they loosen and peel away forms with the solvent of their doubt. The democratic distrust of forms is thus not merely a social instinct but an ontological one.[29]

This desire to see things for oneself gives Americans "an instinctive disbelief in the supernatural," which makes for the great paradox of their religious life. Tocqueville reads Pascal daily; he understands Christianity to be inseparable from supernatural faith. But from the moment of his arrival in America, Tocqueville observes that these same Americans, so suspicious of the supernatural, almost all go to church. Americans are thus deeply conflicted about their belief: "either I am badly mistaken," Tocqueville writes in a letter to a friend early in his American visit, "or there is a great store of doubt" hidden beneath the external forms of American religious observance. That great store of doubt is the restless core of the democratic mind. In religious life, it helps explain why Americans change, found, and re-found churches so often: they are embarked on a quest for a faith purged of pious posturing, a quest that is frequently disappointed but ever renewed.[30]

This impatience with established ways of doing things also gives Americans an abiding suspicion of the thought of the past. Americans take tradition not as an authority but "merely as information"—an indication of how things were done, not of how they should be done. Innovation, not perpetuation, leads to success in a democratic society, which gives democratic peoples an instinctive preference for the new, not the old. As Mill put it: "As the people in general become aware of the recent date of the most important physical discoveries, they are liable to form a rather contemptuous opinion of their ancestors." Every new round of technological innovation helps "carry the feeling of admiration for modern and disrespect for ancient times down even to the wholly uneducated classes." Democratic human beings are intellectual progressives by default and find in the denial of the authority of tradition an easy way to assert their independence.[31]

Such assertions of intellectual independence, however, turn out to be self-undermining. When we move beyond the ambition to think for ourselves and seriously attempt to do so, we discover that it is no simple business. Questions crowd the mind: How should I live? What is happiness? What are my duties? Is there a God? Does that God ask anything of me? Is the world created, or is it the product of chance? Answers to such questions—indeed, even robust articulations of such questions—turn out to be dauntingly difficult to find. The obvious way to begin to seek them would be to study the thought of those who have investigated such questions before us. Such study proves laborious. Moreover, particularly for beginners, it requires intellectual deference: a young mind cannot begin to judge a basic element of moral philosophy such as Aristotle's catalog of the virtues until it has dwelt for some time with the very word "virtue"—a word democratic human beings tend not to use. That word must be considered in relation to the other elements of Aristotle's philosophic vocabulary, such as "happiness," "soul," and "activity." One cannot judge Aristotle without understanding him; one cannot understand him without seeing what he sees—that is, without becoming an Aristotelian, at least temporarily. Such intellectual apprenticeship repulses the mind that longs for independence: Must I cease thinking for myself in order to learn to think for myself?[32]

The quest for immanent contentment is thus conjoined to a suspicion of forms and intellectual authorities that makes the democratic mind leery of putting itself in tutelage to the great names of the religious and philosophic canons. Insofar as the desire for immanent contentment leads us to try to grasp happiness, here and now, it is also conjoined to an impatience that makes us recalcitrant not only to intellectual authorities but to the experience of serious and sustained thought. To philosophize, to lose oneself in thinking, is to forget time. Democratic human beings never forget time. We cannot afford to: the equality of conditions means that we have no fixed station. If we are not seeking to get ahead, we can be sure that our numberless competitors are stealing a march on us, taking advantage of our inertia. For the same reason, we are impatient for action. We need tangible results for our efforts—something to show for ourselves, something that can help us make our mark on the world. We resist philosophy because we fear that it might cause us to miss out on life, that the happiness we could seize here and now might pass us by while we are transfixed by thinking.[33]

Human beings on the hunt for immanent contentment are constantly drawn out of themselves and into the urgencies of the practical. Attracted by the sight of some striking movement in the agitated social landscape that surrounds them, their heads are always turning. Part of us knows very well that this constant diversion is a problem, but we have an instinct, grounded in Montaignean skepticism, to placate our existential worries by diverting ourselves from them. We must therefore struggle against ourselves to train our minds to the steady contemplation of anything. "The habit of inattention must be considered the greatest vice of the democratic mind," Tocqueville writes. Though the digital age has rightly been called an "age of distraction," recent attention-diverting technologies only exacerbate a long-standing tendency. "There is nothing less conducive to meditation than the interior of a democratic society." Busyness and distraction disperse and deform our attention.[34]

Though our social state encourages the human desire to seek happiness in the light of what individual reason alone can discover, that same social state makes the formation of the rational faculty, through philosophic study and meditation, an undertaking that goes profoundly against the grain. The democratic social state does, however, give rise to its own form of rationalistic genius. While the Americans of his time had not founded a single philosophic school of their own, or discovered a single general law of physics, Tocqueville notes, they invest tremendous energy in the applications of science, and invented the steamboat, a machine that is "changing the face of the world." Their railways are the world's longest; their canals monumental feats of engineering. "The American people sees itself marching across this wilderness, draining swamps, straightening rivers, peopling solitude, mastering nature." Stories of such nature-mastering feats, from Lewis and Clark to Thomas Edison to Steve Jobs, lie at the heart of Americans' poetic self-image as a people at the leading edge of history.[35]

But the Americans' technological genius only deepens their philosophic difficulties. For it calls the ultimate standard of rationalism, nature itself, into question. A technological people regards nature not as a formative standard but as a "standing reserve," in Heidegger's language—a "resource" to be exploited for human purposes rather than a source of purposes that might help us get our bearings in the world. Having seen so much time and distance annihilated by its inventions, a technological people regards natural limits as negotiable rather than as a permanent framework to which individuals must conform their lives. In the risks taken by those who truly push the frontiers, technological genius has its heroism; it is also a source of countless mercies, comforts, and conveniences for everyone. But that heroism and those mercies come at the price of alienation from nature as humanity's formative guide.[36]

Doubting the supernatural basis of their religion even as they make their way to church, desiring to think for themselves yet lacking the time and the taste for meditation, deconstructing the forms and formulae that might help them learn to reason, excelling in practical science but alienated from nature by the technological outlook that pragmatism encourages, democratic human beings have innumerable causes for doubt, "the sentiment I think I see visibly ruling in the depths of everyone's soul." Tocqueville's visit to America dropped him suddenly into a world in which "belief and doubt had exchanged places," as Sheldon Wolin has observed. In democratic modernity, doubt assumes the default governance of moral life, stepping into the role belief long occupied.[37]

When accompanied by the hope that we might acquire knowledge, doubt can form a life with determinate direction— the life of a Socrates or an Augustine. Citizens of modern democracy, however, lack the time and the taste necessary to make doubt into a fruitful mode of existence. Although we have plenty of reservations about the whirlwind of proximate diversions into which our desire for immanent contentment draws us, although we often experience that our distractions do not make us happy, we lack the disposition to think these misgivings through and fall back into the gravity well of the fleeting. Doubt disarms us before the great opportunity that the equality of conditions affords, that of guiding our own lives. The freedom to doubt without the courage to hope then comes to seem less like a sunny prospect than an oppressive cloud.[38]

Self-Scrutiny

In a world where spiritual dogmas and theological virtues were potent political and social forces, Montaignean skepticism suggested the possibility of easing up, giving the despised and neglected desires of the body their due, and allowing for a bit of playfulness on the margins of a world thick with duties. Tocqueville remarks that had he been born in a century like Montaigne's, where spiritual authorities "held souls as if benumbed in the contemplation of another world," he too would have sought to turn our attention toward the pursuit of material well-being. In America, he beholds how the liberation of men's material desires, and the encouragement of their practical industriousness, can produce the welcome spectacle of a prosperity more widespread than history has ever seen. Feeding the engine of that prosperity encourages us to bring our imaginations down from heaven and direct them toward an endless variety of bodily needs and wants. As we lower the horizon of our thoughts, however, we eventually occlude the prospect of the spiritual from our view.[39]

The materialism of the modern middle class can thus prove as constraining as the spiritualism it sought to replace. "Democracy favors the taste for material enjoyments," Tocqueville writes, and "this taste, if it becomes excessive, soon disposes men to believe that everything is only matter." To human beings constantly concerned with tangible acquisition, prone to doubt, and suspicious of forms and of the supernatural, the very idea of a soul—which Aristotle describes as the "living form" of an organic being—can come to seem as fantastic as a fairy godmother. But a living being without such a unifying principle eludes every effort to grasp it. Our reluctance to entertain the possibility of the soul causes us to stall at the entryway to self-understanding.[40]

This spiritual incredulity undermines our sense of our own agency. Commenting on the tendencies of democratic historians of his age, Tocqueville notes that they typically describe human affairs in great chains of cause and effect, subordinating human action to the dictates of "blind fatality." They imagine a world made up only of matter, whose motions are determined by an unbreakable causal sequence extending to the beginning of time, in which active, potent, human souls shaping the world through reflection, choice, and action are reduced to epiphenomena. We come to wonder whether we are nothing more than "powerless transient being[s] in an organically generated cyberspace," as a proponent of this view puts it. The doubt that liberated the human soul from the hegemony of spiritual powers eventually brings it to doubt everything spiritual—including its own existence.[41]

Such a view deepens the existential conundrum of modern man Pascal first identified. Pascal wondered why he had been thrust into a world in which he could find no sensible indication of the purpose of his life. In America, this cosmic unease permeates society; one fears that his fate is to be, as Peter Lawler writes, a "miserable accident perceiving himself as such." Our pursuit of happiness is hamstrung by the persistent urge to deny the effective reality of the very selves we seek to satisfy.[42]

Without self-knowledge to guide it, the quest for the good life becomes a slapdash sequence of locations, vocations, and vacations:

> A man, in the United States, carefully builds a house in which to spend his old age, and he sells it while the ridgepole is being set; he plants a garden and he rents it as he is about to taste its fruits; he clears a field, and he leaves to others the trouble of gathering the harvest. He embraces a profession, and he leaves it. He settles in a place that he soon leaves in order to carry his changing desires elsewhere. If his private affairs give him some respite, he immediately plunges into the whirl of politics. And when, near the end of a year filled with work, he still has a little leisure, he takes his restless curiosity here and there across the vast limits of the United States.[43]

Montaigne self-consciously designed a life without unified form and direction. Democratic human beings, discouraged by so many factors from thinking steadily about what they are and what they long for, inhabit formless lives by default.

This exhausting succession of aims and activities leaves us longing for a point of fixity and rest—somewhere or someone to come home to. But it is difficult to pin our hazily defined selves down or bring them into meaningful relation with one another. Our natural desire for home and for deep human connection can take on a desperate edge as we seek to find these secure supports while beset by existential self-doubt.

Loneliness and the Longing for
Unmediated Approbation

The restlessness of our quest for connection to place and persons is fueled by many factors: our geographic and social mobility, our distrust of forms and expectations, our capacity for imagining relations with the widest variety of people. Our unsettled seeking for stability and social meaning is hard to calm, for all of these factors have roots in justly revered elements of our social order.

The equality of conditions that defines modern democracy requires mobility, both geographic and social. For that equality to have any economic meaning, a man must be able to reap the fruits of his own labor; the condition of his birth should set no limit on his opportunity for success. Democracy teaches us to see work as "the necessary, natural, and honest condition of humanity" and holds labor in high esteem. For people to reap the just rewards for their work, they must rise and fall on the social scale according to the measure of their exertions. They must be flexible and mobile, following the opportunity to deploy their labor profitably wherever it may lead.[44]

Loneliness, however, awaits those who make the effort to rise as far as their merits may take them, for they must leave the near, dear, and familiar behind. On democracy's frontier, in the American West, Tocqueville observes a world in which inhabitants are present but society does not exist. There, "men hardly know one another, and each ignores the history of his closest neighbor." This description might now be applied to neighborhoods all over America. Geographically transient, and never knowing what to expect from others in a social world always in flux, democratic human beings crave the reassurance of their fellows' approbation, which proves to be as elusive as their whereabouts.[45]

In the aristocratic world, one found oneself living in a web of social permanence that would define one throughout one's life, wherever one stood on the social scale. The immobility of such societies was often literal: one might dwell in the very home of one's ancestors, amid their furniture and their clothing, their tombstones not far away. One's place in the order of birth gave one a permanent persona—a role to play, which one could interpret in different ways but never simply abandon. This web of permanence extended beyond the family and into the broader social order. In a letter to one of his nephews, Tocqueville describes the quintessentially aristocratic experience of profound rootedness in the first person:

> I have traced the line of our ancestors back over nearly four hundred years, finding them always at Tocqueville and their history intertwined with that of the population that surrounds me. There is a certain charm in thus treading the earth that one's forbears walked on and in living among people whose very origins are mingled with our own.[46]

To be born into the democratic world is to see that web of permanence dissolved. Democratic human beings learn at a young age that their families, places, and roles are temporary arrangements, open to radical revision or outright rejection. Parents place the prospect of independence and its duties before their children as the definitive challenge of the adult life for which they are preparing. Whether to make a family and what form to give it are choices, now more than ever. To cross the country to make a fortune on the frontier was normal in Tocqueville's time; to cross the country in search of better work, academic prestige, or lower living costs is normal now. If ties will bind us, we must knot them ourselves.

Who does not prefer it that way? The aristocratic world of defined roles had more losers than winners by definition. When compared to the naturalness of democratic mores, those roles can seem hopelessly inauthentic. But to have no given role is to have to build a life from scratch. Where we will live, what we will do, whether and whom we will marry, what political allegiances we will have, if any, whether we will take part in "organized religion"—all of it is up to us. We constantly remake and dissolve the relations that define us. As a result, as Mill puts it, "the members of a democratic community are like the sands of the seashore, each very minute, and no one adhering to any other."[47]

And so democratic human beings turn inward. Politics, the question of the common good, can seem to them a distraction from the real and demanding business of life—making one's way, pursuing one's career, starting some kind of family, creating some kind of home. This dedication to private concerns can bring with it a troubling detachment from common concerns. Tocqueville observes this phenomenon in his own sister-in-law, finding that in a moment of political crisis "both [her] mind and heart were solely concerned with the good God, her husband, her children and especially her health, with no interest left over for other people. She was the most respectable woman and the worst citizen one could find." Though modern democracy universalizes citizenship as never before, it paradoxically tends to drain the moral energy from public life.[48]

Though democratic individualism can undermine citizenship, it is also the foundation of democratic compassion. Democratic human beings are not like Mme de Sévigné: it requires only the simplest and most natural movement of their imaginations to put themselves in the place of others. They are kind, principally because they do not imagine themselves invulnerable to anyone else's ills. They experience their own isolation, vulnerability, and doubt too consistently for that. Readily commiserating with others, they often hold themselves duty-bound to do something to relieve whatever human suffering they learn of, even on the far side of the planet. The fellow feeling democratic compassion evokes, however, becomes thinner as it extends. For although democratic human beings can sympathize with anyone, that sympathy tends to take the form of small and easy kindnesses rather than large and costly ones: a surface softness of manner, small donations to charity, declarations of solidarity with beleaguered people far away. Kind though they may be, these are not the striking acts of a Regulus or an Antigone. Indeed, universal sympathy may be inversely proportional to particular dedication to city or family. As Joshua Mitchell has put it, "God's love may be infinite, but man's is not: concern and solicitude perennially directed over the horizon diminishes what is available for the neighbor who stands in front of you." Because Tocqueville's Americans experience neediness and loneliness so often themselves, they want to be kind. Because they are preoccupied with the cultivation of their own fragile fortunes and ties, they do not want to overcommit themselves.[49]

Democratic loneliness therefore both feeds democratic compassion and determines its limits. Envy, which is compassion's dark Janus-face, hardens the edge of that loneliness. By bringing all human beings within a single scope, democracy makes everyone both potentially pitiable and potentially enviable. As Tocqueville writes, "As long as the bourgeois were different from the nobles, they were not jealous of the nobles, but of one another." If a man is so far above one's own status that one cannot imagine entering into his place, one does not envy him—he is another kind of being, not an incarnation of one's own possibilities. Envy is a passion reserved for people like oneself.

"If we plumb the depths of our hearts, won't we all be frightened to discover what envy makes us feel about our neighbors, friends, and relatives? We are not jealous of these people because they are neighbors, friends, and relatives, but because they are our likes and equals." For the same reason they can pity anyone, democratic human beings can be jealous of anyone. The sentiment of human resemblance, which is compassion toward the suffering, is envy toward the successful.[50]

This envy embitters the democratic pursuit of happiness, as Lucien Jaume notes: "Like men in general according to Pascal, the citizens of 'democracy' do not know themselves, and unfortunately they turn their drive for equality, in which they believe as a source of ultimate joy, against their own lives." Envious contemplation of the contentment of others sours their own contentment. By teaching them to regard all around them as potential rivals, it also hardens the loneliness that necessarily attends upon a mobile life.[51]

The manners of a mobile people thus take on a certain coldness. Tocqueville sees this coldness at work as he observes the newly emerging industrial economy of the 1830s, noting that the bosses of these industries rarely live among their workers, which makes it easier to use them and discard them without too much fuss. Globalization extends this principle so far as to locate executives on the other side of the world from the workers whose low wages make their profits possible. At home, human resources offices staff themselves with professionals trained in the art of firing people nicely, by the book, without ever getting angry. Business does not profit from emotional ugliness.[52]

This businesslike coldness is a universal temptation of democratic souls and penetrates into life's most intimate recesses: the breakup by text message, the simple silence that allows an old friend to slide out of one's life. Democratic human beings are not willfully cold, much less harsh or vindictive. They simply need to move on, to husband their wasting commodities of time and attention. Niceness and coldness grease the skids of democratic mobility, allowing people to slide through one another's lives without the friction of enmity or attachment.

But that friction turns out to be something human beings crave. And modern peoples, who systematically break down conventional ties to particular places and persons, find themselves in a social world in which the unmediated approbation of Montaignean friendship has become the only game in town. Montaigne thought a friendship such as he found with La Boétie was a stroke of fortune that arrived only once in three centuries, flashing out unexpectedly from the monotonous generational succession ensured by more conventional social ties. Modern life liberates us from those monotonous conventional ties—making the quest to find a La Boétie into an urgent necessity.

Because such an idiosyncratic merger of souls is the only mode of human relation we understand to be legitimate, we expect it to bear the weight of our whole social edifice. This impossible demand gives rise to conflicting expectations—we want marriage, for example, to be both utterly liberated from conventional expectations and utterly reliable as a bedrock social institution. As Montaigne knew, however, soulmates are as rare and fleeting as they are precious. A world built on such bonds is a fragile one, in which many will endure a frightful loneliness. And even those who manage to reap the fruits of this new order will find it difficult to perpetuate.

The Politics of Immanence and
the Recovery of Prudence

Tocqueville's insight into the American soul shows that demo-cratizing the Montaignean quest for immanent contentment does not universalize the life of Montaignean nonchalance. An "immanent frame" can be a constricting one, leaving us as rest-less and uneasy as ever. Our frantic scramble for satisfactions and status markers, our haunted search for elusive soulmates with whom to build a life—all of it continually collides with limits that seem arbitrary and test our patience. This frustration with limits eventually rattles our thinking about politics. For it turns against the architecture of separations that is the hallmark invention of liberal prudence.[53]

From the heart of an illiberal political-religious order, in which the Church's constant presence made transcendent con-cerns impossible to ignore, Montaigne sought to carve out a space in which to pursue the satisfactions of immanent content-ment. His proto-liberal stance encouraged his contemporaries to take the prudent step of according one another the liberty of a private life—a little latitude in which an embodied human being might attend to his visceral needs and pleasures, an *arrière-boutique* in which a soul might roam freely through its doubts and dreams. Later thinkers such as John Locke would elaborate a full-blown political theory that rested on the pru-dent recommendation of limits: arguments, now familiar to all, for constraining the scope of government to the immanent concerns of prosperity and security, and leaving exploration of the transcendent largely up to the individual. In their dif-ferent ways, Montaigne and Locke both invent separations and limitations—the characteristic strategy of the modern political art.[54]

The liberal order embodied in America's constitutional architecture is a great achievement of this kind of political prudence. By turns conservative and inventive, daring and compromising, it bespeaks a profound awareness of the manifold and conflicting dimensions of human life and of the consequent challenges of self-government: how to allow majorities to rule without permitting them to tyrannize, how to secure public order while protecting private liberty, how government might be at once limited in scope and energetic in execution. As Tocqueville remarks, this American system dealt in a particularly adroit way with the historically clashing concerns for immanence and transcendence, according to each a secure but limited place. Religion, he remarks, "never directly takes part in the government of society," but it must "nonetheless be considered as the first of [American] political institutions," for it helps men learn to use their liberty well and keeps them from believing the dangerous doctrine that "everything is allowed in the interests of society." By negotiating this fruitful if tense alliance between "the *spirit of religion* and the *spirit of liberty*," the American political order allows each concern to complement the other while keeping it in its place.[55]

If a more and more significant portion of the democratic public comes to believe that immanent goals are the only sensible and legitimate goals, however, the immanent perspective will come to dominate both private and public life, and the separations that thinkers such as Montaigne, Locke, and Madison devised will lose their force. Transcendent principles, both revealed and natural, will come to seem increasingly suspect. Immanence, once a limiting force, will become an invasive one—a "pervasive and encompassing *anticulture*," as Patrick Deneen has put it. Limits on the individual's pursuit of immanent goals, whether traditional, moral, or religious, will come to seem like relics of a disingenuous and oppressive past. When that happens, politics will change its character. Liberalism will no longer call forth the creative yet cautious genius characteristic of its greatest statesmen. It will instead call forth those with the cunning and ruthlessness necessary to drive our demands through.[56]

Prosperity, security, and consent—unpretentious notions once evoked to circumscribe the ambitions of politics—prove to have expansive implications. Boundless economic growth comes to be expected; small risks come to seem intolerable; autonomy comes to defy every limit. Our desires for these things are not consistent, or even compatible—human life cannot be at once limitlessly free, absolutely safe, and ever more prosperous. We therefore find ourselves making strange demands: to be compelled to choose our insurance, buckle our seatbelts, and affirm our consent. For we want to be, at once, completely in charge and perfectly taken care of, "more than kings and less than men."[57]

When we train our attention obsessively on the tangible stuff of property, place, and privilege, politics in its Aristotelian sense—reasoned if intense negotiation between conflicting, plausible, and earnestly held ideas about the good—ceases to make sense. Public argument comes to seem a performative gesture intended to divert attention away from the conflicts of material interests that really drive everyone. Institutions, including the very liberal institutions we created to mediate our differences, now look like the mechanisms of class self-advancement rather than the hard-won fruit of compromise between legitimately opposing perspectives. Antinomian suspicion becomes all-pervasive. Even the most consummate insiders—New York real estate moguls, Silicon Valley tech billionaires, Hollywood celebrities, Ivy League academics—seek to graft themselves onto it. Showboaters and lone wolves, united only by their lack of respect for formalities and willingness to advance themselves and their causes at any cost, dominate the political scene.[58]

When we cease to believe that people are motivated by the principles they invoke, we treat them differently. Conservatives see liberals not as people earnestly if misguidedly working to alleviate entrenched injustice but as insular cultural elites signaling their virtue; liberals see conservatives not as people sincerely if mistakenly working to preserve traditional morality but as rich white men perpetuating their privilege. People on both the right and the left come to despise those who successfully advance through our institutions, calling them "the establishment"—a word that itself seems to justify our contempt. To ears accustomed to hearing one's enemies described in sinister terms, those who invoke principles that might limit political conflict sound weak or duplicitous. For to abide by such limits, we fear, is to be duped into observing arbitrary constraints on one's latitude for action that will not trouble one's adversaries.[59]

Vulgarity comes to be the political vernacular favored by all sides. Crude words are honest and give those who use them the legitimating imprimatur of hardheaded authenticity. Ridicule, always politically potent, becomes less veiled and more common. Violence, too, enjoys an ever-greater measure of legitimacy. For those who deploy it show that they are not fooled by deceptive appearances and get right to the heart of the matter. As every restraint comes to seem a velvet glove hiding the iron fist of power, we feel increasingly compelled to take our own gloves off, and fight fire with fire.[60]

The small, basic courtesies that define moral life fall into disuse—a change that few of us actively desire but to which many of us passively acquiesce. For such niceties are everyday expressions of a reverence for the selves of others we find hard to maintain, haunted as we are by doubts about the reality of our own selves. Why, after all, should we respect persons? Why should we refrain from invading their personal space? Why look away from their embarrassments? Why not interrupt them when they talk? Why not just go where we feel like going, look where we feel like looking, talk when we feel like talking? We observe such limits when we understand other human beings as bearers of dignity, somehow standing apart from the meaningless ebb and flow of matter. But to believe that we are anything more than the matter that makes us up, we must believe in the reality of something more than matter. Our reflexive hostility to forms saps our capacity for perceiving the very thing that constitutes the person—making a living, acting, thinking, being out of inert material stuff, God only knows how. For it is the active and organizing principle of form that transforms the transient stuff we eat into the enduring persons we are; it is when form fails that we return to dust and ashes. As Edmund Spenser put it, transforming Aristotle into poetry: "For of the soul the body form doth take; / for soul is form, and doth the body make." We *are* forms; to fail to respect them is to fail to respect us.[61]

When skepticism about form undermines our sense of the reality of the self, the human beings we deal with come to seem like crude masses to be moved and manipulated by whatever means necessary. There is no particular need to handle them with delicacy or respect, or to allow them the freedom to seek a truth that cannot be seared into their brains by social pressure. A political order that began by separating out some room in which the self might freely maneuver ceases, against its own deepest wisdom, to understand the need for that room.

Politics in the immanent frame then comes to reflect the loneliness and existential unease of souls that inhabit that frame. That unease drives our political imprudence, abets our hostility to restraint, animates our ever-increasing vulgarity, rawness, and fascination with violence, and explains our growing impatience with other human beings, whom we find it ever more difficult to regard as separate and serious realities we are bound to respect. The defense of immanence, an ingenious invention of prudence that once helped mark off the space that freedom and individuality require, comes to breed a new form of imprudence, bent upon collapsing all such spaces. The deepest source of that imprudence is our increasingly oversimplified understanding of ourselves.[62]

CONCLUSION

Liberal Education and the Art of Choosing

On Spending One's Chips

Law school or a PhD? The young fixate on such questions. Trying to be prudent, they investigate them by deploying the modes of analysis they have been taught to use: looking up countless opportunities, tabulating pluses and minuses, making spreadsheets to keep track of it all. But the question of how to live cannot be answered by aggregating quantities. We must rather think about it by attending to the strange and contradictory qualities that make us human—that we are free, rational, and open to the divine but also frail, fallible, and subject to death. How can such a patchwork being pull itself together to make a meaningful life? If education, insistently focused on immanent goods, refuses to help us think through the questions of our nature that yawn beneath our practical alternatives, life's significant choices will seem groundless.[1]

Such a prospect often paralyzes young people, especially those with a bounty of options to consider. As an exceptionally gifted young man once remarked to us in class, what he dreaded most was "spending his chips": investing all his carefully cultivated potential into any particular course of life, converting a hazy but infinitely promising *might be* into a definite and limited *is*. His classmates fell silent at his confession, for he had given voice to the perplexity of their own hearts. On the threshold of adult life, many of the young instinctively shrink back, seeking to remain as long as possible in the condition of stem cells, conveniently malleable, ever ready to employ their talents in whatever way might be called for.[2]

How did we arrive at this strange condition, in which long and expensive education fails to prepare the young to deal with the plain necessity of choosing to become something? Why does this love of indeterminacy persist into adult life, as we try to be super-parents, CEOs, and Samaritans, all at once? In these pages, we have followed the argument of the French *moralistes* about the conception of happiness that we believe inspires this discordant restlessness. Montaigne makes a charming case for this conception, painting a portrait of a capacious life that he contrasts compellingly to the pigheaded quarreling of his pharisaical contemporaries. Fencing off the mind's dangerous forays beyond the immanent frame, Montaigne makes himself at home amid unpretentious pleasures. Taking nothing too seriously, he flits like a butterfly around the garden of his life, never lingering too long over any single flower.

Montaigne's motives are admirable, his practical genius impressive, and his portrait of his own life winsome. But Montaignean humanism begets a strangely inhuman world, a world where we find ourselves alienated from our own self-transcending nature. While that humanism promises a society of diverse individuals pursuing various ways of life side by side, it produces a crowd of similar human beings monotonously fixated on variety. And it afflicts us with the anxiety that comes from having to make life's weightiest choices without the guidance of existential reason: reason familiar with the architecture of transcendent questions in which our practical choices are situated.[3]

The personal disorders brought on by the immanent perspective are described in poignant detail by Pascal and Rousseau. Pascal reveals the misery that haunts the quest for immanent contentment like a shadow. That misery—carefully hidden but constantly revealed in the love of diversion so characteristic of modern men and women—is the enduring sign of the mismatch between the kind of happiness we pursue and the kind of beings we are. Rousseau demonstrates, perhaps against his own intention, that no doubling down on one or another element of the Montaignean vision will allow us to find our wholeness within it. When we see our lives confined to the plane of immanence, stretched out horizontally between the pole of solitude and the pole of society, we are tempted to seek contentment by gathering all of our energies at one or the other extreme. But we can never make ourselves whole by immersing ourselves in either of these alternatives, for something within us always remains drawn to the other pole. If immanence is our standard, dividedness is our fate.[4]

The political disorders of a society oriented toward immanent contentment are laid bare in Tocqueville's portrait of American democracy. When this idea of happiness becomes the tacit goal of a democratic majority, the restlessness that shadows the quest for it eventually comes to unsettle the nation's political arrangements. Although immanent contentment was first imagined as part of an effort to form a defensive barrier around private life and limit the reach of politics, it becomes an invasive principle that draws politics into its service, leaving nothing untouched in its efforts to transform the human and natural world so that we might finally feel at home. Immanence then shows itself to be as mad a master as transcendence had been.[5]

The Philosopher's Plank

The immanent frame is cracking, whether we like it or not. Even our prosaic policy debates are permeated by existential passion; we argue over health care and immigration as if salvation hung in the balance. At the same time, searching souls among the young recognize that their longings will not be satisfied by think-tank white papers and reach instead for a new tribe or an old god. For an older generation, accustomed to think within the confines of Lockean, Enlightenment rationalism or the "public reason" of John Rawls, this movement of the young is terrifying. For to minds so trained, what lies beyond the immanent frame looks like the grotesques at the edges of a medieval map.[6]

Navigating an age in which transcendent claims will again be openly contested requires that we reawaken reason's powers to help us negotiate among them. This must begin with a reconsideration of our assumption that only chaos lies beyond the confines of immanence. Montaigne makes the case for this assumption in the founding document of modern philosophic skepticism, his "Apology for Raymond Sebond." To convince us that reason is incompetent to deal with the questions of the gods, of human nature, and of the good, Montaigne forces us to confront the sheer proliferation of positions on these questions, piling up the most absurd arguments next to the most reasonable ones until our heads spin. "Now trust in your philosophy," he challenges the reader, and "boast that you have found the bean in the cake, when you consider the clatter of so many philosophical brains!"[7]

Montaigne's rhetorical strategy, as T. S. Eliot notes, is like a gas—it is an atmosphere we breathe in, rather than an argument we consider. It is a kind of intellectual fear-mongering, intended to induce a mental vertigo that Montaigne evokes in the image of a philosopher walking a plank between the towers of Notre Dame cathedral, terrified by the sight of his great and precarious distance from broad and solid ground. Though his reason may insist that his path is wide enough for his passage, its protests are powerless to overcome his fear. Montaigne wants us all to feel that if we step out beyond the immanent frame, our intellectual lives will be as unsupported as that of his quaking philosopher.[8]

Montaigne has a point—dealing with the question of our nature, our happiness, and the ultimate source of all things is indeed a perilous passage. But the risks of asking such questions are built into the finite character of human life. By the time we come to ask them, we find ourselves already in motion, with the past fixed behind us and no possibility of turning back. We see dangers to either side, in the form of the many ways in which we might waste our lives. And we have no choice but to step forward, with our eyes wide open, focused on the decisive task of making our way.[9]

With a small but critical shift in perspective, however, traversing the uncertain passage of a human life looks less like needless risk-taking than purposeful adventure. Pascal, who never supposed for a moment that he could be comfortably at home in this world, lives a life of such reflective daring. While few can hope to rival Pascal's astonishing genius, his incandescence is for all of us the flare that illuminates the far reaches of human possibility. Armed not only with doubt but also with reason, honesty, and relentless hope, Pascal burns away every petty attachment in his search for real knowledge, solid happiness, and genuine love. He shows us that the true adventure of the human soul begins not on study abroad but right here— alone in our rooms.[10]

The essential equipment for this adventure of solitude is the thought of other times. When Pascal embarks on the intellectual voyage that will issue in the *Pensées*, he brings the voices of the past along with him: prophets such as Daniel and Isaiah, philosophers such as Epictetus and Montaigne. Conversing with such thinkers compels us to go beyond the clichés of our day and to encounter the framework of abiding questions that structures human life. From that vantage point, we can hope not merely to reflect our moment but to shape it. Whether the work of our age consists in renewing our liberal order or finding a new foundation for our common life, only those with a foothold in the thought of the past will have the perspective necessary to guide it.[11]

The natural places for such vital encounters with the past are our universities—which should be islands of patience in a culture of haste. If they were true to this countercultural role, universities would cease to demand, as the price of admission and advancement, that young people keep themselves forever in motion. With a firmer grasp on their own purpose, they would cease to stamp the elites who emerge from them with the vices that come with not knowing how to sit still: distraction, anxiety, and the merely reactive pragmatism that consists of swaying with the rhythm of prevailing opinion. They would instead offer genuine liberal education, which is ultimately an education in the art of choosing.

Our privileged class is enslaved by an excess of options; although many of us have experienced the delight that arrives when our activities are unexpectedly canceled, we lack the courage to cancel them ourselves. A richer anthropology would teach us not only to appreciate the manifold goods of our existence but to rank them, distinguishing the optional accessories from the worthy crowns of a life. Learning to perceive the height of our existence as well as its breadth is what can transform our hectic dabbling into work with steady purpose. The art of choosing cannot bring our restless hearts to a standstill. But it may help us turn our pointless busyness into a pointed quest.

ACKNOWLEDGMENTS

"Don't publish a book before you're forty"—so said a senior professor at the University of Chicago's Committee on Social Thought, where we both were studying when we met. Without fully understanding the risk this advice entailed for aspiring academics, we followed it, and somehow survived. It is one of the many countercultural lessons we are grateful to have learned from that singular institution.

Because we have taken our time in writing this short book, our debts go back many years. We give thanks first to our teachers: Larry Goldberg, whose capacious love of the wisdom of old books, and genial affection for the liveliness of young minds, has been an enduring model to us; Leon R. Kass, who took us more seriously than we took ourselves and showed us that a life of upright dignity may partake of a higher playfulness; and the late Peter Augustine Lawler, who demonstrated that Pascalian Christianity can allow one to see the greatness and misery of human life with distinctive clarity.

At the University of North Carolina at Chapel Hill, Anne Hall taught young Ben a bit of much-needed sobriety on the cusp of adult life. At Boston University, Geoffrey Hill's patient, persistent green pen taught Jenna reverence for the written word, and Liah Greenfeld helped her to hear the foundational ideas of modern thought echoing in the mundane corners of contemporary life. At the University of Chicago, Nathan Tarcov humbled us with his unnerving questions while unfailingly supporting our fledgling academic careers, and the late Herman Sinaiko, who embodied the wide-ranging spirit of that university, showed us how plain observations of incontestable facts can provoke a sudden encounter with the strangeness of existence. Mark Lilla taught us both how to write, giving us advice we perpetually repeat to ourselves and others. The late Marc Fumaroli of the Academie Française generously introduced Ben first to the cornucopian *Essays* of Montaigne, and then to the still greater abundance of France. While we were in that wonderful country, Pierre Manent graciously hosted us both at his seminar table and demonstrated how one may write for the public without sacrificing depth, complexity, or honesty.

An "Enduring Questions" grant from the National Endowment for the Humanities supported the development of a course that laid the groundwork for this book. We have learned a great deal about the authors discussed here at colloquia sponsored by the Liberty Fund, and are grateful to Christine Dunn Henderson, who brought us to that table many times. At Furman University, we have enjoyed the generous support of our chairs and colleagues in the Department of Politics and International Affairs, particularly Ty Tessitore, Brent Nelsen, Jim Guth, Danielle Vinson, and Liz Smith, as well as our deans John Beckford, Ken Peterson, and Jeremy Cass. At Princeton University, Robby George and Brad Wilson at the James Madison Program sponsored us for a yearlong sabbatical, putting the splendid resources of that university at our fingertips, immersing us in a wonderful community of friends, and stalwartly supporting us in all our endeavors.

Many friends and colleagues from around the country have contributed to this project. Daniel DiSalvo at the City College of New York; Paul Kerry and Father Richard Finn at Oxford

University; Harvey Flaumenhaft, Karin Eckholm, Hannah Hintze, and Joe McFarland at St. John's College; Patrick Deneen, Carter Snead, Mary Keys, Catherine Zuckert, Phillip Munoz, and Sue Collins at the University of Notre Dame; Will Jordan and Charlotte Thomas at Mercer University; Jim Ceaser and Rita Koganzon at the University of Virginia; Robert Jackson at the Institute for Classical Education; Alex Duff, then of the College of the Holy Cross and now of the University of North Texas; and Hugh Liebert of the United States Military Academy at West Point have all sponsored lectures out of which this book grew, generously supporting our efforts with their time and their conversation. Others have offered their wise counsel, practical help, and philosophic insight at many points over the years: Bill McClay, Yuval Levin, Cheryl Miller, Adam Keiper, Dan Gerstle, Dan Mahoney, Diana Schaub, Ralph Hancock, Ann Hartle, Ryan Hanley, Jean Yarbrough, Christopher Nadon, John T. Scott, David Morse, Svetozar Minkov, Rana Liebert, Catherine Borck, Franck Dardenne, Arnaud Odier, Tom and Jacquie Merrill, David Oakley, David Fink, Jon McCord, Father Jay Scott Newman, and the late Jonathan B. Hand, who taught us that a good teacher is "part priest, part lawyer, and part comedian," and some of whose spirit we hope remains alive in these pages.

Conversations with students at Furman University and at the Hertog Program in Washington, DC, have shaped our writing, our thinking, and our lives. In particular, we would like to thank Will Walker, Martin Gramling, Barret Bowdre, Cary Fontana, Raul Rodriguez, Sarah Burnett, Orlin Sergev, Thomas Hydrick, Brian Boda, Andrew Smith, Alise Alexander, Amaya Gunasekera, Bethlehem Belachew, Sara DeSantis, Cecily Kritz, Julia Roberts, Nathan Thompson, Jonathan Kubakundimana, Emma Zyriek, Robin Cooper, Carol Lewis, J. P. Burleigh, Matthew Deininger,

Ben Wirzba, Mason Davis, Evan Myers, Kaiming Zhang, Naomi LaDine, Thomas Moore, Jonathan McKinney, Price St. Clair, Erica Daly, Abigail Smith, Luke Kelly, and Beckett Rueda. Adam Thomas, Josh King, Matthew Story, and Eli Simmons read the manuscript and gave us thoughtful criticism and advice; Cameron Lugo worked meticulously on the notes and bibliography.

We are grateful to Rob Tempio and Eric Crahan of Princeton University Press, who persistently believed in this project from its early days and had the patience to guide us as first-time authors. The Press's anonymous reviewers and first-rate editorial team gave us extensive, charitable, and valuable help in improving the manuscript.

Most importantly, to our families: our parents, Judy and Bill Storey, who created a world in which reading, thinking, and wit were treasured; and Lynn and Ted Silber, who imparted the courage and gentleness necessary for philosophic conversation. And to our own children, Elinor, Rosalind, and Charles, who patiently kept a household running while mom and dad sequestered themselves in the study, talking over an argument or searching for the right word. For fourteen years, they have brought laughter, wonder, and depth to our lives—reminding us that love, not accomplishment, is the proper purpose of living and that grace, not merit, is our ultimate source and end.

SUGGESTED READINGS

We have sought faithfully to capture the texture of the thought of the authors we consider here, but there is no substitute for a firsthand encounter with them. Here we suggest a brief selection of texts through which one might approach the thought of each.

Montaigne's *Essays* consist of chapters of varied lengths, some as short as a single page. An initial approach to the *Essays* might include book 1, chapters 1, 3, 8, 20, 28, 31, and 39; book 2, chapters 6, 16, and 17; and book 3, chapters 2, 10, and 13.

Pascal's *Pensées* consist of fragments varying from a single line to several pages; those fragments have been differently numbered and arranged by his many editors. Using the numbering of Philippe Sellier (which Roger Ariew uses in his excellent translation), a reader could begin with fragments S1–410, 452–60, 494, 669–71, 680–90, and 739–44.

Rousseau's *Discourse on the Origin and Foundations of Inequality among Men* is a brief but major statement of this thought.

A concise study of Tocqueville's two-volume *Democracy in America*, which is also composed of mostly short chapters, might include volume 1, introduction; part 1, chapters 2, 3, and 5; part 2, chapters 7, 9, and 10; volume 2, part 1, chapters 1–3, 5–11, 15–17, and 20; part 2, chapters 1–2, 8–13, 15, and 18–20; part 3, chapters 1 and 8–12; and part 4, chapters 6–8.

NOTES

Prologue

1. Pascal, *Pensées*, S114/L79. References to the *Pensées* give fragment numbers according to Philippe Sellier's numbering (S), as well as that of Louis Lafuma (L), following the practice of Roger Ariew's English translation (Indianapolis: Hackett, 2004). For the French text, we use that of the *Oeuvres complètes* of Henri Gouhier and Louis Lafuma (Paris: Editions du Seuil, 1963). Translations of French texts are from the English editions cited, or our own.

2. Daniel Markovits's *The Meritocracy Trap: How America's Foundational Myth Feeds Inequality, Dismantles the Middle Class, and Devours the Elite* (New York: Penguin, 2019) and William Deresiewicz's *Excellent Sheep: The Miseducation of the American Elite and the Way to a Meaningful Life* (New York: Free Press, 2014) are two of many recent books that have described the unhappiness, miseducation, and leadership failures of American elites. Other recent books, such as *Deaths of Despair and the Future of Capitalism*, by Anne Case and Angus Deaton (Princeton: Princeton University Press, 2020), and Robert Putnam's *Our Kids: The American Dream in Crisis* (New York: Simon and Schuster, 2016), have drawn attention to the growing gap between our elites and our lower class, sounding alarm bells about the dysfunction and despair of the latter. We seek here to examine the vision of happiness that motivates our elites, arguing that our upper class is flailing in ways that do not show up in statistics. That flailing does much to explain the leadership failures of that class and the way in which they perpetuate disorder in the lives of those they govern.

3. Plato, *Republic*, trans. G. M. A. Grube, from *Plato: The Complete Works*, ed. John M. Cooper (Indianapolis: Hackett, 1997), 544d. The restless malaise we describe here may be understood as an aspect of the broader problem of decadence Ross Douthat has recently examined, arguing, as we do, that "the decadent society is, by definition, a victim of its own success" (Douthat, *The Decadent Society: How We Became the Victims of Our Own Success* [New York: Avid Reader Press, 2020], 9).

4. Alexis de Tocqueville, *Democracy in America*, ed. Eduardo Nolla, trans. James T. Schleifer (Indianapolis: Liberty Fund, 2010), II.ii.13, 942–943. We will cite

this edition of Tocqueville, which includes both the French text and an English translation, throughout. Roger Boesche, in *The Strange Liberalism of Alexis de Tocqueville* (Ithaca: Cornell University Press, 1987), and Peter Augustine Lawler, in *The Restless Mind* (Lanham, MD: Rowman and Littlefield, 1993), have identified the centrality of restlessness to Tocqueville's thought, and this book is much indebted to those studies. Boesche situates Tocqueville's thought amid that of an entire "restless generation"; Lawler treats restlessness as the key to understanding Tocqueville's view of liberty. Our aim here is to show that this restlessness is intimately related to a particular ideal of happiness we will call *immanent contentment*, an ideal powerfully articulated by the French tradition of *moralistes* to which, we argue, Tocqueville must be understood to belong.

Introduction

1. Tocqueville, *Democracy in America*, II.i.2.712–17. In a recent defense of liberal democratic pluralism, William Galston notes that "although liberal democracy is the most capacious form of political organization, it is not equally hospitable to all ways of life" but "presupposes, and to some extent nurtures, a distinctive outlook and political psychology" (Galston, *Anti-Pluralism: The Populist Threat to Liberal Democracy* [New Haven: Yale University Press, 2018], 6, 128).

2. As Charles Taylor argues, investigating modern identity through characteristic thinkers need not imply any claim that these thinkers are the "unacknowledged legislators of mankind"; instead, it involves "giving an account of the new identity to make it clear what its appeal was," a question that "can be explored independently of the question of diachronic causation" (Taylor, *Sources of the Self* [Cambridge, MA: Harvard University Press, 1989], 203–7). On the significance of the French term *moraliste*, see Robert Pippin, *Nietzsche, Psychology, and First Philosophy* (Chicago: University of Chicago Press, 2010), 6–8, and *Le grand Robert de la langue française*, s.v. "moraliste" (Paris: Éditions le Robert, 2017), http://grand-robert.lerobert.com. Our inclusion of Tocqueville among the *moralistes* is somewhat novel but justified by Tocqueville's own self-understanding. In a letter to his friend Charles Stöffels, he testifies to his dedication to the self-study characteristic of the *moralistes* with a hyperbole that inscribes him in the tradition of Montaigne and Rousseau: "no matter what you do you will never penetrate the obscurity of the human heart, and you will never see its depths clearly enough to classify systematically what lurks within. . . . Perhaps no other human being has sought as tenaciously as I have to observe the workings of his own mind and follow all the movements of his own heart" (letter dated September 13, 1832, cited in Lucien Jaume, *The Aristocratic Sources of Liberty*, trans. Arthur Goldhammer [Princeton: Princeton University Press, 2013], 183–84). Parallel claims for unrivaled dedication to self-study can be found in Montaigne,

Essais, III.2.805–6 [741], and Rousseau, *Confessions*, preface, 3 [1]. References to Montaigne's *Essais* give book, chapter, and page numbers for Pierre Villey's French edition (Paris: Presses Universitaires de France, 1924), followed, in brackets, by page numbers for the translation of Donald M. Frame in his *Complete Works of Michel de Montaigne* (New York: Everyman's Library, 2003). References to Rousseau give the volume and page number of the Pléiade edition of the *Oeuvres complètes* [*OC*], ed. Bernard Gagnebin and Marcel Raymond (Paris: Gallimard, 1959), followed, in brackets, by a page number for the relevant English translation. In the case of the *Confessions*, we will cite the translation of Christopher Kelly (Hanover, NH: Dartmouth College, 1995). See also Arthur Goldhammer, "Tocqueville's Literary Style," in Alexis de Tocqueville, *Recollections: The French Revolution of 1848 and Its Aftermath*, ed. Olivier Zunz, trans. Arthur Goldhammer (Charlottesville: University of Virginia Press, 2016), xxix–xxxvi. The relation between the authors we consider here, and in particular the influence of the earlier authors in this tradition on their successors, has been widely discussed. See Charles-Augustin Sainte-Beuve, *Port-Royal* (Paris: La Conaissance, 1926), 3:5–13; Leon Brunschvicg, *Descartes et Pascal: Lecteurs de Montaigne* (New York: Brentano's, 1944), 157–217; Marc Fumaroli, preface to Pascal's *L'art de persuader, précédé de l'art de conférer de Montaigne* (Paris: Rivages poche, 2001), 29–48; Thomas M. Hibbs, *Wagering on an Ironic God* (Waco, TX: Baylor University Press, 2017), chaps. 2 and 4; Graeme Hunter, *Pascal the Philosopher: An Introduction* (Toronto: University of Toronto Press, 2013), 11–21; Isabelle Olivo-Poindron, "Du moi humain au moi commun; Rousseau lecteur de Pascal," *Les études philosophiques* 95, no. 4 (January 2010): 557–95; Daniel Cullen, "Montaigne and Rousseau: Ou, les solitaires," in *No Monster of Miracle Greater than Myself: The Political Philosophy of Michel de Montaigne*, ed. Charlotte C. S. Thomas (Macon, GA: Mercer University Press, 2014), 161–85; Mark Hulliung, "Rousseau, Voltaire, and the Revenge of Pascal," in *The Cambridge Companion to Rousseau*, ed. Patrick Riley (Cambridge: Cambridge University Press, 2001), 59–75; Hugh Brogan, *Alexis de Tocqueville: A Life* (New Haven: Yale University Press, 2006), 69; Jaume, *Aristocratic Sources of Liberty*, 160–73; Lawler, *The Restless Mind*, 73–87; and Matthew Maguire, *The Conversion of the Imagination: From Pascal through Rousseau to Tocqueville* (Cambridge, MA: Harvard University Press, 2006). We aim to contribute to that literature by showing that these *moralistes* are engaged in a sustained argument about happiness, as well as about the restlessness that accompanies the typically modern pursuit of it.

3. The quotation is from Bernard Levin and is cited in Sarah Bakewell, *How to Live, or, A Life of Montaigne, in One Question and Twenty Attempts at an Answer* (New York: Other Press, 2010), 6. In *The Social Animal*, David Brooks cites the historian Johan Huizinga's description of the shock of recognition we may experience in encountering the writers of the past: "A feeling of immediate contact with the past is a sensation as deep as the purest enjoyment of art; it is an almost ecstatic sensation of

no longer being myself, of overflowing into the world around me, of touching the essence of things, of through history experiencing the truth" (Brooks, *The Social Animal: The Hidden Sources of Love, Character, and Achievement* [New York: Random House, 2011], 234).

Our focus on Montaigne and the French tradition that follows him is intended to draw attention to a particularly attractive picture of a distinctively modern view of happiness. As such, it is meant as a complement and alternative to portrayals of the modern quest for happiness that focus on English sources. Excellent studies have been done on the modern English manner of thinking about happiness as something that can be captured in reductive or even quantifiable terms. See, for example, Darrin McMahon's treatment of the "blessed isle" in *Happiness: A History* (New York: Atlantic Monthly Press, 2006), 175–96; David Wooton, *Power, Pleasure, and Profit: Insatiable Appetites from Machiavelli to Madison* (Cambridge, MA: Harvard University Press, 2018); Richard Kraut, "Two Conceptions of Happiness," *Philosophical Review* 88, no. 2 (April 1979): 167–97; and Martha Nussbaum, "Mill between Aristotle and Bentham," *Daedalus* 133, no. 2 (Spring 2004): 62. But the emphasis on English sources in scholarship on the modern conception of happiness can encourage the assumption, noted by Bernard Reginster to be widespread among contemporary philosophers, that the serious study of happiness belongs exclusively to the ancients (Reginster, "Happiness as a Faustian Bargain," *Daedalus* 133, no. 2 [Spring 2004]: 53). While the work of philosophers such as Alasdair MacIntyre and Julia Annas has resulted in a valuable resuscitation of premodern understandings of happiness, their work does not examine the characteristically modern way of pursuing happiness as a genuinely compelling alternative (MacIntyre, *Ethics in the Conflicts of Modernity: An Essay on Desire, Practical Reasoning, and Narrative* [Cambridge: Cambridge University Press, 2017], 197–98; Annas, *The Morality of Happiness* [Oxford: Oxford University Press, 1993], 4–5, 10–11, 16–17; Aristotle, *Nicomachean Ethics*, ed. Arthur Rackham [Cambridge, MA: Harvard University Press, 1934], 1098a16–20). On the difference between Western and Eastern conceptions of happiness, see Diana Lobel, *Philosophies of Happiness: A Comparative Introduction to the Flourishing Life* (New York: Columbia University Press, 2017). By focusing on Montaigne and his followers, we aim to elaborate and examine a non-reductive and thus distinctly compelling form of the modern, Western pursuit of happiness.

4. Montaigne, *Essais*, III.13.1105–15 [1034–44]. Our portrait of the modern ideal of happiness, which goes hand in hand with the development of the conception of the *self*, bears significant relation to Mark Edmundson's portrayal of the nature and aims of the modern self in *Self and Soul: A Defense of Ideals* (Cambridge, MA: Harvard University Press, 2015), especially 12–14 and 200–201. Whereas Edmundson contrasts what he sees as the sadly constrained aims of the modern self with the soaring ideals of the premodern soul, our work seeks to understand why the vision

of the quest for happiness associated with the modern self has seemed so compelling to so many. Our account of Montaigne's conception of human flourishing as a variegated psychic equilibrium follows Virginia Woolf, who remarks that Montaigne "achieved happiness" through a "miraculous adjustment of all [the] wayward parts that constitute a human soul" (Woolf, *The Common Reader* [New York: Harcourt Brace, 1932], 100). Our concentration on Montaigne's substantive conception of the good life contrasts with depictions of him that focus on his skeptical individualism. For this latter view, see the work of Sissela Bok, who follows Judith Shklar in appreciating Montaigne as a thinker who "could survey the luxuriating proliferation of quests for happiness and wisdom all around him with a generous tolerance for every form of diversity" (Bok, *Exploring Happiness: From Aristotle to Brain Science* [New Haven: Yale University Press, 2010], 29; Shklar, *Ordinary Vices* [Cambridge, MA: Harvard University Press, 1984], 36).

5. Montaigne, *Essais*, I.28.183–95 [164–76]. Alexander Nehamas gives an account of what we are calling the unmediated character of modern friendship in *On Friendship*, arguing that "Montaigne, in fact, was the first philosopher to realize a truth that is absolutely central to love and friendship: that any effort to explain why we love particular people by citing their virtues, their accomplishments, or anything else about them is bound to fail": friendship must be unmediated if it is to be truly friendship. Such friendship comes to constitute an integral part of each friend's being and is thus inseparable from their happiness (Nehamas, *On Friendship* [New York: Basic Books, 2016], 117–20; see also Aristotle, *Nicomachean Ethics*, 1155b17–20, and Jacques Derrida, *The Politics of Friendship*, trans. George Collins [New York: Verso, 2005]).

6. Taylor, *Sources of the Self*, 23, 177–84. In our focus on the determinedly thisworldly aims of the Montaignean ideal, we follow Taylor and McMahon, who see modern happiness as taking place within an "immanent frame" (Taylor, *A Secular Age* [Cambridge, MA: Harvard University Press, 2007], 539; McMahon, *Happiness: A History*, 11–13). Taylor and McMahon both argue that the modern "affirmation of ordinary life" derives from a secularization of the Protestant endeavor to estimate one's worth in God's eyes by taking stock of the fruitfulness of one's worldly endeavors. They thus understand Christian ideals to give the modern quest for happiness much of its force and argue that we must reconnect our contemporary search for happiness to its Christian roots to understand and grapple with our frustrations with that quest. For Taylor, acknowledging the theological "sources" of the modern self will make our contemporary quest for meaning more properly holistic and compelling; for McMahon, grasping the theological history of our ideal can allow those who no longer think that worldly happiness is indicative of God's grace to moderate their desires (Taylor, *Sources of the Self*, 13, 23; McMahon, *Happiness: A History*, 168–75, 265). In contrast to both, we present a picture of modern happiness that is self-consciously articulated as an alternative to a life lived in the light of the transcendent.

In seeing Montaigne's humanist conception of happiness as a carefully considered departure from the classical and Christian tradition, we follow Tzvetan Todorov and Pierre Manent (Todorov, *Imperfect Garden: The Legacy of Humanism*, trans. Carol Cosman [Princeton: Princeton University Press, 2002]; Manent, *Montaigne: La vie sans loi* [Paris: Flammarion, 2014]). Drawing on the language of Montaigne and Rousseau, Todorov argues that modern humanism develops a conception of happiness that is at once "imperfect" or "frail" and yet basically adequate to our needs— the conception of happiness we here call immanent contentment (Todorov, *Imperfect Garden*, 90, 236). Manent points out that Montaigne, unlike his fellow early moderns Machiavelli and Calvin, speaks to the large number of human beings "who do not care about either the salvation of their city or that of their soul"—the sizable niche audience of people interested in a form of happiness that is at once immanent and private (Manent, *Montaigne*, 19).

The literature on Montaigne's contributions to modernity is vast. His role in the development of modern moral and political philosophy—through the elaboration of values such as humanity, authenticity, egalitarianism, and moral individualism, and through the elevation of private life, as well as the establishment of the groundwork for later arguments for toleration—has been detailed by authors such as Manent and Shklar, as well as Stephen Toulmin (*Cosmopolis: The Hidden Agenda of Modernity* [Chicago: University of Chicago Press, 1990]), David Lewis Schaefer (*The Political Philosophy of Montaigne* [Ithaca: Cornell University Press, 1990]), David Quint (*Montaigne and the Quality of Mercy* [Princeton: Princeton University Press, 1998]), Alan Levine (*Sensual Philosophy* [Lanham, MD: Lexington Books, 2001]), Biancamaria Fontana (*Montaigne's Politics: Authority and Governance in the* Essais [Princeton: Princeton University Press, 2008]), and, most recently, Douglas I. Thompson (*Montaigne and the Tolerance of Politics* [Oxford: Oxford University Press, 2018]). His place in the history of modern philosophy has been described, in different ways, by Ann Hartle (*Montaigne and the Origins of Modern Philosophy* [Evanston, IL: Northwestern University Press, 2013]) and Richard Popkin (*History of Skepticism from Erasmus to Spinoza* [Berkeley: University of California Press, 1979]). Georges Gusdorf and Karl Joachim Weintraub have given accounts of Montaigne's place in the history of the modern self, particularly insofar as that history is related to the rise of the literary genre of autobiography. See Gusdorf, "Conditions and Limits of Autobiography," in *Autobiography: Essays Theoretical and Critical*, trans. and ed. James Olney (Princeton: Princeton University Press, 1980), and Weintraub, *The Value of the Individual: Self and Circumstance in Autobiography* (Chicago: University of Chicago Press, 1978). Here, we synthesize many of the valuable insights of these scholars under the rubric of happiness and then consider the history of this Montaignean conception of happiness in the later tradition of the *moralistes*.

7. George Huppert, *Les Bourgeois Gentilshommes* (Chicago: University of Chicago Press, 1977), 4–5; Nannerl Keohane, *Philosophy and the State in France: The Renaissance to the Enlightenment* (Princeton: Princeton University Press, 1980), 283–89.

8. Pascal, *Pensées*, S149/L117, S192/L160. Our reading of Pascal draws upon the work of Graeme Hunter, who makes a compelling case that Pascal understood philosophy to be his central concern and puts him in conversation with other philosophers, such as Montaigne, Epictetus, and Socrates, as we do here (Hunter, *Pascal the Philosopher*, 9–37, 216–22). We join Thomas Hibbs in reading the *Pensées* as an effort to raise the question of the good life and to speak to the "universal human desire for happiness" (*Wagering on an Ironic God*, 10), a claim that can be usefully contrasted to Leszek Kolakowski's description of what he calls "Pascal's sad religion" (Kolakowski, *God Owes Us Nothing: A Brief Remark on Pascal's Religion and on the Spirit of Jansenism* [Chicago: University of Chicago Press, 1995], 113). Peter Kreeft calls the *Pensées* the first book of Christian apologetics intended "to speak to modern pagans, not medieval Christians"; we here contend that the influence of Montaigne on both Pascal and his anticipated audience decisively shaped the distinctively modern character of his project (Kreeft, *Christianity for Modern Pagans* [San Francisco: Ignatius Press, 1993], 12). Michel Le Guern helps define the specifically modern element of Pascal's approach by noting that he seems to be the first author to have asked the essential modern question, "What is the self?" (Qu'est-ce que le *moi*?), at least in French, a development we believe can be partially accounted for by Montaigne's elevation of the self, or *moi*, to the status of a legitimate object of philosophic inquiry. See Le Guern, *Études sur la vie et les Pensées de Pascal* (Paris: Honoré Champion, 2015), 73. Similarly, John McDade argues that Pascal's theology, which he describes as woven in a "deliberately rough cloth," is particularly suited to an age dominated by "postmodern accounts of a fragmented self" (McDade, "The Contemporary Relevance of Pascal," *New Blackfriars* 91, no. 1032 [February 2010]: 185–96). We will treat Pascal as the first and perhaps still greatest critic of the modern self's pursuit of an immanent, Montaignean vision of happiness, as well as the first analyst of the specifically modern form of restlessness that afflicts those who orient their lives toward happiness so understood—a critique that resounds, in opposed ways, in the thought of Rousseau and Tocqueville.

9. Kolakowski, *God Owes Us Nothing*, 103; Sainte-Beuve, *Port-Royal*, 1:xiii.

10. Rousseau, *Émile* (*OC*, 4:249 [40]); bracketed references to this text refer to the English translation of Allan Bloom (New York: Basic Books, 1969). Pankaj Mishra, following Isaiah Berlin, critiques Rousseau's anti-bourgeois stance as the work of "the greatest 'militant lowbrow' in history." See Mishra, *Age of Anger: A History of the Present* (New York: Farrar, Straus, and Giroux, 2017), 21; Berlin, *Political Ideas in the Romantic Age: Their Rise and Influence on Modern Thought*, ed. Henry

Hardy, intro. Joshua L. Cherniss (Princeton: Princeton University Press, 2008), 107. While this characterization of Rousseau is surely plausible, we here aim to show that, for all of his oddities, Rousseau's experiment with the extreme possibilities of modern philosophic anthropology powerfully displays that anthropology's limits.

11. Rousseau, *Rêveries du promeneur solitaire* (*OC*, 1:1047 [69]); bracketed references to this text refer to the English translation of Charles Butterworth (Indianapolis: Hackett, 1992); Carol Blum, *Rousseau and the Republic of Virtue* (Ithaca: Cornell University Press, 1986), 31; Jean Starobinski, *Transparency and Obstruction*, trans. Arthur Goldhammer (Chicago: University of Chicago Press, 1988). John T. Scott and Robert Zaretsky note that Rousseau's influence was not merely a matter of shaping public opinion but of helping to "create" that force in the first place, by reaching an audience of unprecedented size with philosophic works presented in the form of novels such as *Julie* and *Émile* (Scott and Zaretsky, *The Philosophers' Quarrel: Rousseau, Hume, and the Limits of Human Understanding* [New Haven: Yale University Press, 2009], 181).

For other works that deal with the question of the relation between Rousseau's thought and that of Pascal and Montaigne, see note 6 in this chapter. David Gauthier (*Rousseau: The Sentiment of Existence* [Cambridge: Cambridge University Press, 2006]) and Pierre Burgelin (*La philosophie de l'existence de J.-J. Rousseau* [Paris: Presses Universitaires de France, 1952) identify what Rousseau calls the "sentiment of existence" as the center of his conception of happiness. As Jeffrey A. Smith argues, the sentiment of existence often seems to consist of "feelings of happiness connected to immediate physical experience"; like Montaignean immanent contentment, it depends upon an equilibrium between our capacities and our desires, whose standard is provided by "man's original nature" (Smith, "Natural Happiness, Sensation, and Infancy in Rousseau's *Emile*," *Polity* 35, no. 1 [Autumn 2002]: 98). Rousseau gives us several autobiographical pictures of happiness so understood: amid the circle of his simple round of activities at Les Charmettes in the *Confessions* and, most notably, on St. Peter's Island in the *Rêveries*. Both are pictures of what Ann Hartle calls "calm sensuality," but a calm sensuality that depends upon a radical break with prevailing social mores, and even physical isolation. See Hartle, *The Modern Self in Rousseau's Confessions: A Reply to St. Augustine* (South Bend, IN: University of Notre Dame Press, 1983), 59, as well as Christopher Kelly, *Rousseau's Exemplary Life: The Confessions as Political Philosophy* (Ithaca: Cornell University Press, 1987), 156. Drawing on Joseph H. Lane's "Reverie and the Return to Nature: Rousseau's Experience of Convergence," *Review of Politics* 68, no. 3 (Summer 2006): 474–99, as well as John T. Scott's "Rousseau's Quixotic Quest in the *Rêveries du promeneur solitaire*," in *The Nature of Rousseau's Rêveries: Physical, Human, Aesthetic*, ed. John C. O'Neal (Oxford: Voltaire Foundation, 2008), 139–52, we here present Rousseau's whole moral system as an attempt to vindicate Montaignean immanence and naturalism in the face of

Pascal's critique and argue that the tragic character of Rousseau's system raises important doubts about the ideal of immanent contentment as such.

12. J. S. Mill, "De Tocqueville on Democracy in America," in *Collected Works of J. S. Mill*, vol. 18, ed. J. M. Robson and Alexander Brady (Toronto: University of Toronto Press, 1977), 167. As Pascal Bruckner writes, "As soon as the goal of life is no longer to do one's duty but rather to enjoy oneself, the slightest discomfort strikes us as an affront . . . the persistence of suffering . . . [becomes] an absolute obscenity" (Bruckner, *Perpetual Euphoria: On the Duty to Be Happy*, trans. Steven Rendall [Princeton: Princeton University Press, 2010], 35; see also McMahon, *Happiness: A History*, xii).

13. *Democracy in America*, II.2.13.942–43; Mark Lilla, *The Shipwrecked Mind: On Political Reaction* (New York: New York Review of Books, 2016), xiv.

14. *Democracy in America*, introduction, 32. Patrick Deneen (*Why Liberalism Failed* [New Haven: Yale University Press, 2018]) and Mark Lilla (*The Stillborn God: Religion, Politics, and the Modern West* [New York: Knopf, 2007]) have drawn attention to the question of modern philosophic anthropology, and our work is indebted to both. Deneen and Lilla approach modern self-understanding from roughly opposite points of view, and the account of modern philosophic anthropology we offer here is meant to be more sympathetic than Deneen's and more critical than Lilla's. We aim to show why modern philosophic anthropology has proven such a compelling mode of self-understanding for so many, while also suggesting that our long experiment in living in the light of that anthropology has at this point revealed its serious limitations.

Chapter 1

1. Geralde Nakam, *Montaigne et son temps* (Paris: Gallimard, 1993), 213–15, 248–50.

2. *Essais*, III.12.1046 [974], II.12.527 [476]. As Philippe Desan points out, because he died without male issue, Montaigne was not only the first of his family to call himself by the name "Montaigne"—he was also the last. Desan, *Montaigne: A Political Biography* (Princeton: Princeton University Press, 2017), 253.

3. Lilla, *The Stillborn God*, 7; Levine, *Sensual Philosophy*, 195; Shklar, *Ordinary Vices*, 7–8.

4. *Essais*, I.3.15 [9–10]; Levine, *Sensual Philosophy*, 151.

5. Eugene F. Rice Jr. and Anthony Grafton, *The Foundation of Early Modern Europe, 1460–1559* (New York: W. W. Norton, 1994), 87–89; Sainte-Beuve, *Port-Royal*, 3:26. Elsewhere, Sainte-Beuve remarks that "it was scarcely thirty years ago that whenever the sixteenth century was mentioned it was spoken of as a barbarous epoch, Montaigne only excepted" (Sainte-Beuve, *Literary and Philosophical Essays:*

French, German and Italian, ed. Charles W. Eliot [New York: P. F. Collier and Sons, 1914], 108). Tzvetan Todorov distinguishes Montaignean humanism from the "proud humanism" of Alberti and Pico. Though it is surely true that Montaigne has a lower estimate of man than Pico, he nonetheless affirms the self-sufficiency of the human and natural dimension, independent of any action of grace. See Todorov, *Imperfect Garden,* 52–53.

6. Mark Edmundson ascribes to Shakespeare, whom he calls "the ultimate poet of worldliness," a similar role in the elevation of the self that we here ascribe to Montaigne (Edmundson, *Self and Soul,* 138–40). Jacob Burkhardt finds a similar attentiveness to the details of worldly life in earlier, Italian humanism (Burkhardt, *The Civilization of the Renaissance in Italy,* trans. S. G. C. Middlemore [Vienna: Phaidon Press, 1950], 171–83).

7. *Essais,* III.2.805 [740].

8. Gusdorf, "Conditions and Limits of Autobiography," 33; Taylor, *Sources of the Self,* 285–86. Nicholas Carr has a fascinating account of how the technological development of the book helped spread the experience of sustained, solitary reflection, mediated by a written text, that is so typified by Montaigne (Carr, *The Shallows: What the Internet Is Doing to Our Brains* [New York: W. W. Norton, 2010], 67–72).

9. Thompson, *Montaigne and the Tolerance of Politics,* 21; Desan, *Montaigne: A Political Biography,* xxi; Fumaroli, *La querelle des anciens et des modernes* (Paris: Gallimard, 2001), 9; Bakewell, *How to Live,* 215–20, 277, 327; Ralph Waldo Emerson, "Montaigne, or, The Skeptic," in *Complete Writings of Ralph Waldo Emerson* (New York: Wm. H. Wise & Co., 1929), 1:375; Woolf, *The Common Reader,* 87–100. The Melville quotation from *Billy Budd* is cited in Robert Eden, "The Introduction to Montaigne's Politics," *Perspectives on Political Science* 20, no. 4 (Fall 1991): 211. Keohane, too, notes that Montaigne's book "was read by almost all educated persons in the seventeenth and eighteenth centuries" (*Philosophy and the State in France,* 98).

10. Keohane, *Philosophy and the State in France,* 98–99; Huppert, *Les Bourgeois Gentilshommes,* 90, 4–5; Desan, *Montaigne: A Political Biography,* 615.

11. *Essais,* III.2.805 [740], III.9.994 [925]; Emerson, "Montaigne, or, The Skeptic," 375; Manent, *Montaigne,* 52; see also Thompson, *Montaigne and the Tolerance of Politics,* 3, and Pierre Hadot, *Philosophy as a Way of Life: Spiritual Exercises from Socrates to Foucault,* ed. Arnold I. Davidson (Malden, MA: Wiley-Blackwell, 1995).

12. *Essais,* III.10.1011 [940].

13. Augustine, *Confessions,* trans. R. S. Pine-Coffin (New York: Penguin, 1961), 21; Plato, *Symposium,* trans. Alexander Nehamas and Paul Woodruff (Indianapolis: Hackett, 1989), 207a.

14. *Essais,* II.11.435 [385], II.12.450–68 [401–18]; Shklar, *Ordinary Vices,* 13–14.

15. Rousseau, *Discourse on Inequality* (*OC,* 3:165–66 [92]), bracketed citations to the *Discourse on Inequality* refer to the English translation of John T. Scott in *The Major*

Political Writings of Jean-Jacques Rousseau (Chicago: University of Chicago Press, 2012); Leon Kass, *The Hungry Soul: Eating and the Perfection of Our Nature* (New York: Free Press, 1994), 120. As Fontana writes, Montaigne sees that, "in his struggle to elevate himself above his original near-animal condition, man could only magnify the most perverse features of his nature such as greed, deceit, cruelty, and ambition" (*Montaigne's Politics*, 150); see also Quint, *Montaigne and the Quality of Mercy*, 61–65.

16. *Essais*, II.12.460 [408], III.12.1049 [978]. M. A. Screech notes in Montaigne a suspicion of the "ecstatic" and "daemonic" in the thought of Plato and others that reflects the centrality he accords to the untrustworthy faculty of imagination (Screech, *Montaigne & Melancholy: The Wisdom of the* Essays [Selinsgrove, PA: Susquehanna University Press, 1983], 160).

17. Luke 10:42.

18. Plato, *Apology of Socrates*, trans. Thomas G. West and Grace Starry West (Ithaca: Cornell University Press, 1984), 38a; Plato, *Gorgias*, from *Plato Gorgias and Aristotle Rhetoric*, trans. Joe Sacks (Indianapolis: Hackett, 2009), 512e; *Essais*, I.37.229–32 [205–8]; Matthew 13:45–46.

19. *Essais*, III.2.805–9 [741–45], II.6.379 [332].

20. Manent, *Montaigne*, 18.

21. *Essais*, III.13.1108 [1036]; Job 5:7. As Shklar, Quint, and Bok all note, this affirmation of the goodness of life in its ordinariness is the converse of Montaigne's rejection of cruelty (Shklar, *Ordinary Vices*, 37; Quint, *Montaigne and the Quality of Mercy*, 57; Bok, *Exploring Happiness*, 29).

22. *Essais*, I.20.81 [67], I.23.116–17 [101–2], II.12.538, 544, 577 [488, 495, 529], I.50.303 [268].

23. *Essais*, II.16.622 [572], III.13.1072 [1000]. Karl Weintraub argues that this shift in our understanding of self-knowledge from a question about human nature in general to a focus on a particular individual makes the *Essays* a "pivotal document in the gradually growing consciousness of man's individuality" (*Value of the Individual*, 167).

24. *Essais*, "Au lecteur," 3 [2], II.6.378 [331]; Marc Fumaroli, *La diplomatie de l'esprit* (Paris: Hermann, 2001), 395; on Pascal's coinage of the term *le moi*, see note 30 in chapter 2. Charles Taylor describes this turn from the general to the particular as follows: "We seek self-knowledge, but this can no longer mean just impersonal lore about human nature as it could for Plato. Each of us has to discover his or her own form. We are not looking for the universal nature; we each look for our own being" (*Sources of the Self*, 181).

25. *Essais*, III.2.811 [746], III.13.1096, 1101 [1024, 1030], II.10.413 [364–65]. As Karl Weintraub puts it, in Montaigne, "thoughts were not thought for their independent beauty but were self-communings by which a self tested itself" (*Value of the Individual*, 180). Autobiographical writing such as Montaigne's, Gusdorf notes, is "a second reading of experience, truer than the first because it adds to experience itself

consciousness of it" and thereby does not merely record the self but helps constitute it ("Conditions and Limits of Autobiography," 38).

26. *Essais*, III.12.1009 [939], II.18.665 [612]; Weintraub captures this harmony of the given and the chosen as follows: "nature and artfulness blend in the grace with which a man masters the situations into which life throws him" (*Value of the Individual*, 194).

27. *Essais*, III.2.813 [748].

28. Lionel Trilling, *Sincerity and Authenticity* (Cambridge, MA: Harvard University Press, 1971), 4–5; *Essais*, III.2.805–6 [741], III.13.1097 [1026], III.1.792 [728], III.5.889 [824], III.12.1061–62 [990]. As Jacob Zeitlin remarks, Montaigne's implicit message is as follows: "Behold how sensibly and humanely I have borne myself amidst the troubles of our time! How steadfastly and courageously I have learned to face misfortune and death, with the artlessness of the peasants and the heroism of Socrates! So successful have I been in integrating my actions according to a principle that Nature has implanted within me that my honesty and goodwill shine forth in my countenance and even my enemies are ashamed to do me an injury." Montaigne does not put matters so boldly, but that is plainly his point. Zeitlin, *Essays of Montaigne* (New York: Knopf, 1934), 3:430.

29. *Essais*, I.26.172 [155], II.1.790 [726]. Thompson notes that Montaigne's *nonchalance* is related to the *sprezzatura* celebrated in Baldesar Castiglione's *Book of the Courtier* (Thompson, *Montaigne and the Tolerance of Politics*, 134).

30. *Essais*, I.20.89 [74]. Biancamaria Fontana emphasizes the degree to which this nonchalance is an accomplishment: "feelings of rage, disgust, indignation, [and] outrage" are "carefully mastered under the smooth surface of an easy, meandering prose" (*Montaigne's Politics*, 14), which explains how Montaigne combines his famous detachment with his tremendous intellectual energy. As Todorov puts it, accepting that "the garden remains forever imperfect" is "what allows us to live in truth" (*Imperfect Garden*, 236–37).

31. *Essais*, I.26.157 [140–41], II.12.450 [399]; Friedrich Nietzsche, *The Gay Science*, trans. Walter Kaufmann (New York: Random House, 2010), sections 277, 223.

32. *Essais*, I.20.94 [79].

33. *Essais*, I.26.152 [135]. As Todorov writes, "The activity of the mind itself must be freed from the grip of tradition in order to rely solely on its own forces. That is the reason why Montaigne prefers to educate 'understanding and conscience' rather than to 'fill our memory.' . . . a parrot can repeat what the Ancients have to say; human beings must judge and act on their own" (*Imperfect Garden*, 49–50).

34. *Essais*, I.37.229 [205], II.10.418–19 [370], II.32.725 [665]; Donald M. Frame, *Montaigne: A Biography* (San Francisco: North Point Press, 1984), 143.

35. *Essais*, I.1.8 [4], III.11.1029 [958]. Pierre Manent comments on the magnitude of this shift: "The morality of the moderns . . . for which [Montaigne] pleads and

preaches by example, moves the line of demarcation between ordinary evil and extraordinary evil, shifting ordinary evil, in sum, onto the side of good, or rather gathering both in the reassuring immensity of the 'human,' and throwing out the human extreme evil which becomes, properly, the inhuman" (*Montaigne*, 165).

36. *Essais*, III.2.807 [742].

37. *Essais*, II.17.646 [595], I.31.210 [189]; Shklar, *Ordinary Vices*, 1, 7. David Quint suggests that Montaigne is engaged in a "retreat from the cruelty of virtue" (*Montaigne and the Quality of Mercy*, 57), which might explain his decision not to deploy the term "virtue" with respect to his own best qualities.

38. *Essais*, III.2.807–9 [743–45]; Aristotle, *Nicomachean Ethics*, 1129b32–1130a4.

39. Manent, *Montaigne*, 215–16.

40. Woolf, *The Common Reader*, 100.

41. *Essais*, III.13.1107 [1036]; Rousseau, *Reveries of the Solitary Walker* (*OC*, 1:1047 [69]).

42. *Essais*, I.8.33 [25], I.39.241 [215]. Philippe Desan questions the veracity of Montaigne's account of the solitary and contemplative character of his retirement, pointing out that the period after his retirement from the Bordeaux Parlement was also a period of impressive political advance, including Montaigne's reception of the Order of St. Michel in 1571 and his being named Ordinary Gentleman of the King's Chamber in 1573—honors for which Montaigne seems to have striven (Desan, *Montaigne: A Political Biography*, 193–237). However, such advancements are not incompatible with periods of solitude and even depression, and it is that experience that Montaigne analyzes in this passage of the *Essays*.

43. *Essais*, I.39.241 [214–15].

44. Sarah Bakewell notes that Montaigne's coolness and silence on the subject of his own family is more intelligible when we remember that he wrote in the aftermath of the deaths of La Boétie, his father, and a brother; that his marriage was arranged; and that he and his wife, Françoise, had lost five children in infancy (Bakewell, *How to Live*, 162–63).

45. *Essais*, I.39.246 [220].

46. *Essais*, III.5.849–50 [783], III.13.1107 [1036]; William Hazlitt, "Bibliographical Notice of the Editions of Montaigne," in *The Works of Michel de Montaigne*, ed. William Hazlitt (London: Templeton, 1845), lxviii. Stephen Toulmin sees Montaigne's "relaxed attitude toward his sexual experience" as characteristic of sixteenth-century humanism and contrasts it with the concern with "respectability" and the separation of mind and body characteristic of Descartes and the seventeenth-century founders of modern science (Toulmin, *Cosmopolis*, 40–44). We think there is a greater continuity between Montaigne's relaxed attitude not only toward sex but toward the good itself and modern science and technology, and that the seventeenth-century reaction to it embodied by Pascal is driven by deeper concerns than respectability.

47. *Essais*, III.13.1107 [1036].

48. *Essais*, III.3 passim; Hartle, *Montaigne and the Origins of Modern Philosophy*, 38. As Fontana remarks, Montaigne "did not write in order to reach an audience so much as to create one, in the same way in which he had fashioned himself through his book" (*Montaigne's Politics*, 25).

49. John Locke, *Essay Concerning Human Understanding*, ed. Peter H. Nidditch (Oxford: Oxford University Press, 1975), 269. Commenting on Montaigne's political virtues, Douglas I. Thompson notes that Montaigne "offers a rich affirmation of pleasure and enjoyment" of engagement with diverse people; this delight in diversity as a positive good reflects Montaigne's variegated but distinct vision of the good life (Thompson, *Montaigne and the Tolerance of Politics*, 46).

50. *Essais*, I.28.184, 188 [165, 169]; Nehamas, *On Friendship*, 119.

51. *Essais*, I.28.183–95 [164–76]. Nakam describes the *Essays* as the "empty tomb" of La Boétie: Montaigne tells us that he originally intended to place *On Voluntary Servitude* at the center of book 1 but later withdrew it for political reasons, and simply left chapter 29 vacant (Nakam, *Montaigne et son temps*, 230).

52. Nehamas, *On Friendship*, 114–21; compare Plato, *Symposium*, 210a–212b. While Aristotle's view of friendship is more down-to-earth than Plato's, it retains the view that friendship is necessarily mediated by some third term, be it pleasure, utility, or virtue (Aristotle, *Nicomachean Ethics*, 1155b17–20).

53. Erich Auerbach, *Mimesis: The Representation of Reality in Western Literature* (Princeton: Princeton University Press, 1953), 38.

54. See, for example, Psalm 139.

55. *Essais*, I.23.119 [104], I.54.313 [275].

56. *Essais*, I.56.318 [278]; Hartle, *Montaigne and the Origins of Modern Philosophy*, 31; Desan, *Montaigne: A Political Biography*, 16, 603–9; *Journal de Voyage* (from the *Oeuvres complètes*), 1206–7, 1248.

57. Pascal, *Pensées*, S559 / L680; *Logique de Port-Royal*, cited in the Villey edition of the *Essais*, 06; *Essais*, III.2.816 [752], I.31.212 [192], II.12.521–22 [471], 532 [482], II.27.701 [643], I.56.318–20 [279–81]. Marie de Gournay defends the *Essays* from charges of heresy in her "Long Preface" of 1595 (Gournay, *Preface to the Essays of Michel de Montaigne by His Adoptive Daughter, Marie le Jars de Gournay*, trans. Richard Hillman and Colette Quesnel, from the edition prepared by François Rigolot, Medieval & Renaissance Text & Studies 193 (Tempe, AZ: Medieval & Renaissance Texts & Studies, 1998), 55–57. The *Essays* were included in the Index beginning in 1676; Bakewell attributes the impetus for placing them there to Antoine Arnauld and Pierre Nicole, two of Pascal's Jansenist collaborators (Bakewell, *How to Live*, 151–52). See also Schaefer, *Political Philosophy of Montaigne*, 269; Henri Busson, *Literature et théologie* (Paris: Presses Universitaires de France, 1962), 72–73.

58. Emerson, "Montaigne, or, The Skeptic," 377; *Essais*, II.12.445 [394], 527 [477].

59. Ann Hartle, *Michel de Montaigne: Accidental Philosopher* (Cambridge: Cambridge University Press, 2003), 4; *Essais*, III.10.1010 [939], II.12.553 [503], 575 [526], III.12.1059 [988], III.13.1073 [1001]; Michel Adam, *Études sur Pierre Charron* (Bordeaux: Presses Universitaires de Bordeaux, 1991), 21.

60. *Essais*, II.12.491 [440], III.2.812–13 [748–49]; Matthew 4:19; Mark Lilla, "The Hidden Lesson of Montaigne," *New York Review of Books*, March 24, 2011, https://www.nybooks.com/articles/2011/03/24/hidden-lesson-montaigne/; Friedrich Nietzsche, *Ecce Homo*, from *On the Genealogy of Morals and Ecce Homo*, trans. Walter Kaufmann (New York: Vintage, 1989), 215. As Weintraub writes, for Montaigne, the "rules of life should enable us to play the game of life; that is all we can and should expect of them. . . . the Church, the state, the customs of his land were a given order, which, like the order of nature, enabled the individual to exist" (*Value of the Individual*, 191).

61. Edmund Burke, *Reflections on the Revolution in France*, ed. J. G. A. Pocock (Indianapolis: Hackett, 1987), 76; Yuval Levin, *The Great Debate: Edmund Burke, Thomas Paine, and the Birth of Right and Left* (New York: Basic Books, 2014), 136–37; *Essais*, I.23.116–117 [101].

62. *Essais*, I.23.115 [100], III.13.1072 [1000], III.9.957 [888]. In "Our Feelings Reach Out beyond Us," Montaigne does refer to democracy as the "most natural and equitable" form of government but only in the course of stating that the superstition to which democratic peoples are prone almost leads him to "irreconcilable hatred" against it (*Essais*, I.3.20 [14]).

63. Niccolò Machiavelli, *The Prince*, trans. Harvey C. Mansfield (Chicago: University of Chicago Press, 1988), 98; Alexander Hamilton, James Madison, and John Jay, *The Federalist*, ed. Jacob E. Cooke (Hanover, NH: Wesleyan University Press, 1961), 3; *Essais*, III.9.956–59 [887–89].

64. Marc Fumaroli, "First Gentleman of Gascony: Montaigne's Liberal Antidotes to the Hubris of Democracy," *Times Literary Supplement*, October 15, 1999, 8. François Rigolot nicely contrasts the eloquence of Montaigne to the eloquence of his poetic contemporary Ronsard: whereas Ronsard used his poetic energies to cause his French readers to identify more closely with their king and to more fully commit themselves to his cause, Montaigne deploys his eloquence to detach his readers from politics for the sake of the social and interior life of the self. Rigolot, *Les métamorphoses de Montaigne* (Paris: Presses Universitaires de France, 1988), 57.

65. *Essais*, III.10.1012 [941], I.42.266 [236]. According to Desan, Montaigne's patron the Marquis de Trans saw in him "an ideal intermediary who was clearly a Catholic but also a man of dialogue," though Desan credits him with little success as a negotiator (*Montaigne: A Political Biography*, 232). Bakewell's account of Montaigne's political activity credits him with a more significant role as a go-between during the so-called War of the Three Henrys (*How to Live*, 258–73). As Fontana notes, "When

[Montaigne] died, those who had known him were unanimous in paying tribute to his ability to handle with confidence and experience 'les affaires du monde'" (*Montaigne's Politics*, 7). Douglas I. Thompson has recently offered a systematic account of Montaigne's virtues as a negotiator in his *Montaigne and the Tolerance of Politics*, particularly chapters 1 and 5.

66. Benjamin Constant, "The Liberty of the Ancients Compared with That of the Moderns," in *Political Writings*, trans. Biancamaria Fontana (Cambridge: Cambridge University Press, 1988), 308–28; Adam Gopnik, "Montaigne on Trial," *New Yorker*, January 16, 2017. Alan Levine nicely summarizes Montaigne's relationship to liberalism: "Montaigne's indifference to particular political institutions disqualifies him from being called a liberal, but his desire to promote all the freedom possible without jeopardizing the political stability that serves as its base clearly situates him as a protoliberal" (*Sensual Philosophy*, 168).

Chapter 2

1. Sainte-Beuve, *Port-Royal*, 3:29; T. S. Eliot writes, similarly, that Montaigne gives voice "to the skepticism of *every* human being" (Eliot, "The *Pensées* of Pascal," in *Selected Essays* [New York: Harcourt, Brace, & World, 1932], 363).

2. Keohane, *Philosophy and the State in France*, 283–89.

3. Henry A. Grubbs, *Damien Mitton (1618–1690): Bourgeois Honnête Homme* (Princeton: Princeton University Press, 1932), 57; Jean Mesnard, *Pascal* (Paris: Hatier, 1962), 51; Kolakowski, *God Owes Us Nothing*, 159.

4. Pascal, *Pensées*, S164/L131. On Pascal as physicist, see Daniel C. Fouke, "Pascal's Physics," in *The Cambridge Companion to Pascal*, ed. Nicholas Hammond (Cambridge: Cambridge University Press, 2003), 75–101; on the echoes of Hobbes in Pascal's analysis of politics, see Erich Auerbach, *Scenes from the Drama of European Literature: Six Essays* (New York: Meridian Books, 1959), 125–27.

5. François de Chateaubriand, *Génie du Christianisme* (Paris: Garnier-Flammarion, 1966), 1:425; Chateaubriand's reading of Pascal emphasizes the "*immensity*" of his thought.

6. Gilberte Périer, *Vie de monsieur Pascal*, in *Oeuvres complètes*, ed. Henri Gouhier and Louis Lafuma (Paris: Editions du Seuil, 1963), 18–19. Ben Rogers gives an excellent short overview of Pascal's life in "Pascal's Life and Times," in *The Cambridge Companion to Pascal*, ed. Nicholas Hammond (Cambridge: Cambridge University Press, 2003), 4–19; Marvin O'Connell's *Blaise Pascal: Reasons of the Heart* (Grand Rapids, MI: Eerdmans, 1997) and Mesnard's *Pascal* offer fuller treatments of his biography.

7. As Hans Jonas writes, "Among the features determining [the spiritual situation of modern man] is one which Pascal was the first to face in its frightening implications and to expound with the full force of his eloquence: man's loneliness in the

physical universe of modern cosmology" (Jonas, *The Gnostic Religion: The Message of the Alien God and the Beginnings of Christianity* [Boston: Beacon Hill Press, 2001], 322). Although Pascal's thought is frequently opposed to that of Descartes, Roger Ariew notes substantial overlap between their conceptions of science and causality, notable particularly in Pascal's "Discourse on the Machine" (Ariew, "Descartes and Pascal," *Perspectives on Science* 15, no. 4 [2007]: 397–409).

8. *Pensées*, S57/L23. The Jansenists were truly austere; Sainte-Beuve describes one of their so-called "solitaries," M. de Pontchateau, killing himself through an excess of fasting (*Port-Royal*, 1:xxiv–xxv). John McDade notes that the very term "Jansenist" was a name given to Jansenius's followers by their enemies; he calls them simply Augustinians. We retain the traditional denomination for ease of understanding, but McDade's point seems well-founded, particularly in the light of the case made by Kolakowski that in condemning the doctrine of the Jansenists, the Church condemned the doctrine of St. Augustine himself. See McDade, "The Contemporary Relevance of Pascal," and note 11 in this chapter.

9. Mesnard, *Pascal*, 27–28; O'Connell, *Blaise Pascal*, 53–65, 138–39; Jacques Attali, *Blaise Pascal, ou, Le génie français* (Paris: Fayard, 2000), 224.

10. Kolakowski, *God Owes Us Nothing*, 59.

11. Sainte-Beuve, *Port-Royal*, 3:43–44; Mesnard, *Pascal*, 74; Hunter, *Pascal the Philosopher*, 7. The five propositions are as follows:

> Some of God's commandments are impossible for just people—with the forces they actually have—who will and try [to fulfill them]; and they lack the grace whereby those commandments would become possible.
>
> In the state of fallen nature one never resists interior grace.
>
> In the state of fallen nature, in order to earn a merit or to lose it, freedom from necessity is not required in man; freedom from compulsion is enough.
>
> The semi-Pelagians admitted the necessity of prevenient internal grace for all particular acts including the beginning of faith; and they were heretics because they wanted this grace to be such that the human will could resist or obey it.
>
> It is semi-Pelagian to say that Christ died or shed his blood for all men in general.

We here use Kolakowski's translation of the five propositions in Innocent X's Bull of 1653, *Cum Occasione*, which condemns them as heretical. As Kolakowski points out, both sides of the controversy were, in a sense, right: the Jesuits were right that the five propositions are in Jansenius, which Pascal and the Jansenists denied; Pascal and the Jansenists were right that the five propositions are also to be found in St. Augustine. In siding with the Jesuits, "the Church was in effect condemning—without, of course, stating it explicitly—Augustine himself, its own greatest theological authority." Kolakowski sums up the stakes of the recondite controversy as follows: "Ultimately the whole problem boils down to the perplexing difficulty in reconciling two tenets of Christianity: God is omnipotent and it is impossible to imagine that His will might be foiled by men; men are responsible for their salvation or damnation" (*God Owes Us Nothing*, 5–24).

12. Charles M. Natoli, *Fire in the Dark: Essays on Pascal's Pensées and* Provinciales (Rochester: University of Rochester Press, 2005), 57.

13. Pascal, *Lettres Provinciales*, in *Oeuvres complètes*, 399, 408, 392–93, 388, 420; English translation by Thomas M'Crie (New York: Modern Library, 1941), 375, 434, 390, 410, 472 (references to this English translation appear hereafter in brackets). As Mesnard points out, Pascal relied heavily on Arnauld and Nicole for the research behind the *Provinciales* and submitted his drafts to them for judgment (Mesnard, *Pascal*, 74).

14. Richard Parish, "Pascal's *Lettres provinciales*: From Flippancy to Fundamentals," in *The Cambridge Companion to Pascal*, ed. Nicholas Hammond (Cambridge: Cambridge University Press, 2003), 182–83.

15. Attali, *Pascal*, 266–69.

16. Attali, *Pascal*, 259–61, 285; O'Connell, *Blaise Pascal*, 133–34.

17. *Provinciales*, 387 [374], 418 [463]; Kolakowski, *God Owes Us Nothing*, 58–59.

18. *Provinciales*, 423 [480–81].

19. Harold Nicholson, *Sainte-Beuve* (Garden City, NY: Doubleday, 1956), 140–45.

20. Jacques Chevalier, *Pascal*, cited in Attali, *Pascal*, 298; on Voltaire's role in shaping the reception of Pascal, see Attali, *Pascal*, 433–35, and Sainte-Beuve, *Port-Royal*, 3:394–413.

21. Kreeft, *Christianity for Modern Pagans*.

22. Étienne Périer, "Preface [de l'édition de Port-Royal]," in Blaise Pascal, *Pensées*, ed. Michel Le Guern (Paris: Gallimard, 2004), 41–43; Mesnard, *Pascal*, 127.

23. Périer, "Preface," 44; *Pensées*, S163/L130. That Pascal had such rhetorical aims in mind as he worked on his *Apology* is well attested. Pierre Nicole writes that "the late M. Pascal knew as much true rhetoric as any man ever." As his sister Gilberte puts it, Pascal "conceived of eloquence as a means for saying things in a manner that all those to whom one spoke could understand them without pain and with pleasure," an art that consists in knowledge of "certain relations which must be found between the heart and the mind of those to whom one speaks, and the thoughts and expressions which one uses." Pascal knew that his audience prided itself on the *esprit de finesse*. Indeed, he had been forced to endure the contempt of Mitton and Méré on this subject during a famous country excursion in the carriage of Pascal's friend Arthus de Roannez, during which, on Méré's telling, the three savvy men of the

world introduced the young, awkward, mathematically inclined Pascal to the truths of human life. It seems possible that Mitton and Méré first inspired Pascal's direct engagement with Montaigne. Périer, *Vie de Monsieur Pascal*, 23; Pierre Viguié, *L'honnête homme au XVIIe siècle: Le Chevalier de Méré (1607–1684)* (Paris: Editions Sansot, 1922), 46; Fumaroli, "Preface," 31–36.

24. Montaigne, *Essais*, III.4.830–31 [764–65]; Pascal, *Pensées*, S33/L414.

25. *Pensées*, S168/L136.

26. *Pensées*, S168/L136. Pierre Nicole describes Pascal's engagement with this young prince, Charles-Honoré de Chevreuse, who would later become governor of Guyenne, in his introduction to a text of his redaction that records lectures Pascal gave to that prince, titled *Trois discours sur la condition des grands* (Pascal, *Oeuvres*, ed. Gérard Ferreyrolles and Philippe Sellier [Paris: Classiques Garnier, 2004], 746–47). Nicole claims that Pascal thought nothing more important than this project and would have "willingly sacrificed his life" to it. In his *discours*, Pascal advises his pupil not to "dominate [his subjects] by force, or treat them with harshness," but to "satisfy their just desires, solace them in their necessities," and "find [his] pleasure in being beneficent." Doing so much, however, will not ensure one's salvation but only allow one to "damn oneself as an honest man." Nicole reports that all were surprised to find that there was no written text of Pascal's remarks found among his papers upon his death; he reconstructed the discourses from memory, perhaps consulting some of the *Pensées* as he worked.

27. *Pensées*, S168/L136, S20/L401; Montaigne, *Essais*, I.20.81 [67], III.13.1073 [1001].

28. *Pensées*, S242/L210, S646/L792.

29. *Pensées*, S743/L978.

30. *Pensées*, S567/L688; Le Guern, *Études*, 73.

31. Montaigne, *Essais*, I.28.188–89 [169].

32. *Pensées*, S15/L396.

33. *Pensées*, S494/L597.

34. Keohane, *Philosophy and the State in France*, 99.

35. *Pensées*, S94/L60; A. J. Beitzinger, "Pascal on Justice, Force, and Law," *Review of Politics* 46, no. 2 (April 1984): 212–13; Montaigne, *Essais*, II.12.439 [388].

36. *Pensées*, S135/L103; Kreeft, *Christianity for Modern Pagans*, 92. Auerbach, *Scenes from the Drama of European Literature*, 103–28, contains a riveting analysis of this line of argument but one that radicalizes Pascal's view so far as to say that, for Pascal, might is "pure evil, which one must obey unquestioningly" (129). Such a view, however, can hardly make sense of the life and thought of a man who was unmistakably willing to confront unjust power when he thought it necessary, as Pascal did at significant personal risk with *The Provincial Letters*.

37. *Pensées*, S457/L533.

38. *Pensées*, S454/L525.

39. *Pensées*, S94/L60; see also Augustine, *City of God*, trans. R. W. Dyson (Cambridge: Cambridge University Press, 1998), IV.27.176. Pierre Manent critiques Leo Strauss on this point: "I have never been able to understand the figure Strauss sketches of a philosopher who would fulfill his being by completely abandoning all interest in human things, who would leave all human interests behind. I find more humanity in religion, in the religious person, than in the philosopher as I conceive him, or rather as I cannot manage to conceive him, a philosopher above all human things, for whom justice becomes a secondary consideration and for whom human bonds are of no real interest" (Manent, *Seeing Things Politically: Interviews with Benedict Delorme-Montini*, trans. Ralph C. Hancock [South Bend, IN: St. Augustine's Press, 2015], 48–49).

40. *Essais*, I.54.312–313 [275–76]; *Pensées*, S94/L60; Manent, *Montaigne*, 284.

41. *Essais*, II.17.645 [594].

42. As Chateaubriand points out, modern thought has tended to emphasize only the low side of Pascal's human paradox: "The insults we have prodigally bestowed on human nature by philosophy have been more or less taken from Pascal. But, in stealing from this rare genius the *misery* of man, we have not known how to perceive, like him, man's *greatness*" (*Génie du Christianisme*, vol. 1, 428).

43. *Pensées*, S146–49/L114–17; Friedrich Nietzsche, *Thus Spoke Zarathustra*, trans. Walter Kaufmann (New York: Penguin, 1978), 88.

44. *Pensées*, S147/L115, S150/L118.

45. *Pensées*, S145/L113, S231/L200.

46. *Pensées*, S230/L199, S339/L308; see also C. S. Lewis, *Miracles: A Preliminary Study* (New York: Collier, 1947), 12–24.

47. *Pensées*, S145/L113, S230/L199.

48. *Pensées*, S164/L131.

49. *Pensées*, S192/L160.

50. *Pensées*, S1, S172–79/L140–46.

51. Sainte-Beuve, *Port-Royal*, 3:5; O'Connell, *Blaise Pascal*, 106–18.

52. Fontaine's redaction of the *Entretien avec M. de Saci* is considered by scholars to be sufficiently faithful to the Pascal we know from works written in his own hand—particularly *Pensées* S164/L131 and S172–79/L140–46—to be customarily included among Pascal's works. We cite the text here from the *Oeuvres complètes*, 291–97.

53. *Entretien avec M. de Saci*, 292.

54. *Entretien avec M. de Saci*, 296; Hunter, *Pascal the Philosopher*, 13.

55. *Entretien avec M. de Saci*, 292–293.

56. *Entretien avec M. de Saci*, 294–296.

57. *Entretien avec M. de Saci*, 296; *Pensées*, S164/L131. As the evocation of the evil demon suggests, Pascal may have had his contemporary rival Descartes as much in mind in the conversation with Saci as Montaigne and Epictetus. See Hunter, *Pascal the Philosopher*, 16–19. See also Hans Jonas's account of the genealogy of gnosticism, which finds in Stoicism an unstable midpoint between the sense of meaningful participation in a "divinely ordered whole" he associates with the classical *polis* and the radical sense of alienation that characterized the gnostic movement, of which Jonas sees echoes in Pascal. Jonas, *The Gnostic Religion*, 248–49, 330.

58. *Entretien avec M. de Saci*, 296; Hibbs, *Wagering on an Ironic God*, 172.

59. As Hunter indicates, for Pascal, transcending rationalism does not mean leaving reason behind. His apologetics seeks "to win non-Christians over to Christianity by making them think it offers the most reasonable and the most attractive explanation of their lives" (*Pascal the Philosopher*, 25–26).

60. Périer, "Préface," 44–45; *Pensées*, S235–53/L203–20.

61. *Pensées*, S252/L219, S86/L53, S375/L343; G. K. Chesterton, *The Everlasting Man* (Nashville: Sam Torode Book Arts, 2014), 126.

62. *Pensées*, S241–42/L209.

63. *Pensées*, S694/L454, S692/L452, S276/L244, S493/L593.

64. *Pensées*, S693/L453.

65. *Pensées*, S738/L502, S288/L256.

66. *Comparaison des Chrétiens des premiers temps avec ceux d'aujourd'hui*, from *Oeuvres complètes*, 360–62; *Pensées*, S680/L418; O'Connell, *Blaise Pascal*, 88–89.

67. *Pensées*, S186/L153, S39/L5; Tocqueville, *Democracy in America*, II.ii.9.928 note d; Tocqueville here refers to fragment S6/L387, often taken to summarize "The Wager." For a helpful discussion of the scholarly objections to the "The Wager" and some insightful responses to those objections, see Hunter, *Pascal the Philosopher*, 104–8, 125–29.

68. *Pensées*, S680/L418. The sentence Ariew translates as "this will make you believe naturally and mechanically" is "Naturellement même cela vous fera croire et vous abêtira"; the final word is derived from *bête*, beast. With a little license, one might render it "by the way of nature itself this will make you believe and reduce your disquiet reason to a bestial but fitting silence." Daniel Garber presents three objections to this aspect of the Pascalian approach: (1) that it is a form of self-deception; (2) that it is "non-cognitive," working on the passions rather than reason to persuade; and (3) that it could work just as well for a number of different beliefs (Garber, *What Happens after Pascal's Wager: Living Faith and Rational Belief* [Milwaukee: Marquette University Press, 2009], 32–33). Pascal's answers to the first and second objections appear in the next several paragraphs of our main text. The third is correct insofar as "The Wager" does not make the case for the specifically Christian vision of God, except insofar as the Christian promise of eternal life is in itself distinctive; for that

case, one must look to Pascal's larger account of the nature of man, the character of the Christian revelation, and the correspondence between the two.

69. *Pensées*, S680/L418; Hibbs, *Wagering on an Ironic God*, 146–48, 157–58. For a secular analogue to this Christian process of moral transformation, see Mark Van Doren, *Don Quixote's Profession* (New York: Columbia University Press, 1958), in which Van Doren argues that Don Quixote is an actor, who succeeds to a surprising degree in bringing about new realities by acting as if they already existed. Although much of the world violently refuses to play along with the Don's imagination, those who do, such as Sancho Panza, actually get a better life out of the bargain. As Lilla comments, "The Knight of the sorrowful face is absurd but noble, a suffering saint stranded in the present who leaves those he meets improved, if slightly bruised" (*The Shipwrecked Mind*, 144).

70. *Pensées*, S201/L170.

71. *Pensées*, S46/L12, S680/L418.

72. *Pensées*, S275/L242, S682/L429, S734/L487; letter to the Roannez, October 1656, in *Oeuvres complètes*, 267; Jonas, *The Gnostic Religion*, 327. McDade describes these four stages through which God becomes both more revealed and more hidden at once in "The Contemporary Relevance of Pascal," 192. Pascal's conception of God as hidden inscribes him in what Cornel West calls "a particular tradition of faith" that understands that "doubt is inscribed within that faith" (West, "The Indispensability yet Insufficiency of Marxist Theory," in *The Cornel West Reader* [New York: Basic Books, 1999], 215–16).

73. *Pensées*, S182/L149; Hibbs, *Wagering on an Ironic God*, 151; Hunter, *Pascal the Philosopher*, 25–27.

74. Hibbs, *Wagering on an Ironic God*, 151; *Pensées*, S742/L913; Abraham Joshua Heschel, *God's Search for Man* (New York: Farrar, Straus, and Giroux, 1955), 136.

75. *Pensées*, S36/L417; *Entretien avec M. de Saci*, 296; Thomas More, *The Sadness of Christ*, trans. Clarence Miller (New York: Scepter, 1993), 13–16, 75; Louis W. Karlin and David R. Oakley, *Inside the Mind of Thomas More: The Witness of His Writings* (New York: Scepter, 2018), 96; Kreeft, *Christianity for Modern Pagans*, 47.

76. Montaigne, *Essais*, III.13.1107 [1035]; Levine, *Sensual Philosophy*, 160; *Pensées*, S252/L219.

77. *Pensées*, S680/L423, S142/L110; Mesnard defines the heart as a "sort of instinct for truth" (*Pascal*, 141), perhaps parallel to Aristotle's *nous* (*Nicomachean Ethics*, 1139b15ff.).

78. *Pensées*, S329/L298.

79. *Pensées*, S339/L308, S142/L110, S124/L90.

80. *Pensées*, S405/L373, S408/L376, S392/L360.

81. *Pensées*, S742/L913, S471/L564.

82. *Pensées*, S55/L21, S457/L534; Hibbs, *Wagering on an Ironic God*, 33.

83. *Pensées*, S389/L357.

84. Montaigne, *Essais*, III.4.834 [767]; *Pensées*, S680/L418; Hibbs, *Wagering on an Ironic God*, 171.

85. Périer, *La vie de monsieur Pascal*, 30.

86. *Pensées*, S759/L931.

87. O'Connell, *Blaise Pascal*, 174–75. In spite of the Jansenist position in the quarrel over the five propositions (see note 11 in this chapter), McDade notes that Pascal advises all of us to believe that we are of the elect, and to believe the same of everyone on earth, for the mystery of salvation shrouds the secret of election from us, and we live best by hoping for it for ourselves and wishing for it for others (McDade, "The Contemporary Relevance of Pascal," 192).

88. *Pensées*, S742/L913; Tocqueville, *Democracy in America*, II.1.10.782, II.1.17.840; Lawler, *The Restless Mind*, 69.

89. Kolakowski, *God Owes Us Nothing*, 197; Kreeft, *Christianity for Modern Pagans*, 47; McMahon, *Happiness: A History*, 11.

90. Sainte-Beuve, *Port-Royal*, 3:xiii. On the reception of Montaigne among the *philosophes*, see Dudley M. Marchi, *Montaigne among the Moderns: Reception of the Essais* (Providence, RI: Berghahn Books, 1994), and Eliane Martin Haag, "Diderot et Voltaire lecteurs de Montaigne: Du jugement suspendu à la raison libre," *Revue de métaphysique et de morale*, no. 3 (1997): 365–83.

Chapter 3

1. Even within the world of Catholic thought to which Pascal understands himself to belong, many in the Thomistic tradition would hold that Pascal's account of the fall is far too severe, and the Church itself put his works on the Index of Forbidden Books. See Kolakowski, *God Owes Us Nothing*, 154.

2. Voltaire, *Lettres philosophiques*, vingt-cinquième lettre, "sur les *Pensées* de M. Pascal," and *Le Mondain*, both from *Mélanges*, ed. Jacques Van Den Heuvel (Paris: Gallimard, 1961), 104–34, 207–10; Hulliung, "Rousseau, Voltaire, and the Revenge of Pascal," 57.

3. Specifically, in an anonymous pamphlet published in Geneva under the title *Sentiments des citoyens*, Voltaire helps publicize both Rousseau's religious unorthodoxy and the fate of his five children, whom Rousseau and his companion (and eventual wife) Thérèse Levasseur abandoned at the gate of a foundling home. He also makes a groundless accusation that Rousseau murdered his mother-in-law, who was alive and well at the time. Voltaire's accusations precipitate the stoning of Rousseau's house in Môtiers, not far from Geneva. For his part, Rousseau writes

bluntly to Voltaire, "I hate you." See Scott and Zaretsky, *The Philosophers' Quarrel*, 57, 67–70, 91.

4. *Confessions*, 214 [179] and Book VII, "Neufchatel Preface to the *Confessions* of J.-J. Rousseau," 1150–51 [586–87].

5. *Confessions*, 351 [294]; Charles L. Griswold, "Genealogical Narrative and Self-Knowledge in Rousseau's *Discourse on the Origin and the Foundations of Inequality among Men*," *History of European Ideas* 42, no. 2 (2016): 292; Arthur Melzer, "Rousseau and the Modern Cult of Sincerity," in *The Legacy of Rousseau*, ed. Clifford Orwin and Nathan Tarcov (Chicago: University of Chicago Press, 1996), 282.

6. *Confessions*, 351 [294], 361–64 [303–4], 389–90 [327], 401 [337]. Rousseau will reluctantly return to Paris in 1772, but never renounces his preference for living elsewhere, and seeks to simulate a country life even in the heart of the capital: *Reveries of the Solitary Walker*, 1003 [13].

7. *Confessions*, 401 [337], 362 [304]; Kelly, *Rousseau's Exemplary Life*, 195. Ourida Mostefai notes that "the posture of the author"—his refusal of a royal pension, his decision to earn his bread as a music copyist, his insistence on signing his works, his modes of dress—was as central to the controversy over Rousseau in his own time as the content of his works (Mostefai, "Un auteur paradoxal: Singularité et exemplarité de la carrière de Rousseau," *Romantic Review* 103, nos. 3–4 [2013]: 427–37). Pankaj Mishra notes the centrality of Paris as a symbol of Rousseau's quarrel with the Enlightenment's *philosophes*, one that resonates still in the populist revolts against cosmopolitanism of our time. See Mishra, *Age of Anger*, 90–93.

8. Laurence D. Cooper, "Nearer My True Self to Thee: Rousseau's New Spirituality—and Ours," *Review of Politics* 74, no. 3 (2012): 465–88.

9. On Rousseau's interest in experiments, see *Discourse on Inequality*, 123–24 [52–53]; in his *Reveries of the Solitary Walker*, he describes his autobiographical activity as "apply[ing] the barometer to [his] soul" (1000–1001 [7]).

10. J. L. Talmon, *The Origins of Totalitarian Democracy* (New York: Praeger, 1960), 43; François Furet, "Rousseau and the French Revolution," in *The Legacy of Rousseau*, ed. Clifford Orwin and Nathan Tarcov (Chicago: University of Chicago Press, 1997), 179. As Leo Strauss remarks, "The question is . . . not how [Rousseau] solved the conflict between the individual and society but how he conceived of that indissoluble conflict" (Strauss, *Natural Right and History* [Chicago: University of Chicago Press, 1950], 255).

11. Although the political philosophy of Rousseau is often contrasted to those of thinkers such as John Locke and Thomas Hobbes, who more obviously shape our American political order and culture, Rousseau claims that he merely extends the principles of those thinkers to their logical conclusions. At the outset of the *Discourse on Inequality*, he remarks that "the philosophers who have examined the foundations of society, have all felt the necessity of going back to the state of Nature, but none of them has reached it"; to reach the "pure" state of nature is of course the project of

that book (*Discourse on Inequality*, 132 [62]). The radicalism of Rousseau's thought has been extensively discussed (see, for example, Furet, "Rousseau and the French Revolution," 179; Blum, *Rousseau and the Republic of Virtue*, 13–19; Judith Shklar, *Men and Citizens: A Study of Rousseau's Social Theory* [Cambridge: Cambridge University Press, 1985], 13; and Jonathan Marks, *Perfection and Disharmony in the Thought of Jean-Jacques Rousseau* [Cambridge: Cambridge University Press, 2005], 11). Here, we add to that discussion by noting that the radicalism of Rousseau's thought can be understood to result from his attempt to revindicate the principles of Montaignean immanent naturalism in response to Pascal's Augustinian critique.

12. *Émile*, 322 [92]; *Discourse on Inequality*, 202 [127].

13. Gauthier, *Rousseau*, chap. 1; Griswold, "Genealogical Narrative and Self-Knowledge," 278; Christopher Kelly, *Rousseau as Author: Consecrating One's Life to Truth* (Chicago: University of Chicago Press, 2003), 2. In a letter to Christophe de Beaumont, the archbishop of Paris responsible for the condemnation of *Émile* and *The Social Contract*, Rousseau makes clear that he intended to explain what the Bible and the Church merely invoked as a mystery (939 [173]).

14. *Discourse on Inequality*, 143–44 [73–74]. In his *Perfection and Disharmony in the Thought of Jean-Jacques Rousseau*, Jonathan Marks argues that history would never begin were Rousseau's solitary as content as Rousseau makes him out to be (5–7). But that view seems to us compatible with Rousseau's stated expectation that his reader will take the contentment of natural man as a standard (*Discourse on Inequality*, 135 [63]).

15. *Discourse on Inequality*, 134–42 [65–73].

16. *Discourse on Inequality*, 167–68, 146–51 [94, 75–80].

17. *Discourse on Inequality*, 165–66, 170 [92, 96]. Ryan Patrick Hanley, "Rousseau's Virtue Epistemology," *Journal of the History of Philosophy* 50, no. 2 (April 2012): 239–63, emphasizes the importance of the comparative faculty as a driver of human development.

18. *Discourse on Inequality*, 171–77 [97–103].

19. *Discourse on Inequality*, 171, 174–75, 219 [97, 100–101, 147]. As Bruckner puts it, "pleasure is no longer a promise but a problem" (*Perpetual Euphoria*, 49).

20. *Émile*, 245 [37].

21. *Discourse on Inequality*, 193 [116–17].

22. *Discourse on Inequality*, 138, 162–63 [69, 89–90].

23. See Arthur Melzer, *The Natural Goodness of Man* (Chicago: University of Chicago Press, 1990), 91. Melzer identifies two possible ways forward in Rousseau's thought, one solitary, the other social; we here distinguish four such ways on a continuum from social to solitary, and further such subdivisions are probably possible. See also Benjamin Storey, "Rousseau and the Problem of Self-Knowledge," *Review of Politics* 71, no. 2 (Spring 2009), 251–274.

24. *Rousseau, Judge of Jean-Jacques*, 935 [213]; bracketed citations of this text refer to the English translation of Judith R. Bush, Christopher Kelly, and Roger D. Masters (Hanover, NH: University Press of New England, 1990). *Discourse on Inequality*, 207 [133]; *Émile*, 249–50 [40].

25. Although he wrote in genres ranging from treatise to novel to opera, and although his thought often seems at odds with itself in ways both great and small, Rousseau insists on its consistency and coherence, calling it a "sad and great system" and a "true but distressing system." *Rousseau, Judge of Jean-Jacques*, 930 [209]; *Preface of a Second Letter to Bordes* (*OC*, 1:105–6 [108–9]); bracketed citations of this text refer to the English translation of Victor Gourevitch in *The Discourses and Other Early Political Writings* (Cambridge: Cambridge University Press, 1997).

26. *Confessions*, 351 [294–95].

27. *Confessions*, 351 [294–95]; *Discourse on the Sciences and the Arts*, 14–15 [19–20]; bracketed citations for this text refer to the English translation of John T. Scott in *The Major Political Writings of Jean-Jacques Rousseau* (Chicago: University of Chicago Press, 2012). Rousseau would most likely have recalled the story of Fabricius as it is told in Plutarch's *Life of Pyrrhus*, sections 20–21.

28. *Confessions*, 9 [8].

29. As Christopher Kelly notes, Rousseau's highly deliberate practice of signing his books was exceptional and controversial in times when men often wrote anonymously or under pseudonyms. He signed the *Discourse on the Sciences and the Arts* simply as "a citizen of Geneva" but would go on thereafter to sign all those he thought politically salutary with both his name and his citizenship (Kelly, *Rousseau as Author*, 18, 42–43).

30. *Confessions*, 351 [295], 416 [350]; Kelly, *Rousseau's Exemplary Life*, 194; Ruth Grant (*Hypocrisy and Integrity: Machiavelli, Rousseau, and the Ethics of Politics* [Chicago: University of Chicago Press, 1997]) highlights the significance of integrity in Rousseau's moral thought.

31. *Confessions*, 404 [340]; *Discourse on Political Economy*, 254–62 [15–23] in *Basic Political Writings*, ed. Donald A. Cress (Indianapolis: Hackett, 2011); Keohane, *Philosophy and the State in France*, 279–81.

32. *Discourse on Political Economy*, 248 [10].

33. Grant, *Hypocrisy and Integrity*, 60; Rousseau, *The Social Contract*, 364 [176] in Scott, *Major Political Writings*.

34. *Considerations on the Government of Poland*, 966 [179] in *The Plan for Perpetual Peace, On the Government of Poland, and Other Writings on History and Politics*, trans. Chrstopher Kelly and Judith Bush, edited Christopher Kelly (Hanover, NH: Dartmouth College Press, 2005).

35. *Considerations on the Government of Poland*, 1019 [222]; *Confessions*, 416 [350].
36. *Émile*, 249 [40].
37. *Confessions*, 395–96 [332–33]; *Émile* 251 [41].

38. *Émile*, 484 [205]; *Discourse on Inequality*, 180 [105]. In his *Perfection and Disharmony in the Thought of Jean-Jacques Rousseau* (38–55), Jonathan Marks argues that the understanding of nature presented in *Émile* is, contrary to scholarly consensus, teleological, an argument that has influenced our account.

39. *Discourse on Inequality*, 171 [97].

40. *Discourse on Inequality*, 157–59, 167–68 [85–88, 94–95]. Susan Meld Shell points out the decisive role of women in bringing about this first, domestic revolution. See Shell, "*Émile*: Nature and the Education of Sophie," in *The Cambridge Companion to Rousseau*, 280.

41. Shell, "*Émile*: Nature and the Education of Sophie," 281–83.

42. Shell, "*Émile*: Nature and the Education of Sophie," 282–84.

43. *Rousseau, Judge of Jean-Jacques*, 112. Laurence D. Cooper points out the centrality of what Rousseau calls "the desire to extend our being" at work in the development in the family described here in his "Between Eros and Will to Power: Rousseau and 'the Desire to Extend Our Being,'" *American Political Science Review* 98, no. 1 (2004): 105–6.

44. *Discourse on Inequality*, 169–74 [95–101]; *Émile*, 656 [329]; Stendhal [Marie-Henri Beyle], *On Love*, ed. C. K. Scott-Moncrieff (New York: Grosset and Dunlap, 1947), 5–34.

45. *Émile*, 487–88 [207–8].

46. *Discourse on Political Economy*, 259 [20]; *Émile*, 656 [329].

47. *Émile*, 692–693 [357]; Shell, "*Émile*: Nature and the Education of Sophie," 284.

48. *Émile*, 703–21 [365–78].

49. *Émile*, 809–13 [439–41].

50. *Émile*, 720 [377]; Shell, "*Émile*: Nature and the Education of Sophie," 291.

51. *Émile*, 503 [221], 691 [355]; Tzvetan Todorov, *Frail Happiness: An Essay on Rousseau*, trans. John T. Scott and Robert D. Zaretsky (University Park: Pennsylvania State University Press, 2001), 66.

52. At the same time, the story of Émile and Sophie has drawn significant criticism, particularly from feminists who see in Rousseau's description of Sophie's education a betrayal of the case for natural individualism of the human species he makes so powerfully in *Discourse on Inequality*. See, for example, Susan Moller Okin, *Women in Western Political Thought* (Princeton: Princeton University Press, 1979), 99–100. Rousseau's barbed one-liners on the differences between the sexes, his mean-sounding mockery of female writers—all of it was calculated to offend in the eighteenth century and is positively painful to read in the twenty-first. He surely overemphasizes sexual differences and underestimates the possibility of friendship between the sexes. Nonetheless, Rousseau speaks to a problem inherent in modern thought, indeed all thought that begins from the solitary and self-sufficient individual: How does one make a social whole out of beings who think of self-sufficiency as both natural and desirable?

53. *Émile et Sophie, ou, Les Solitaires*, in *OC*, 4:881–924.

54. *Émile et Sophie*, 4:881–924.

55. *Émile et Sophie*, 4:884–85; Pascal, *Pensées*, S15/L396; see also Pierre Burgelin's introduction to "Émile and Sophie," in *OC*, 4:cliii–clxvii.

56. *Confessions*, 52, 221–22 [44, 186]; *Julie*, in *OC*, 2:676 [555]. Bracketed page numbers for this work refer to *Julie, or the New Heloise*, trans. Philip Stewart and Jean Vaché, ed. Jean Vaché (Hanover, NH: Dartmouth College Press, 1997). See also Jennifer Einspahr, "The Beginning That Never Was: Mediation and Freedom in Rousseau's Political Thought," *Review of Politics* 72 (2010): 437–61, and Benjamin Storey, "Self-Knowledge and Sociability in the Thought of Rousseau," *Perspectives on Political Science* 41, no. 3 (August 2012): 150, the argument of which we recapitulate here.

57. *Confessions*, 225 [189].

58. In his "Rousseau and the Recovery of Human Nature," Roger Masters gives one form of the objection to Rousseau's picture of man as naturally solitary, arguing that "recent scientific research in ethnology, neuroscience, and behavioral ecology leads to a paradoxical criticism of Rousseau: humans are innately social animals whose psychology and politics are more clearly understood by the ancient tradition of Plato and Aristotle than by modern political philosophy" (in *The Legacy of Rousseau*, ed. Clifford Orwin and Nathan Tarcov [Chicago: University of Chicago Press, 1996], 111).

59. *Confessions*, 573–91 [480–94]. As Trilling puts it, "The ideal of authentic personal being stands at the very center of Rousseau's thought" (*Sincerity and Authenticity*, 93). But an authentic human being is not necessarily an amiable one: as Scott and Zaretsky point out, Rousseau was an impossibly demanding friend and one of the world's most difficult guests, and thereby decisively contributed to the conditions that required him to constantly relocate. See *The Philosophers' Quarrel*, chap. 9. Mostefai nicely summarizes the paradoxical place of Rousseau in the minds of his contemporaries: "Celebrity put into circulation and juxtaposition incoherent images of the author, whose books are burned even while children are being raised according to the principles of *Émile*" ("Un auteur paradoxal," 436).

60. *Émile*, 560, 566–67 [262, 266–67].

61. *Émile*, 564–65, 609–10 [266, 297].

62. *Émile*, 567–68 [267–68]. Montaigne might, of course, defend the compatibility of Pyrrhonism and practical life: see *Essais*, II.12.505 [454]. But the Vicar could point out, in response, that for all his professed skepticism, Montaigne himself gives a definite answer to the question of the human good: the standard of immanent contentment we described earlier.

63. *Émile*, 570, 574 [270, 272]; Pascal, *Pensées*, S142/L110.

64. *Émile*, 589 [282]; Kolalowski, *God Owes Us Nothing*, 39.

65. *Émile*, 594 [286].

66. Pascal, *Pensées*, S94/L60; Montaigne, *Essais*, I.23.115 [100]; *Émile*, 569 [269], 598–599 [289].

67. *Émile*, 618–619 [302–303].

68. *Émile*, 589–90 [282–83].

69. *Émile*, 589, 587, 564–65, 592 [282, 281, 266, 284].

70. *Émile*, 554–55, 610, 625–29 [257, 297, 307–9].

71. *Émile*, 558–61 [260–63].

72. *Émile*, 614–17, 607 [295, 300–301].

73. See Pascal, *Pensées*, S690/L447. The "Profession of Faith" might be the original formulation of what has come to be called "Moralistic Therapeutic Deism." See Christian Smith and Melinda Lundquist Denton, *Soul Searching: The Religious and Spiritual Lives of American Teenagers* (Oxford: Oxford University Press, 2009), chap. 4.

74. *Confessions*, 455 [382].

75. *Pensées*, S168/L136.

76. *Confessions*, 427 [359].

77. *Confessions*, 426–27 [358].

78. *Confessions*, 421, 440 [354, 370]. This episode illustrates the self-destructive power of the Rousseauan imagination Eve Grace describes as follows: "Imagination is fueled by the expansiveness of our 'desire to exist': we do not only seek more powerful means to preserve ourselves; we also seek to strengthen and to expand the 'sentiment of our existence' . . . by fashioning new ends to which our energy can be put. Imagination thereby gains a demonic potency through which it works the transformation of man from an animal with limited needs to a being with limitless dreams of happiness, a being who seeks to exist as the image he creates" (Grace, "The Restlessness of 'Being': Rousseau's Protean Sentiment of Existence," *History of European Ideas* 27 [2001]: 148).

79. *Rêveries*, 1040–49 [62–71].

80. *Rêveries*, 1047 [69]. Although the experience of the sentiment of existence is most self-sufficient when felt alone, it is not necessarily a solitary experience; indeed, all of Rousseau's social ideals rely on extending one's being over a larger whole, with both the satisfactions and the dangers that entails.

81. *Rêveries*, 1048 [70].

82. *Rêveries*, 1065, 1044 [95, 66].

83. *Rêveries*, 1041–42 [64].

84. *Rêveries*, 1069–71 [99–101]; Joseph Lane points out this passage as exemplifying Rousseau's awareness of the limits of any human return to nature in his "Reverie and the Return to Nature," 493.

85. Charles Butterworth, preface to the *Reveries of the Solitary Walker*, vii; *Rêveries*, 1001, 1042 [7, 64]; Scott, "Rousseau's Quixotic Quest in the *Rêveries du promeneur solitaire*," 139–52.

86. *Confessions*, 362 [304], *Rêveries*, 995[1]. Rousseau erroneously believes he is "never much inclined to amour-propre" (*Rêveries*, 1079 [115]). As Scott and Zaretsky show, Rousseau prefers to express his affection for others with the immediacy of

gestures, which he trusts much more than language, since he sees language as riddled with obfuscation from its origin. He wants others to reciprocate in kind and is furious when they cannot or will not meet his emotional demands (*The Philosophers' Quarrel*, 157; see also Starobinski, *Transparency and Obstruction*, 137–40).

87. See Grace, "The Restlessness of 'Being,'" 150.

88. See note 25 in this chapter.

Chapter 4

1. Herodotus, *The History*, trans. David Grene (Chicago: University of Chicago Press, 1987), I.32; Aristotle, *Nicomachean Ethics*, 1100a10; McMahon, *Happiness: A History*, 4–9.

2. Montaigne, *Essais*, I.3.17 [11].

3. Mill, "De Tocqueville on Democracy in America," 167; *Democracy in America*, II.ii.13.943, I.i.4.97. Pascal Bruckner succinctly encapsulates the transformation of contentment from exception to norm: "Our societies put into the category of the pathological what other cultures consider as normal—the preponderance of pain—and put into the category of the normal and even the necessary what others see as exceptional—the feeling of happiness" (*Perpetual Euphoria*, 65).

4. *Democracy in America*, introduction, 16; Aristotle, *Politics*, trans. Carnes Lord (Chicago: University of Chicago Press, 2013), 1328b1–2. Catherine Zuckert helpfully enumerates three parts of Tocqueville's new political science: (1) a history of the advance of the equality of conditions in Europe over the course of seven centuries; (2) an account of the "material and intellectual condition" of a people that Tocqueville calls the "social state"; and (3) "an attempt to isolate and explain the operation of the factors that determined whether the political outcome of this new social condition would be free or despotic." Zuckert argues that "the three most important factors . . . were geography, laws, and mores." We follow her in holding that "mores [are] the most decisive" and concentrate our analysis on that element of Tocqueville's thought (Zuckert, "Tocqueville's 'New Political Science,'" in *Tocqueville's Voyages: The Evolution of His Ideals and Their Journey beyond His Time*, ed. Christine Dunn Henderson [Indianapolis: Liberty Fund, 2014], 142–76).

5. Boesche, *Strange Liberalism of Alexis de Tocqueville*, 159.

6. David Lewis Schaefer has also explored this connection between Montaigne and Tocqueville on the subject of skepticism; see Schaefer, "Montaigne, Tocqueville, and the Politics of Skepticism," *Perspectives on Political Science* 31, no. 2 (2002): 204–12.

7. Letter to E. V. Childe, December 12, 1856, from *Tocqueville on America after 1840: Letters and Other Writings*, ed. Aurelian Craiutu and Jeremy Jennings (Cambridge: Cambridge University Press, 2009), 190; Brogan, *Alexis de Tocqueville*, 454.

8. The phrase "to teach democracy to know itself" comes from a letter Tocqueville wrote to Silvestre de Sacy in October 1840, which he may never have sent. Cited in André Jardin, *Tocqueville: A Biography*, trans. Lydia Davis and Robert Hemenway (New York: Farrar, Straus, and Giroux, 1988), 272–73. As Alan S. Kahan remarks, "As a moralist Tocqueville aspired to be not merely democracy's political guru, but its spiritual director" (Kahan, *Tocqueville, Democracy, and Religion: Checks and Balances for Democratic Souls* [Oxford: Oxford University Press, 2015], 3). As noted earlier, we follow Lawler and Boesche in seeing restlessness as the central Tocquevillean theme but aim to deepen our understanding of that restlessness by considering its relationship to the distinctive modern manner of pursuing happiness we have traced back to the time of Montaigne. See Lawler, *The Restless Mind*, 4–6, 73–87; Boesche, *Strange Liberalism of Alexis de Tocqueville*, 27–41.

9. Pierre Manent, *Cours familier de philosophie politique* (Paris: Fayard, 2001), 9.

10. Rousseau, *Discourse on Inequality*, 144 [74]. Seymour Drescher nicely formulates this point, writing that one must view "from without what one wishes to understand within" (Drescher, "Tocqueville's Comparative Perspectives," in *The Cambridge Companion to Tocqueville*, ed. Cheryl B. Welch [Cambridge: Cambridge University Press, 2006], 21–48).

11. Brogan, *Alexis de Tocqueville*, 25; Eduardo Nolla, editor's introduction to the Liberty Fund edition of *Democracy in America*, li; Tocqueville, *Souvenirs*, from *OC*, vol. 3, ed. François Furet and Françoise Mélonio (Paris: Gallimard, 2004), English translation ed. J. P. Mayer and A. P. Kerr (New Brunswick, NJ: Transaction Publishers, 2009), 912, 1249, [217n4], page numbers in brackets refer to the English translation. As Boesche notes, Tocqueville's aristocratic manners could at times be debilitating and ridiculous: "Imagine this man who occasionally called himself a democrat, but who once, while wanting to leave a gathering, felt compelled to remain because he could not find a doorman to open the door for him!" (*Strange Liberalism of Alexis de Tocqueville*, 169). Though his mores may have been aristocratic, Tocqueville did not believe himself set apart from the common run of humanity. One sees this in a letter he wrote to his wife, Mary Mottley, dated December 26, 1837: "Who can understand the many trivialities that fill my soul and yet the vast, boundless taste that ever draws it toward greatness? A thousand times I have wished that God had not allowed me to see the wretchedness and limitations of our nature, or that he had shown them to me from on high. But no, I belong to humanity, to the most common and vulgar humanity, and yet I glimpse something above and beyond humanity" (cited in Jaume, *Aristocratic Sources of Liberty*, 182).

12. Charles Loyseau, *A Treatise on Orders*, in *The Old Regime and the Revolution*, University of Chicago Readings in Western Civilization, vol. 7, ed. Keith Michael Baker (Chicago: University of Chicago Press, 1987), 13–31; Brogan, *Alexis de Tocqueville*, 4.

13. Mill, "De Tocqueville on Democracy in America," 167; Tocqueville to Louis de Kergolay, June 29, 1831, in *Selected Letters on Politics and Society*, ed. Roger Boesche,

trans. James Toupin and Roger Boesche (Berkeley: University of California Press, 1985) 39, 51; David Foster Wallace, "This Is Water," http://bulletin-archive.kenyon .edu/x4280.html.

14. For objections to the pertinence of Tocqueville's observations in his own time, see Gary Wills, "Did Tocqueville 'Get' America?" *New York Review of Books*, April 29, 2004, 52–56. For objections to its continued pertinence in our time, see Helen Andrews, "Tocqueville in the Gutter," *First Things*, January 2017, 64, and Daniel Choi, "Unprophetic Tocqueville: How *Democracy in America* Got the Modern World Completely Wrong," *Independent Review* 12, no. 2 (Fall 2007): 165–78.

15. Rousseau, *The Social Contract*, 361–62n [173]. Tocqueville regarded slavery as "the most horrible of social evils" (letter to Theodore Sedgwick, April 13, 1857, in *Tocqueville on America after 1840*, 226). Diana Schaub describes both the power and the limits of the view of the questions of race and slavery Tocqueville shared with his friend and coauthor, Gustave de Beaumont. Both Tocqueville and Beaumont saw that race prejudice would long outlive slavery itself because of their penetrating analysis of the problem of public opinion; neither saw any plausible solution to America's racial problem. Schaub estimates their pessimism on this point as both understandable in the context of the 1830s and a real failure of moral imagination (Schaub, "On Slavery: Beaumont's *Marie* and Tocqueville's *Democracy in America*," *Legal Studies Forum* 22, no. 4 [1998]: 607–26). As Craiutu and Jennings note, Tocqueville's pessimism only increased as he observed America's failures on the slavery question in the 1850s (Craiutu and Jennings, "The Third *Democracy*: Tocqueville's Views of America after 1840," in *Tocqueville on America after 1840*, 28–33). Tocqueville's treatment of colonialism is equally complex and controverted. Cheryl B. Welch argues that Tocqueville's views on European imperialism, particularly in the case of French policy in Algeria, run afoul of his own arguments about the dangers of despotism within the European context and that Tocqueville contradicts himself because he neglects to "apply fully" his European analysis in the colonial case (Welch, "Tocqueville on Fraternity and Fratricide," in *The Cambridge Companion to Tocqueville*, ed. Cheryl B. Welch [Cambridge: Cambridge University Press, 2006], 303–36). Ewa Atanassow notes these same contradictions but argues that they are less intellectual failures on Tocqueville's part than contradictions inherent to the advance of egalitarian modernity itself, which has, as she puts it, a "dark side": a tendency toward violent conflict with non-democratic forms of social and political organization both within and without the Western world (Atanassow, "Colonization and Democracy: Tocqueville Reconsidered," *American Political Science Review* 111, no. 1 [2017]: 83–96).

16. *Democracy in America*, II.iii.1.991–92. As Ewa Atanassow and Richard Boyd point out, however, modernization can give rise to "new inequalities and exclusions" on these edges of democracy. These inequalities and exclusions can be particularly harsh, for to exclude people from a regime of rights understood to be universal is to

dehumanize them (Atanassow and Boyd, *Tocqueville and the Frontiers of Democracy* [Cambridge: Cambridge University Press, 2013], 4).

17. *Democracy in America*, II.iii.5.1014; Manent, *Cours familier de philosophie politique*, 63; Todorov, *Imperfect Garden*, 30.

18. Rousseau, *Discourse on Inequality*, 166 [92].

19. Manent, *Cours familier de philosophie politique*, 65; Tocqueville, *Democracy in America*, introduction, 14.

20. Letter to Louis de Kergolay, June 29, 1831, in *Selected Letters*, 55; *Democracy in America*, introduction, 10; II.iv.6.1282.

21. Sheldon Wolin, *Tocqueville between Two Worlds: The Making of a Political and Theoretical Life* (Princeton: Princeton University Press, 2001); *Democracy in America*, introduction, 28.

22. *Democracy in America*, II.i.1.701, II.1.5.750, II.iii.8.1036.

23. Montaigne, *Essais*, I.20.96 [81], III.13.1085 [1013], III.9.988 [919]; Manent, *Montaigne*, 302–3.

24. Pascal, *Pensées*, S78/L44; Scott and Zaretsky, *The Philosophers' Quarrel*, 3. As Jean Starobinski writes, "Nothing is more revealing than certain extremes of Rousseau's behavior" (*Transparency and Obstruction*, 170).

25. Adrian Vermeule, "Liturgy of Liberalism," *First Things*, January 2017, 57–60.

26. *Democracy in America*, introduction, 28.

27. Edmundson, *Self and Soul*, 12.

28. Todorov, *Imperfect Garden*, 30; *Democracy in America*, II.i.1.699, 701.

29. *Democracy in America*, II.i.1.701. As Jean M. Yarbrough puts it, "The widespread tendency to doubt whatever individual reason cannot confirm leads circuitously back to materialism" (Yarbrough, "Tocqueville on the Needs of the Soul," *Perspectives on Political Science* [Spring 2018]: 6).

30. *Democracy in America*, II.i.2.717; letter to Louis de Kergolay, June 29, 1831, in *Selected Letters*, 49.

31. *Democracy in America*, II.i.1.699; Mill, "De Tocqueville on Democracy in America [II]," 196. Edmundson notes that the "self has a difficult time imagining that there could be other ways to live" (*Self and Soul*, 19). As Ralph C. Hancock comments, "the bondage of the mind is," at least to some degree, "the natural and inevitable condition of humanity"; democracy works a change "in the character of this bondage" rather than a release from mental bondage as such (Hancock, *The Responsibility of Reason: Theory and Practice in a Liberal-Democratic Age* [Lanham, MD: Rowman and Littlefield, 2011], 257–58).

32. Rousseau did exactly that and shows how intellectual apprenticeship can be a preparation for intellectual independence. Remarking on the solitary studies through which he developed his mind during the years he spent living in the countryside with Mme de Warens, he writes:

I began with some book of philosophy, such as the *Logic* of Port-Royal, Locke's *Essay*, Malebranche, Leibnitz, Descartes, and so on. I soon noticed that all these authors were in almost perpetual contradiction with each other, and I formed the chimerical project of reconciling them, which tired me out very much and made me lose a lot of time.... Finally renouncing this method also, I acquired an infinitely better one, to which I attribute all the progress I have been able to make, in spite of my lack of capacity; for it is certain that I have always had extremely little for study. While reading each Author, I made it a law for myself to adopt and follow all his ideas without mixing in my own or those of anyone else, and without ever disputing with him.... Then when trips and business deprived me of the means of consulting books, I amused myself by thinking over and comparing what I had read, by weighing each thing in the scale of reason, and sometimes by judging my masters. I did not find that my faculty of judging had lost its vigor because it had been put into use late, and when I published my own ideas, I was not accused of swearing *in verba magistri*. (*Confessions*, 237–38 [199])

33. Zuckert describes the mixed blessing of democratic education as follows: "Partly as a result of the ideas that spread from the Puritan settlements to the other colonies, primary education is available to everyone, but it is almost impossible for anyone to acquire higher education.... As a result, in America one encounters a great number of individuals with basically the same ideas about 'religion, history, the sciences, political economy, legislation, and government'" ("Tocqueville's 'New Political Science,'" 155–56).

34. Brogan, *Alexis de Tocqueville*, 297; *Democracy in America*, II.iii.15.1084, II.i.10.779. See also Matthew Crawford, *The World beyond Your Head: On Becoming an Individual in an Age of Distraction* (New York: Farrar, Straus, and Giroux, 2016); Alan Jacobs, *The Pleasures of Reading in an Age of Distraction* (Oxford: Oxford University Press, 2011); Mark Bauerlein, *The Dumbest Generation: How the Digital Age Stupefies the Young and Threatens Our Future* (New York: TarcherPerigee, 2009); and Carr, *The Shallows*, 115–43. As Wilfred McClay writes, the digital revolution is "perhaps best understood as a *continuation* of ... the gradual but pervasive process of democratic leveling that Tocqueville described" (McClay, "The Tocquevillean Moment ... and Ours," *Wilson Quarterly* 36 [Summer 2012]: 53).

35. *Democracy in America*, II.i.10.784, II.i.17.836–37.

36. Martin Heidegger, "The Question Concerning Technology," in *Basic Writings*, ed. David Farrell Krell (New York: Harper Collins, 1993), 322; Alexander S. Duff, *Heidegger and Politics: The Ontology of Radical Discontent* (Cambridge: Cambridge University Press, 2015), 91; see also Benjamin Storey, "Tocqueville on Technology," *New Atlantis* 40 (Fall 2013): 48–71.

37. Letter to Louis de Kergolay, June 29, 1831, in *Selected Letters*, 49; Wolin, *Tocqueville between Two Worlds*, 85.

38. As Laurence Cooper has put it, "Modern Socratism is the cause of our unsocratic character" (Cooper, "Every Man a Socrates? Tocqueville and the Conceit of Modernity," *American Political Thought* 1 [Fall 2012]: 213). Tocqueville lists doubt as one of three great human evils, surpassed only by death and disease. This is in part because, at sixteen, he lost the faith of his childhood as a result of his explorations of some of the more daring books in his father's library. He describes himself as "overcome by the blackest melancholy, seized by an extreme disgust for the life which I had not even begun, and crushed, as it were, by distress and terror at the sight of the road through the world which lay before me." See Brogan, *Alexis de Tocqueville*, 49–51. Joshua Mitchell, who has written about his experiences teaching Tocqueville to American students at Georgetown and Middle Eastern students in Qatar, notes that his Middle Eastern students think they see nihilism beneath their American counterparts' veneer of cheerful pragmatism and humanitarian moralism. See his *Tocqueville in Arabia: Dilemmas in a Democratic Age* (Chicago: University of Chicago Press, 2013), 52.

39. *Democracy in America*, II.2.15.956, II.2.13.942.

40. *Democracy in America*, II.ii.15.958; cf. Montaigne, *Essais*, II.12.450 [400]; Kass, *The Hungry Soul*, 35–44. As Yarbrough writes, "Although . . . not all schools of philosophical materialism lead to or condone vulgar hedonism, in democratic ages the two tend mutually to reinforce one another" ("Tocqueville on the Needs of the Soul," 4).

41. *Democracy in America*, II.i.20.858; Lee M. Silver, *Challenging Nature: The Clash between Biotechnology and Spirituality* (New York: Harper Perennial, 2006), 62.

42. Lawler, *The Restless Mind*, 74.

43. *Democracy in America*, II.ii.13.944.

44. *Democracy in America*, II.ii.18.969.

45. *Democracy in America*, II.ii.2.884, I.i.3.86. Through his reflections on his American experience, Tocqueville discovers a new type of being, whom Joshua Mitchell calls *homo solus*: man, alone. His discovery of this type results in a paradox: Tocqueville, the first great sociologist, notes that democracy tends not merely to change society but to annihilate it, by breaking the chains that bind human beings together and setting each link apart (Mitchell, *Tocqueville in Arabia*, 43).

46. Letter to Hubert de Tocqueville, February 23, 1857, quoted in Jardin, *Tocqueville: A Biography*, 48; *Democracy in America*, I.i.3.81–83, II.ii.2.883; Mitchell, *Tocqueville in Arabia*, 46.

47. Mill, "De Tocqueville on Democracy in America [II]," 182.

48. Tocqueville, *Souvenirs*, 757 [40]. As Boesche notes, in Tocqueville's generation, many on both the left and the right shared his concerns about individualism

and materialism. Tocqueville distinguishes himself from his contemporaries, however, in suggesting that "the household—the private realm—was a place of servility, and that only a servile society could spring from urging people to seek the bulk of their satisfactions in the private sphere" (*Strange Liberalism of Alexis de Tocqueville*, 35–37, 53). The self-isolating character of democratic individuals will necessarily have political effects, as Zuckert notes: "Because isolated individuals (or families) are weak and unable to protect themselves from others in a democratic social state, as in nature, they will, in fact, need help. Where they have not learned the art of association from participating in local government, they will look primarily to the central government to provide them with the assistance they need" ("Tocqueville's 'New Political Science,'" 170).

49. Mitchell, *Tocqueville in Arabia*, 58.

50. *Democracy in America*, II.iv.3.1203 note d; Jaume, *Aristocratic Sources of Liberty*, 179. As Zuckert puts it, Tocqueville followed Montesquieu in emphasizing "the softening effects of commerce on mores" but also notes that this effect concerns the nation's external relations, not its internal ones: "commerce did not have the same unifying effect on the citizens of a particular nation, however; it tended to lead them to compete more than cooperate" ("Tocqueville's 'New Political Science,'" 165).

51. Jaume, *Aristocratic Sources of Liberty*, 162.

52. *Democracy in America*, II.ii.20.984.

53. Taylor, *A Secular Age*, 542.

54. Manent, *Cours familier de philosophie politique*, 23–37.

55. *Democracy in America*, I.ii.9.475, I.i.2.69. Aristide Tessitore identifies Tocqueville's celebration of the tense, complex, yet fruitful "combination of 'the *spirit of religion* and the *spirit of liberty*'" achieved at America's puritan founding as the "nub" of the "American thesis" around which *Democracy in America* is built (Tessitore, "Tocqueville's American Thesis and the New Science of Politics," *American Political Thought* 4 [Winter 2015]: 72–99).

56. Deneen, *Why Liberalism Failed*, 65. As Tessitore puts it, "The danger resides in the possibility that America's philosophic Enlightenment inheritance could completely overwhelm its biblical one, with dangerous consequences for both individual and political freedom." But should it achieve such a dominant position, "Enlightenment philosophy tolerant of everything except serious religious conviction" will find itself opposed by "a variety of 'almost fierce' or 'bizarre' religious sects ungrounded in nature and skeptical of reason" because religion, which "draws its force from the natural 'sentiments, instincts, and passions' of the human soul," can be distorted but not eradicated. Its exclusion from the sphere of what contemporary liberalism, following Rawls, calls "public reason" encourages this fundamentalist mutation (Tessitore, "Tocqueville's American Thesis," 96–97, 82).

57. *Democracy in America*, II.iv.6.1260; L. Joseph Hebert, *More than Kings and Less than Men* (Lanham, MD: Lexington Books, 2010). On the "self-subverting" character of Lockean political principles such as consent, see D. C. Schindler, *Freedom from Reality* (South Bend, IN: University of Notre Dame Press, 2017), 5–6. As Aurelian Craiutu and Jeremy Jennings note, during the last decade of his life, Tocqueville became ever more concerned that "it was in the very nature of democracy, even in the most advanced democratic regime in the world, to transgress its limits and to subvert its own foundations" ("The Third *Democracy*," 28).

58. Aristotle, *Politics*, 1253a1–20, 1280a7–25, 1294a30–1294b40; Jonathan Rauch, "How American Politics Went Insane," *Atlantic Monthly*, July/August 2016, https://www.theatlantic.com/magazine/archive/2016/07/how-american-politics-went-insane/485570/. As Craiutu and Jennings note, in the 1850s, Tocqueville saw that America "risked disappointing the hopes of millions of people for a better future, because it offered in reality the disquieting spectacle of an unstable regime led by incompetent and dishonest leaders," "individuals who lacked moderation, sometimes probity, and above all education, and who resembled mere political adventurers, violent, gross, and devoid of principles" ("The Third *Democracy*," 31, 38).

59. See Yuval Levin, *A Time to Build* (New York: Basic Books, 2020). As Joshua Mitchell writes, "An escalating conflict of ideas that may lead to violence is the inevitable outcome of thought's labor when it is no longer embodied in viable institutions" (Mitchell, *The Fragility of Freedom: Tocqueville on Religion, Democracy and the American Future* [Chicago: University of Chicago Press, 1995], 12).

60. The ascendance of violence and vulgarity also has distressing antecedents. In an 1857 letter to an American correspondent, Tocqueville writes that reports from America indicate that "the part of the population in the States that still has violent mores and uncouth habits increasingly sets the tone for the rest" (Tocqueville to Francis Lieber, October 9, 1857, in *Tocqueville on America after 1840*, 261).

61. These lines, from Edmund Spenser's "A Hymn in Honour of Beauty," are cited in Kass, *The Hungry Soul*, 17. In the first chapter of that book, Kass draws on an Aristotelian understanding of form as the active reality of every living being to argue (1) that such an understanding of form is compatible with the truths of modern biology, and (2) that so basic a biological phenomenon as metabolism is in fact unintelligible apart from the active work of form. See also Aristotle, *De Anima*, in *The Basic Works of Aristotle*, ed. Richard McKeon (New York: Modern Library, 2001), 412a1–415a14.

62. As Daniel J. Mahoney writes, "Philosophical modernity [cannot] ultimately sustain a popular government. . . . One must turn to older and richer spiritual resources in order to renew American republicanism and the democratic world more

broadly" (Mahoney, *The Idol of Our Age* [New York: Encounter Books, 2018], 40).
James W. Ceaser makes a similar point, arguing for the necessity of an "ongoing process of adjustment or supplementation of the modern philosophical doctrine of natural rights, which can take place through creative interpretation of its sources or by introducing other foundational principles to qualify and complement it" (Ceaser, "Alexis de Tocqueville and the Two-Founding Thesis," in *Tocqueville's Voyages,* ed. Henderson, 111–41).

Conclusion

1. Charles Griswold illustrates the connection between reason and happiness by pointing out that happiness, unlike contentment, is "inseparable from a reflective arrangement of one's life . . . because any such arrangement of one's life must be evaluatively linked to a notion of what sort of life is worth living" (Griswold, "Happiness, Tranquility, and Philosophy," in *In Pursuit of Happiness,* Boston University Studies in Philosophy and Religion, vol. 16, ed. Leroy Rouner [South Bend, IN: University of Notre Dame Press, 1995], 28).

2. As Deresiewicz points out, a significant proportion of graduates from America's most elite universities take their first jobs in consulting, work that in many ways allows the young to preserve their protean qualities (Deresiewicz, *Excellent Sheep,* 17). Liah Greenfeld investigates the cases in which this incapacity for choice becomes so severe that it results in mental illness, a "malfunction of the 'acting self'" that manifests itself in chronic depression, bipolar disorder, and schizophrenia. Greenfeld argues that these mental illnesses appear only in modernity and that "it is modern culture—specifically the presumed equality of all the members of the society, secularism, and choice in self-definition, implied in the national consciousness—that makes the formation of the individual identity difficult." She also cites data to show that "these diseases first and most gravely affect the strata whose possibilities of self-realization are least limited and whose members face the largest number of choices" (Greenfeld, *Mind, Modernity, Madness: The Impact of Culture on Human Experience* [Cambridge, MA: Harvard University Press, 2013], 26, 28–29).

3. Edmundson powerfully depicts the contrast between the unity and intensity that invigorates a life devoted to an ideal and the distraction and dissipation that attends a life devoted to what we call immanent contentment (Edmundson, *Self and Soul,* 4, 19–21, 62, 97, 100–101). See Bruckner's parallel analysis of how the skeptical "critique of consumer society" has led "so quickly to the triumph" of a conformist consumerism (Bruckner, *Perpetual Euphoria,* 47–48).

4. Wilfred McClay offers an extended meditation on this claim in the context of a history of American thought on self and society in his book *The Masterless:*

Self and Society in Modern America (Chapel Hill: University of North Carolina Press, 1994).

5. See Mark Lilla, "The Truth about Our Libertarian Age," *New Republic*, June 17, 2014, https://newrepublic.com/article/118043/our-libertarian-age-dogma-democracy-dogma-decline. David Wooton notes one important source of this particularly modern form of immoderation. From the fifteenth century onward, he argues, moral philosophy was systematically reoriented around the term "interest" as an alternative to happiness, and this term crystallizes modern opposition to the Aristotelian ethics of moderation: "the point about interests . . . is that they have no natural limit; their fundamental principle is immoderation," because it is impossible to satiate an interest (Wooton, *Power, Pleasure, and Profit*, 22–24). While the immanent contentment we describe as the aim of the modern pursuit of happiness promises equilibrium, it contains no principle of limitation beyond immanence itself that might check the tendency to immoderation Wooton describes.

6. Isaiah Berlin makes a famous version of the case that reasoned argument about the good is a threat to liberty in his "Two Concepts of Liberty," in *Four Essays on Liberty* (New York: Oxford University Press, 1970), 145–54. The concept of "mere civility" Teresa M. Bejan resuscitates from Roger Williams shows how a free society can make room for serious public argument about the question of the good. Civility so understood is a minimalist "bond of tolerant societies" that can go "hand-in-hand with an unapologetically cacophonous and evangelical approach to toleration," which Bejan contrasts to the prevailing "public reason" approach, which ultimately leaves us only with the choice between "conversion to the fundamentals of political liberalism or silence" (Bejan, *Mere Civility: Disagreement and the Limits of Toleration* [Cambridge, MA: Harvard University Press, 2017], 14–15). Similarly, William Galston argues for an understanding of liberalism as a form of government that is uniquely aware of its own limits, of its "incompleteness," and that does not insist that the human mind reside within those limits. According to Galston, it is only insofar as liberalism retains this awareness of the "incompleteness" of its philosophic anthropology, and is consequently open to richer accounts of our nature, that it "harbors the power of self-correction" (Galston, *Anti-Pluralism*, 126, 1).

7. *Essais*, II.12.516 [465].

8. Eliot, "The *Pensées* of Pascal," 362; *Essais*, II.12.594 [546].

9. Such a vision of life as serious and necessary adventure might help liberate us from what Christy Wampole has described as a malaise of "ironic living." For it requires that we chart a specific course, stepping out of "the ironic frame [which] functions as a shield against criticism" (Wampole, "How to Live without Irony," in *Modern Ethics in 77 Arguments*, ed. Peter Catapano and Simon Critchley [New York: W. W. Norton, 2017], 79–84).

10. David Brooks gives an account of the Pascalian, comet-like life of those who are "brave enough to let parts of their old self die" in his book *The Second Mountain: The Quest for a Moral Life* (New York: Random House, 2019), xii.

11. See Yuval Levin, "Taking the Long Way: Disciplines of the Soul Are the Basis of a Liberal Society," *First Things*, October 2014, 25–31, https://www.firstthings.com/article/2014/10/taking-the-long-way. As Ross Douthat writes, exhausted, repetitive moments in our history can sometimes be revived only by "something else, something extra, that really can come only from outside our present frame of reference" (*The Decadent Society*, 237).

BIBLIOGRAPHY

Adam, Michel. *Études sur Pierre Charron*. Bordeaux: Presses Universitaires de Bordeaux, 1991.

Andrews, Helen. "Tocqueville in the Gutter." *First Things*, January 2017, 63–65.

Annas, Julia. *The Morality of Happiness*. Oxford: Oxford University Press, 1993.

Ariew, Roger. "Descartes and Pascal." *Perspectives on Science* 15, no. 4 (2007): 397–409.

Aristotle. *De Anima*. In *The Basic Works of Aristotle*, edited by Richard McKeon. New York: Modern Library, 2001.

———. *Nicomachean Ethics*. Edited by Arthur Rackham. Cambridge, MA: Harvard University Press, 1934.

———. *Politics*. Translated by Carnes Lord. Chicago: University of Chicago Press, 2013.

Atanassow, Ewa. "Colonization and Democracy: Tocqueville Reconsidered." *American Political Science Review* 111, no. 1 (2017): 83–96.

Atanassow, Ewa, and Richard Boyd, eds. *Tocqueville and the Frontiers of Democracy*. Cambridge: Cambridge University Press, 2013.

Attali, Jacques. *Blaise Pascal, ou, le génie français*. Paris: Fayard, 2000.

Auerbach, Erich. *Mimesis: The Representation of Reality in Western Literature*. Princeton: Princeton University Press, 1953.

———. *Scenes from the Drama of European Literature: Six Essays*. New York: Meridian Books, 1959.

Augustine. *City of God*. Translated by R. W. Dyson. Cambridge: Cambridge University Press, 1998.

———. *Confessions*. Translated by R. S. Pine-Coffin. New York: Penguin, 1961.

Bakewell, Sarah. *How to Live, or, A Life of Montaigne, in One Question and Twenty Attempts at an Answer*. New York: Other Press, 2010.

Bauerlein, Mark. *The Dumbest Generation: How the Digital Age Stupefies the Young and Threatens Our Future*. New York: TarcherPerigee, 2009.

Beitzinger, A. J. "Pascal on Justice, Force, and Law." *Review of Politics* 46, no. 2 (April 1984): 212–43.

Bejan, Teresa M. *Mere Civility: Disagreement and the Limits of Toleration*. Cambridge, MA: Harvard University Press, 2017.

Berlin, Isaiah. *Political Ideas in the Romantic Age: Their Rise and Influence on Modern Thought*. Edited by Henry Hardy, with an introduction by Joshua L. Cherniss. Princeton: Princeton University Press, 2008.

———. "Two Concepts of Liberty." In *Four Essays on Liberty*, 145–54. New York: Oxford University Press, 1970.

Blum, Carol. *Rousseau and the Republic of Virtue*. Ithaca: Cornell University Press, 1986.

Boesche, Roger. *The Strange Liberalism of Alexis de Tocqueville*. Ithaca: Cornell University Press, 1987.

Bok, Sissela. *Exploring Happiness: From Aristotle to Brain Science*. New Haven: Yale University Press, 2010.

Brogan, Hugh. *Alexis de Tocqueville: A Life*. New Haven: Yale University Press, 2006.

Brooks, David. *The Second Mountain: The Quest for a Moral Life*. New York: Random House, 2019.

———. *The Social Animal: The Hidden Sources of Love, Character, and Achievement*. New York: Random House, 2011.

Bruckner, Pascal. *Perpetual Euphoria: On the Duty to Be Happy*. Translated by Steven Rendall. Princeton: Princeton University Press, 2010.

Brunschvicg, Leon. *Descartes et Pascal: Lecteurs de Montaigne*. New York: Brentano's, 1944.

Burgelin, Pierre. *La philosophie de l'existence de J.-J. Rousseau*. Paris: Presses Universitaires de France, 1952.

Burke, Edmund. *Reflections on the Revolution in France*. Edited by J. G. A. Pocock. Indianapolis: Hackett, 1987.

Burkhardt, Jacob. *The Civilization of the Renaissance in Italy*. Translated by S. G. C. Middlemore. Vienna: Phaidon Press, 1950.

Busson, Henri. *Literature et théologie*. Paris: Presses Universitaires de France, 1962.

Carr, Nicholas. *The Shallows: What the Internet Is Doing to Our Brains*. New York: W. W. Norton, 2010.

Case, Anne, and Angus Deaton. *Deaths of Despair and the Future of Capitalism*. Princeton: Princeton University Press, 2020.

Ceaser, James W. "Alexis de Tocqueville and the Two-Founding Thesis." In *Tocqueville's Voyages: The Evolution of His Ideals and Their Journey beyond His Time*, edited by Christine Dunn Henderson, 111–41. Indianapolis: Liberty Fund, 2014.

Chateaubriand, François de. *Génie du Christianisme*. Vols. 1–2. Paris: Garnier-Flammarion, 1966.

Chesterton, G. K. *The Everlasting Man*. Nashville: Sam Torode Book Arts, 2014.

Choi, Daniel. "Unprophetic Tocqueville: How *Democracy in America* Got the Modern World Completely Wrong." *Independent Review* 12, no. 2 (Fall 2007): 165–78.

Constant, Benjamin. "The Liberty of the Ancients Compared with That of the Moderns." In *Political Writings*, translated by Biancamaria Fontana, 308–28. Cambridge: Cambridge University Press, 1988.

Cooper, Laurence D. "Between Eros and Will to Power: Rousseau and 'the Desire to Extend Our Being.'" *American Political Science Review* 98, no. 1 (2004): 105–19.

———. "Every Man a Socrates? Tocqueville and the Conceit of Modernity." *American Political Thought* 1 (Fall 2012): 208–35.

———. "Nearer My True Self to Thee: Rousseau's New Spirituality—and Ours." *Review of Politics* 74, no. 3 (2012): 465–88.

Craiutu, Aurelian, and Jeremy Jennings, eds. *Tocqueville on America after 1840: Letters and Other Writings*. Cambridge: Cambridge University Press, 2009.

Crawford, Matthew. *The World beyond Your Head: On Becoming an Individual in an Age of Distraction*. New York: Farrar, Straus, and Giroux, 2016.

Cullen, Daniel. "Montaigne and Rousseau: Ou, les solitaires." In *No Monster of Miracle Greater than Myself: The Political Philosophy of Michel de Montaigne*, edited by Charlotte C. S. Thomas. Macon, GA: Mercer University Press, 2014.

Deneen, Patrick. *Why Liberalism Failed*. New Haven: Yale University Press, 2018.

Deresiewicz, William. *Excellent Sheep: The Miseducation of the American Elite and the Way to a Meaningful Life*. New York: Free Press, 2014.

Derrida, Jacques. *The Politics of Friendship*. Translated by George Collins. New York: Verso, 2005.

Desan, Philippe. *Montaigne: A Political Biography*. Princeton: Princeton University Press, 2017.

Douthat, Ross. *The Decadent Society: How We Became the Victims of Our Own Success*. New York: Avid Reader Press, 2020.

Drescher, Seymour. "Tocqueville's Comparative Perspectives." In *The Cambridge Companion to Tocqueville*, edited by Cheryl B. Welch, 21–48. Cambridge: Cambridge University Press, 2006.

Duff, Alexander S. *Heidegger and Politics: The Ontology of Radical Discontent*. Cambridge: Cambridge University Press, 2015.

Eden, Robert. "The Introduction to Montaigne's Politics." *Perspectives on Political Science* 20, no. 4 (Fall 1991): 211–20.

Edmundson, Mark. *Self and Soul: A Defense of Ideals*. Cambridge, MA: Harvard University Press, 2015.

Einspahr, Jennifer. "The Beginning That Never Was: Mediation and Freedom in Rousseau's Political Thought." *Review of Politics* 72 (2010): 437–61.

Eliot, T. S. "The *Pensées* of Pascal." In *Selected Essays*. New York: Harcourt, Brace, & World, 1932.

Emerson, Ralph Waldo. "Montaigne, or, The Skeptic." In *Complete Writings of Ralph Waldo Emerson*, 1:371–82. New York: Wm. H. Wise & Co., 1929.

Fontana, Biancamaria. *Montaigne's Politics: Authority and Governance in the* Essais. Princeton: Princeton University Press, 2008.

Fouke, Daniel C. "Pascal's Physics." In *The Cambridge Companion to Pascal*, edited by Nicholas Hammond, 75–101. Cambridge: Cambridge University Press, 2003.

Frame, Donald M. *Montaigne: A Biography*. San Francisco: North Point Press, 1984.

Fumaroli, Marc. *La diplomatie de l'esprit*. Paris: Hermann, 2001.

―――. "First Gentleman of Gascony: Montaigne's Liberal Antidotes to the Hubris of Democracy." *Times Literary Supplement*, October 15, 1999.

―――. Preface to *L'art de persuader, précédé de l'art de conférer de Montaigne*, by Blaise Pascal, 7–48. Paris: Rivages poche, 2001.

―――. *La querelle des anciens et des modernes*. Paris: Gallimard, 2001.

Furet, François. "Rousseau and the French Revolution." In *The Legacy of Rousseau*, edited by Clifford Orwin and Nathan Tarcov, 168–82. Chicago: University of Chicago Press, 1997.

Galston, William. *Anti-Pluralism: The Populist Threat to Liberal Democracy*. New Haven: Yale University Press, 2018.

Garber, Daniel. *What Happens after Pascal's Wager: Living Faith and Rational Belief*. Milwaukee: Marquette University Press, 2009.

Gauthier, David. *Rousseau: The Sentiment of Existence*. Cambridge: Cambridge University Press, 2006.

Gopnik, Adam. "Montaigne on Trial." *New Yorker*, January 16, 2017.

Gournay, Marie de. *Preface to the* Essays *of Michel de Montaigne by His Adoptive Daughter, Marie le Jars de Gournay*. Translated by Richard Hillman and Colette Quesnel, from the edition prepared by François Rigolot. Medieval & Renaissance Texts & Studies 193. Tempe, AZ: Medieval & Renaissance Texts & Studies, 1998.

Grace, Eve. "The Restlessness of 'Being': Rousseau's Protean Sentiment of Existence." *History of European Ideas* 27 (2001): 133–51.

Grant, Ruth. *Hypocrisy and Integrity: Machiavelli, Rousseau, and the Ethics of Politics*. Chicago: University of Chicago Press, 1997.

Greenfeld, Liah. *Mind, Modernity, Madness: The Impact of Culture on Human Experience*. Cambridge, MA: Harvard University Press, 2013.

Griswold, Charles L. "Genealogical Narrative and Self-Knowledge in Rousseau's *Discourse on the Origin and the Foundations of Inequality among Men*." *History of European Ideas* 42, no. 2 (2016): 276–301.

———. "Happiness, Tranquility, and Philosophy." In *In Pursuit of Happiness*, Boston University Studies in Philosophy and Religion, vol. 16, edited by Leroy Rouner, 13–32. South Bend, IN: University of Notre Dame Press, 1995.

Grubbs, Henry A. *Damien Mitton (1618–1690): Bourgeois Honnête Homme*. Princeton: Princeton University Press, 1932.

Gusdorf, Georges. "Conditions and Limits of Autobiography." In *Autobiography: Essays Theoretical and Critical*, translated and edited by James Olney, 28–48. Princeton: Princeton University Press, 1980.

Hadot, Pierre. *Philosophy as a Way of Life: Spiritual Exercises from Socrates to Foucault*. Edited by Arnold I. Davidson. Malden, MA: Wiley-Blackwell, 1995.

Hamilton, Alexander, James Madison, and John Jay. *The Federalist*. Edited by Jacob E. Cooke. Hanover, NH: Wesleyan University Press, 1961.

Hancock, Ralph C. *The Responsibility of Reason: Theory and Practice in a Liberal-Democratic Age*. Lanham, MD: Rowman and Littlefield, 2011.

Hanley, Ryan Patrick. "Rousseau's Virtue Epistemology." *Journal of the History of Philosophy* 50, no. 2 (April 2012): 239–63.

Hartle, Ann. *Michel de Montaigne: Accidental Philosopher*. Cambridge: Cambridge University Press, 2003.

———. *The Modern Self in Rousseau's* Confessions: *A Reply to St. Augustine*. South Bend, IN: University of Notre Dame Press, 1983.

———. *Montaigne and the Origins of Modern Philosophy*. Evanston, IL: Northwestern University Press, 2013.

Hazlitt, William. "Bibliographical Notice of the Editions of Montaigne." In *The Works of Michel de Montaigne*, edited by William Hazlitt, lxvi–lxxxv. London: Templeton, 1845.

Hebert, L. Joseph. *More than Kings and Less than Men*. Lanham, MD: Lexington Books, 2010.

Heidegger, Martin. "The Question Concerning Technology." In *Basic Writings*, edited by David Farrell Krell, 307–43. New York: Harper Collins, 1993.

Herodotus. *The History*. Translated by David Grene. Chicago: University of Chicago Press, 1987.

Heschel, Abraham Joshua. *God's Search for Man*. New York: Farrar, Straus, and Giroux, 1955.

Hibbs, Thomas M. *Wagering on an Ironic God*. Waco, TX: Baylor University Press, 2017.

Hulliung, Mark. "Rousseau, Voltaire, and the Revenge of Pascal." In *The Cambridge Companion to Rousseau*, edited by Patrick Riley, 57–77. Cambridge: Cambridge University Press, 2001.

Hunter, Graeme. *Pascal the Philosopher: An Introduction*. Toronto: University of Toronto Press, 2013.

Huppert, George. *Les Bourgeois Gentilshommes*. Chicago: University of Chicago Press, 1977.

Jacobs, Alan. *The Pleasures of Reading in an Age of Distraction*. Oxford: Oxford University Press, 2011.

Jardin, André. *Tocqueville: A Biography*. Translated by Lydia Davis and Robert Hemenway. New York: Farrar, Straus, and Giroux, 1988.

Jaume, Lucien. *The Aristocratic Sources of Liberty*. Translated by Arthur Goldhammer. Princeton: Princeton University Press, 2013.

Jonas, Hans. *The Gnostic Religion: The Message of the Alien God and the Beginnings of Christianity*. Boston: Beacon Hill Press, 2001.

Kahan, Alan S. *Tocqueville, Democracy, and Religion: Checks and Balances for Democratic Souls*. Oxford: Oxford University Press, 2015.

Karlin, Louis W., and David R. Oakley. *Inside the Mind of Thomas More: The Witness of His Writings*. New York: Scepter, 2018.

Kass, Leon. *The Hungry Soul: Eating and the Perfection of Our Nature*. New York: Free Press, 1994.

Kelly, Christopher. *Rousseau as Author: Consecrating One's Life to Truth*. Chicago: University of Chicago Press, 2003.

———. *Rousseau's Exemplary Life: The Confessions as Political Philosophy*. Ithaca: Cornell University Press, 1987.

Keohane, Nannerl. *Philosophy and the State in France: The Renaissance to the Enlightenment*. Princeton: Princeton University Press, 1980.

Kolakowski, Leszek. *God Owes Us Nothing: A Brief Remark on Pascal's Religion and on the Spirit of Jansenism*. Chicago: University of Chicago Press, 1995.

Kraut, Richard. "Two Conceptions of Happiness." *Philosophical Review* 88, no. 2 (April 1979): 167–97.

Kreeft, Peter. *Christianity for Modern Pagans*. San Francisco: Ignatius Press, 1993.

Lane, Joseph H. "Reverie and the Return to Nature: Rousseau's Experience of Convergence." *Review of Politics* 68, no. 3 (Summer 2006): 474–99.

Lawler, Peter Augustine. *The Restless Mind*. Lanham, MD: Rowman and Littlefield, 1993.

Le Guern, Michel. *Études sur la vie et les Pensées de Pascal*. Paris: Honoré Champion, 2015.

Le grand Robert de la langue française. Paris: Éditions le Robert, 2017. http://grand -robert.lerobert.com.

Levin, Yuval. *The Great Debate: Edmund Burke, Thomas Paine, and the Birth of Right and Left*. New York: Basic Books, 2014.

———. "Taking the Long Way: Disciplines of the Soul Are the Basis of a Liberal Society." *First Things*, October 2014, 25–31. https://www.firstthings.com/article /2014/10/taking-the-long-way.

————. *A Time to Build.* New York: Basic Books, 2020.

Levine, Alan. *Sensual Philosophy.* Lanham, MD: Lexington Books, 2001.

Lewis, C. S. *Miracles: A Preliminary Study.* New York: Collier, 1947.

Lilla, Mark. "The Hidden Lesson of Montaigne." *New York Review of Books,* March 24, 2011. https://www.nybooks.com/articles/2011/03/24/hidden-lesson-montaigne/.

————. *The Shipwrecked Mind: On Political Reaction.* New York: New York Review of Books, 2016.

————. *The Stillborn God: Religion, Politics, and the Modern West.* New York: Knopf, 2007.

————. "The Truth about Our Libertarian Age." *New Republic,* June 17, 2014. https://newrepublic.com/article/118043/our-libertarian-age-dogma-democracy-dogma-decline.

Lobel, Diana. *Philosophies of Happiness: A Comparative Introduction to the Flourishing Life.* New York: Columbia University Press, 2017.

Locke, John. *Essay Concerning Human Understanding.* Edited by Peter H. Nidditch. Oxford: Oxford University Press, 1975.

Loyseau, Charles. *A Treatise on Orders.* In *The Old Regime and the Revolution,* University of Chicago Readings in Western Civilization, vol. 7, edited by Keith Michael Baker, 13–31. Chicago: University of Chicago Press, 1987.

Machiavelli, Niccolò. *The Prince.* Translated by Harvey C. Mansfield. Chicago: University of Chicago Press, 1998.

MacIntyre, Alasdair. *Ethics in the Conflicts of Modernity: An Essay on Desire, Practical Reasoning, and Narrative.* Cambridge: Cambridge University Press, 2017.

Maguire, Matthew. *The Conversion of the Imagination: From Pascal through Rousseau to Tocqueville.* Cambridge, MA: Harvard University Press, 2006.

Mahoney, Daniel J. *The Idol of Our Age.* New York: Encounter Books, 2018.

Manent, Pierre. *Cours familier de philosophie politique.* Paris: Fayard, 2001.

————. *Montaigne: La vie sans loi.* Paris: Flammarion, 2014.

————. *Seeing Things Politically: Interviews with Benedict Delorme-Montini.* Translated by Ralph C. Hancock. South Bend, IN: St. Augustine's Press, 2015.

Marchi, Dudley M. *Montaigne among the Moderns: Reception of the Essais.* Providence, RI: Berghahn Books, 1994.

Markovits, Daniel. *The Meritocracy Trap: How America's Foundational Myth Feeds Inequality, Dismantles the Middle Class, and Devours the Elite.* New York: Penguin, 2019.

Marks, Jonathan. *Perfection and Disharmony in the Thought of Jean-Jacques Rousseau.* Cambridge: Cambridge University Press, 2005.

Martin Haag, Eliane. "Diderot et Voltaire lecteurs de Montaigne: Du jugement suspendu à la raison libre." *Revue de métaphysique et de morale,* no. 3 (1997): 365–83.

Masters, Roger. "Rousseau and the Recovery of Human Nature." In *The Legacy of Rousseau*, edited by Clifford Orwin and Nathan Tarcov, 110–41. Chicago: University of Chicago Press, 1996.

McClay, Wilfred. *The Masterless: Self and Society in Modern America*. Chapel Hill: University of North Carolina Press, 1994.

———. "The Tocquevillean Moment . . . and Ours." *Wilson Quarterly* 36 (Summer 2012): 48–55.

McDade, John. "The Contemporary Relevance of Pascal." *New Blackfriars* 91, no. 1032 (February 2010): 185–96.

McMahon, Darrin M. *Happiness: A History*. New York: Atlantic Monthly Press, 2006.

Melzer, Arthur. *The Natural Goodness of Man*. Chicago: University of Chicago Press, 1990.

———. "Rousseau and the Modern Cult of Sincerity." In *The Legacy of Rousseau*, edited by Clifford Orwin and Nathan Tarcov, 274–95. Chicago: University of Chicago Press, 1996.

Mesnard, Jean. *Pascal*. Paris: Hatier, 1962.

Mill, J. S. "De Tocqueville on Democracy in America." In *Collected Works of J. S. Mill*, vol. 18, edited by J. M. Robson and Alexander Brady, 47–90. Toronto: University of Toronto Press, 1977.

Mishra, Pankaj. *Age of Anger: A History of the Present*. New York: Farrar, Straus, and Giroux, 2017.

Mitchell, Joshua. *The Fragility of Freedom: Tocqueville on Religion, Democracy and the American Future*. Chicago: University of Chicago Press, 1995.

———. *Tocqueville in Arabia: Dilemmas in a Democratic Age*. Chicago: University of Chicago Press, 2013.

Montaigne, Michel de. *Complete Works of Michel de Montaigne*. Translated by Donald M. Frame. New York: Everyman's Library, 2003.

———. *Les Essais*. Edited by Pierre Villey. Paris: Presses Universitaires de France, 1924.

More, Thomas. *The Sadness of Christ*. Translated by Clarence Miller. New York: Scepter, 1993.

Mostefai, Ourida. "Un auteur paradoxal: Singularité et exemplarité de la carrière de Rousseau." *Romanic Review* 103, nos. 3–4 (2013): 427–37.

Nakam, Geralde. *Montaigne et son temps*. Paris: Gallimard, 1993.

Natoli, Charles M. *Fire in the Dark: Essays on Pascal's Pensées and Provinciales*. Rochester: University of Rochester Press, 2005.

Nehamas, Alexander. *On Friendship*. New York: Basic Books, 2016.

Nicholson, Harold. *Sainte-Beuve*. Garden City, NY: Doubleday, 1956.

Nietzsche, Friedrich. *Ecce Homo*. In *On the Genealogy of Morals and Ecce Homo*, translated by Walter Kaufmann. New York: Vintage, 1989.

———. *The Gay Science.* Translated by Walter Kaufmann. New York: Random House, 2010.

———. *Thus Spoke Zarathustra.* Translated by Walter Kaufmann. New York: Penguin, 1978.

Nussbaum, Martha. "Mill between Aristotle and Bentham." *Daedalus* 133, no. 2 (Spring 2004): 60–68.

O'Connell, Marvin. *Blaise Pascal: Reasons of the Heart.* Grand Rapids, MI: Eerdmans, 1997.

Okin, Susan Moller. *Women in Western Political Thought.* Princeton: Princeton University Press, 1979.

Olivo-Poindron, Isabelle. "Du moi humain au moi commun; Rousseau lecteur de Pascal." *Les études philosophiques* 95, no. 4 (January 2010): 557–95.

Parish, Richard. "Pascal's *Lettres provinciales*: From Flippancy to Fundamentals." In *The Cambridge Companion to Pascal,* edited by Nicholas Hammond, 182–200. Cambridge: Cambridge University Press, 2003.

Pascal, Blaise. *Oeuvres complètes.* Edited by Henri Gouhier and Louis Lafuma. Paris: Editions du Seuil, 1963.

———. *Pensées.* Translated and edited by Roger Ariew. Indianapolis: Hackett, 2004.

———. *The Provincial Letters.* Translated by Thomas M'Crie. New York: Modern Library, 1941.

Pascal, Blaise, and Pierre Nicole. *Trois discours sur la condition des grands.* In Blaise Pascal, *Oeuvres,* edited by Gérard Ferreyrolles and Philippe Sellier. Paris: Classiques Garnier, 2004.

Périer, Étienne. "Preface [de l'édition de Port-Royal]." In Blaise Pascal, *Pensées,* edited by Michel Le Guern, 41–62. Paris: Gallimard, 2004.

Périer, Gilberte. *Vie de Monsieur Pascal.* In Blaise Pascal, *Oeuvres complétes,* edited by Henri Gouhier and Louis Lafuma. Paris: Editions du Seuil, 1963.

Pippin, Robert. *Nietzsche, Psychology, and First Philosophy.* Chicago: University of Chicago Press, 2010.

Plato. *Apology of Socrates.* Translated by Thomas G. West and Grace Starry West. Ithaca: Cornell University Press, 1984.

———. *Gorgias.* In *Plato: Gorgias and Aristotle: Rhetoric,* translated by Joe Sacks. Indianapolis: Hackett, 2009.

———. *Republic.* Translated by G. M. A. Grube. In *Plato: Complete Works,* edited by John M. Cooper. Indianapolis: Hackett, 1997.

———. *Symposium.* Translated by Alexander Nehamas and Paul Woodruff. Indianapolis: Hackett, 1989.

Popkin, Richard. *History of Skepticism from Erasmus to Spinoza.* Berkeley: University of California Press, 1979.

Putnam, Robert. *Our Kids: The American Dream in Crisis*. New York: Simon and Schuster, 2016.

Quint, David. *Montaigne and the Quality of Mercy*. Princeton: Princeton University Press, 1998.

Rauch, Jonathan. "How American Politics Went Insane." *Atlantic Monthly*, July/August 2016. https://www.theatlantic.com/magazine/archive/2016/07/how-american-politics-went-insane/485570/.

Reginster, Bernard. "Happiness as a Faustian Bargain." *Daedalus* 133, no. 2 (Spring 2004): 52–59.

Rice, Eugene F., Jr., and Anthony Grafton. *The Foundation of Early Modern Europe, 1460–1559*. New York: W. W. Norton, 1994.

Rigolot, François. *Les métamorphoses de Montaigne*. Paris: Presses Universitaires de France, 1988.

Rogers, Ben. "Pascal's Life and Times." In *The Cambridge Companion to Pascal*, edited by Nicholas Hammond, 4–19. Cambridge: Cambridge University Press, 2003.

Rousseau, Jean-Jacques. *Basic Political Writings*, ed. Donald A. Cress. Indianapolis: Hackett, 2011.

Rousseau, Jean-Jacques. *The Confessions and Correspondence, Including Letters to Malesherbes*. Translated by Christopher Kelly. Edited by Christopher Kelly, Roger D. Masters, and Peter G. Stillman. The Collected Writings of Rousseau, vol. 5. Hanover, NH: Dartmouth College, 1995.

———. *The Discourses and Other Early Political Writings*. Translated by Victor Gourevitch. Cambridge: Cambridge University Press, 1997.

———. *Émile, or, On Education*. Translated and edited by Allan Bloom. New York: Basic Books, 1969.

———. *Julie, or the New Heloise*. Translated by Philip Stewart and Jean Vaché. Edited by Jean Vaché. Collected Writings of Rousseau, vol. 6. Hanover, NH: Dartmouth College Press, 1997.

———. *The Major Political Writings of Jean-Jacques Rousseau*. Translated by John T. Scott. Chicago: University of Chicago Press, 2012.

———. *Oeuvres complètes*. Vols. 1–4. Edited by Bernard Gagnebin and Marcel Raymond. Bibliothèque de la Pléiade. Paris: Gallimard, 1959–69.

———. *The Plan for Perpetual Peace. On the Government of Poland, and Other Writings on History and Politics*. Translated by Chrstopher Kelly and Judith Bush. Edited by Christopher Kelly. The Collected Writings of Rousseau, vol. 2. Hanover, NH: Dartmouth College Press, 2005.

———. *The Reveries of the Solitary Walker*. Translated by Charles Butterworth. Indianapolis: Hackett, 1992.

———. *Rousseau: Judge of Jean-Jacques*. Translated by Judith R. Bush, Christopher Kelly, and Roger D. Masters. Hanover, NH: University Press of New England, 1990.

Sainte-Beuve, Charles-Augustin. *Literary and Philosophical Essays: French, German and Italian*. Edited by Charles W. Eliot. New York: P. F. Collier and Sons, 1914.

———. *Port-Royal*. Vols. 1–7. Paris: La Conaissance, 1926.

Schaefer, David Lewis. "Montaigne, Tocqueville, and the Politics of Skepticism." *Perspectives on Political Science* 31, no. 2 (2002): 204–12.

———. *The Political Philosophy of Montaigne*. Ithaca: Cornell University Press, 1990.

Schaub, Diana. "On Slavery: Beaumont's *Marie* and Tocqueville's *Democracy in America*." *Legal Studies Forum* 22, no. 4 (1998): 607–26.

Schindler, D. C. *Freedom from Reality*. South Bend, IN: University of Notre Dame Press, 2017.

Scott, John T. "Rousseau's Quixotic Quest in the *Rêveries du promeneur solitaire*." In *The Nature of Rousseau's* Rêveries: *Physical, Human, Aesthetic*, edited by John C. O'Neal, 139–52. Oxford: Voltaire Foundation, 2008.

Scott, John T., and Robert Zaretsky. *The Philosophers' Quarrel: Rousseau, Hume, and the Limits of Human Understanding*. New Haven: Yale University Press, 2009.

Screech, M. A. *Montaigne & Melancholy: The Wisdom of the* Essays. Selinsgrove, PA: Susquehanna University Press, 1983.

Shell, Susan Meld. "*Émile*: Nature and the Education of Sophie." In *The Cambridge Companion to Rousseau*, ed. Patrick Riley, 272–301. Cambridge: Cambridge University Press, 2006.

Shklar, Judith. *Men and Citizens: A Study of Rousseau's Social Theory*. Cambridge: Cambridge University Press, 1985.

———. *Ordinary Vices*. Cambridge, MA: Harvard University Press, 1984.

Silver, Lee M. *Challenging Nature: The Clash between Biotechnology and Spirituality*. New York: Harper Perennial, 2006.

Smith, Christian, and Melinda Lundquist Denton. *Soul Searching: The Religious and Spiritual Lives of American Teenagers*. Oxford: Oxford University Press, 2009.

Smith, Jeffrey A. "Natural Happiness, Sensation, and Infancy in Rousseau's *Emile*." *Polity* 35, no. 1 (Autumn 2002): 93–120.

Starobinski, Jean. *Transparency and Obstruction*. Translated by Arthur Goldhammer. Chicago: University of Chicago Press, 1988.

Stendhal [Marie-Henri Beyle]. *On Love*. Edited by C. K. Scott-Moncrieff. New York: Grosset and Dunlap, 1947.

Storey, Benjamin. "Rousseau and the Problem of Self-Knowledge." *Review of Politics* 71, no. 2 (Spring 2009): 251–74.

———. "Self-Knowledge and Sociability in the Thought of Rousseau." *Perspectives on Political Science* 41, no. 3 (August 2012): 146–54.

———. "Tocqueville on Technology." *New Atlantis* 40 (Fall 2013): 48–71.

Strauss, Leo. *Natural Right and History*. Chicago: University of Chicago Press, 1950.

Talmon, J. L. *The Origins of Totalitarian Democracy*. New York: Praeger, 1960.

Taylor, Charles. *A Secular Age*. Cambridge, MA: Harvard University Press, 2007.

———. *Sources of the Self*. Cambridge, MA: Harvard University Press, 1989.

Tessitore, Aristide. "Tocqueville's American Thesis and the New Science of Politics." *American Political Thought* 4 (Winter 2015): 72–99.

Thompson, Douglas I. *Montaigne and the Tolerance of Politics*. Oxford: Oxford University Press, 2018.

Tocqueville, Alexis de. *Democracy in America*. Edited by Eduardo Nolla. Translated by James T. Schleifer. Indianapolis: Liberty Fund, 2010.

———. *Recollections: The French Revolution of 1848 and Its Aftermath*. Edited by Oliver Zunz. Translated by Arthur Goldhammer. Charlottesville: University of Virginia Press, 2016.

———. *Selected Letters on Politics and Society*. Edited by Roger Boesche. Translated by James Toupin and Roger Boesche. Berkeley: University of California Press, 1985.

———. *Souvenirs*. Edited by J. P. Mayer and A. P. Kerr. New Brunswick, NJ: Transaction Publishers, 2009.

———. *Souvenirs*. In *Oeuvres complètes*, vol. 3, edited by François Furet and Françoise Mélonio. Paris: Gallimard, 2004.

Todorov, Tzvetan. *Frail Happiness: An Essay on Rousseau*. Translated by John T. Scott and Robert D. Zaretsky. University Park: Pennsylvania State University Press, 2001.

———. *Imperfect Garden: The Legacy of Humanism*. Translated by Carol Cosman. Princeton: Princeton University Press, 2002.

Toulmin, Stephen. *Cosmopolis: The Hidden Agenda of Modernity*. Chicago: University of Chicago Press, 1990.

Trilling, Lionel. *Sincerity and Authenticity*. Cambridge, MA: Harvard University Press, 1971.

Van Doren, Mark. *Don Quixote's Profession*. New York: Columbia University Press, 1958.

Vermeule, Adrian. "Liturgy of Liberalism." *First Things*, January 2017, 57–60.

Viguié, Pierre. *L'honnête homme au XVIIe siècle: Le Chevalier de Méré (1607–1684)*. Paris: Editions Sansot, 1922.

Voltaire. *Lettres philosophiques*, vingt-cinquième lettre, "sur les Pensées de M. Pascal." In *Mélanges*, edited by Jacques Van Den Heuvel. Paris: Gallimard, 1961.

———. *Le Mondain*. In *Mélanges*, edited by Jacques Van Den Heuvel. Paris: Gallimard, 1961.

Wallace, David Foster. "This Is Water." http://bulletin-archive.kenyon.edu/x4280.html.

Wampole, Christy. "How to Live without Irony." In *Modern Ethics in 77 Arguments*, edited by Peter Catapano and Simon Critchley, 79–84. New York: W. W. Norton, 2017.

Weintraub, Karl Joachim. *The Value of the Individual: Self and Circumstance in Autobiography*. Chicago: University of Chicago Press, 1978.

Welch, Cheryl B. "Tocqueville on Fraternity and Fratricide." In *The Cambridge Companion to Tocqueville*, edited by Cheryl B. Welch. Cambridge: Cambridge University Press, 2006.

West, Cornel. "The Indispensability yet Insufficiency of Marxist Theory." In *The Cornel West Reader*. New York: Basic Books, 1999.

Wills, Gary. "Did Tocqueville 'Get' America?" *New York Review of Books*, April 29, 2004.

Wolin, Sheldon. *Tocqueville between Two Worlds: The Making of a Political and Theoretical Life*. Princeton: Princeton University Press, 2001.

Woolf, Virginia. *The Common Reader*. New York: Harcourt Brace, 1932.

Wooton, David. *Power, Pleasure, and Profit: Insatiable Appetites from Machiavelli to Madison*. Cambridge, MA: Harvard University Press, 2018.

Yarbrough, Jean M. "Tocqueville on the Needs of the Soul." *Perspectives on Political Science* (Spring 2018): 1–19.

Zeitlin, Jacob. *Essays of Montaigne*. Vol. 3. New York: Knopf, 1934.

Zuckert, Catherine. "Tocqueville's 'New Political Science.'" In *Tocqueville's Voyages: The Evolution of His Ideals and Their Journey beyond His Time*, edited by Christine Dunn Henderson, 142–76. Indianapolis: Liberty Fund, 2014.

INDEX